Marion J. Hatchett

SANCTIFYING LIFE, TIME AND SPACE

An Introduction to Liturgical Study

The Seabury Press • *New York*

The Seabury Press
815 Second Avenue
New York, N.Y. 10017

Printed in the United States of America

LIBRARY OF CONGRESS CATALOGING IN PUBLICATION DATA

Hatchett, Marion J
  Sanctifying life, time, and space.

  Bibliography: p.
  Includes index.
  1. Liturgics. 2. Church of England. Book of
common prayer. I. Title.
BV176.H34   264'.007   75-38502
ISBN 0-8164-2396-2
First paperback printing

CONTENTS

Contents

This introductory study has been prepared in response to a number of requests from students, parish clergy, and lay persons for a brief synoptic presentation incorporating results of recent historical studies and theological and pastoral concerns which must be taken into account in a time of liturgical revision.

This work is so arranged that a person interested in one particular rite or aspect (for example, *Initiation*, *Ordination*, *Vestments*, *Music*, the *Eucharist*, the *Liturgical Year*, or *Sacred Buildings*) can easily trace that aspect through the various chapters.

I wish to express my appreciation to the *St. Luke's Journal of Theology* in whose pages a portion of this work was published in an earlier edition ("An Introduction to Liturgical Study," *St. Luke's Journal of Theology*, XV [September, 1972], 19–158). I wish to acknowledge my indebtedness to colleagues on the faculty of the School of Theology, Sewanee, who have patiently read and criticized this work, or portions of it related to their particular academic disciplines: D. S. Armentrout, W. A. Griffin, P. H. Igarashi, J. H. W. Rhys, and C. L. Winters, Jr. I am indebted to many others who have given encouragement and helpful suggestions but particularly to the Very Reverend Urban T. Holmes, Dean of the School of Theology; to two professors of liturgy, the Reverend Doctors L. L. Mitchell of Notre Dame and T. J. Talley of the General Theological Seminary; to the Reverend Doctor H. Boone Porter, Jr., of Roanridge; and to Captain Howard E. Galley, Jr., of the Office for Prayer Book Revision.

SANCTIFYING
LIFE, TIME
AND SPACE

CHAPTER I

INTRODUCTION

In these days when liturgical changes and revisions seem to be inevitable, liturgical study cannot be approached as a how-to course or as an exposition or examination of a fixed rite. Its goals must include the ability to bring intelligent criticism to bear upon both the old and the new; ability to distinguish between that which is basic to a liturgy and that which is peripheral, inconsistent, or antithetical; an awareness of relationships between liturgy and theology, Bible, church history, and pastoralia; an ability to distinguish between responsible experimentation and eccentricity or gimmickry; an ability to assess ceremonial expressions; an awareness of ecumenical and missionary implications; an ability to recognize and label the liturgies of secular life; and an awareness of liturgical voids in community life which are filled by neither churchly nor secular liturgies.

Worship comes from an Anglo-Saxon word *worth-ship*, to place a value upon. The aim of worship is the glorification of God and the sanctification of man. *Rites* are texts associated with worship. *Ceremonies* are actions associated with worship.

In contrast to ascetical theology, which is concerned with the inner life of the individual, liturgics is concerned with the life of the community. From the standpoint of the liturgiologist, personal devotions should derive from and/or feed into the liturgy. Liturgy is the work of the community, not something done for the community. A good liturgy encapsulates and makes operative in the present the heritage and the hopes of the community, its *myth* (a myth is not that which is not true but the truths which are eternal expressed in terms of time, the real expressed in terms of the ideal). The content of a good liturgy is remembrance (*anamnesis*, the opposite of amnesia) and *prolepsis* (anticipation, expectation, foretaste). Liturgy is the work of the people. It is the opposite of lethargy. "Full, conscious, and active participation . . . is demanded by the very nature of the liturgy" *(The Constitution on the Sacred Liturgy*, 14). The Big-Singing at Benton, Kentucky, or a dance in a Shaker colony, for example, may be said to be more liturgical than a non-communicating Low Mass or a choir-dominated Evensong.[1]

There are several possible approaches to liturgical study: (a) the *rubrical*, where the principal concern is the preparation of the correct conduct of the rites (b) the *theological*, where the concern is with the meaning of a rite, and (c) the *historical*, where the concern is with the development.[2] Neither of the first two approaches can be primary in a day of revision and radical rethinking of rites. *Pastoral* modification must always be carried out with the primal and perennial significations in view.

MODELS FROM ANTHROPOLOGY AND COMPARATIVE RELIGION

Liturgical history did not begin with the 1549 Prayer Book, or even with Hippolytus. Man is a liturgical animal,

and to keep liturgical study from degenerating into esoter-
ica, it might best begin with anthropology. Specialists in the
fields of anthropology and comparative religion have provided a number of models which are useful in the study of
Christian liturgies.

Van Gennep finds in the three phases of a journey—separation, transition, and incorporation—an analogy which illu-
mines the rites and ceremonies associated with crises in the
lives of members of a community ("rites of passage"): initiation, excommunication and reinstatement, marriage, childbirth, vocation, sickness, and death.[3]

Norbeck points out that these *crisis rites* affect the
whole of the community, define or re-define, shape or re-
shape the community. Certain aspects of these rites (re-
counting the myth, sacrifices, and meals) are periodically repeated *(cyclic rites)* for the maintenance of the group life,
bringing both the sustenance and the judgment of the myth
upon the community.[4]

Eliade points out that the first of these groups has to do
with the *sanctification of life* and the second with the *sanctification of time*, and he categorizes a third group of rites
having to do with man's relationship to the earth as *sanctification of space*.[5]

Turner has pointed to an aspect of the rites as having to
do with the tension or balance between hierarchy and community, "structure and anti-structure," *liminality*, and he
denotes certain rites or aspects of rites as rites of status
elevation and others as rites of status reversal.[6]

A distinction must be drawn between the *liturgies* (the
cult) and the *magic* (the *occult*) of a society. The *liturgies*
typically encapsulate the heritage and the hopes (the culture, the myth) of the community. They are typically in the
vernacular. A substantial portion of the people are active
participants, with the leadership roles being filled by those
who best personify the culture. The rites are long and complicated, but they are essentially rational. The rites are designed to define, re-define, shape, re-shape, or maintain the
communal life. They establish, re-establish, or strengthen
communication with the god. On the other hand, the *magic*

or occult rites are typically done for rather than by the people, typically by one man who is in some sense an outsider and is possessed of a certain *gnosis*. The rites are typically brief. They typically involve some use of language unknown to the people, though the language and the rite may represent an active or degenerate form of some element(s) from the liturgies of another culture. The rites are aimed at producing supernatural results or individual advantage at manipulating the god.[7]

Turner has provided a model for use in the examination of any rite, appurtenance, or ceremony: *exegesis* (what do [a] the laymen and [b] the ritual experts say about it?); *operation* (when and why did it come into use, how does it function, what does it accomplish, within the culture?); and *position* (what is its position in the liturgical system, and what meaning does that position imply? what additional meanings does it give to or receive from other uses within the system of the same text, appurtenance, or ceremony?).[8] For example:

> The model might be applied to the text of the Collect for the Second Sunday in Advent (Book of Common Prayer [1928 ed.], p. 92): *exegesis:* possibly the words *mark, patience*, and *comfort* need explanation; *operation:* new to the 1549 Prayer Book, this collect ties in with the Renaissance-Reformation emphasis upon the Scriptures; *position:* this new collect provides a different lens through which to read the old lections for the Second Sunday in Advent; also, its position at the beginning of the year may give it more importance than had it been placed, say, on a Sunday after Trinity (does the shift to the Epiphany Season in *Services for Trial Use* alter its importance or its meaning?).

> The model might be applied to an appurtenance such as candles on the altar: *exegesis:* Jesus the light of the world; the human and divine natures; *operation:* they were placed on the altar in the late Middle Ages for light to read by; they may now add a festive note, they may remind people of Christian fathers who gathered before daybreak, or they may have a significatory value; *position:* they may take meaning from the candle which has ritual and ceremonial significance, the Paschal Candle.

The model might also be applied to a ceremony such as the sign of the cross at the end of the creed: *exegesis:* some might interpret this as a special affirmation of belief in the resurrection; *operation:* it came into use in some places at the end of the Middle Ages (Sarum had a bow instead); *position:* signings refer to the basic signation, the one required signation within the Prayer Book, that at baptism; a reaffirmation of our baptismal confession and commitment.

Von Allmen distinguishes four "dimensions" of liturgy: (1) the *rational* dimension (in contrast to the sentimental, the emotionalistic, the nostalgic, or the gnostic), liturgy as a mirror of reality, as revelatory, as a source of light and life; (2) the *acoustical*—the spoken word; the sung word (music as functional, conveying the word, and as sacramental, transforming the word); and silence;[9] (3) the *visual*, art, color, architecture, iconography, vesture, movement as revelatory or sacramental; and (4) the *kinetic*, postures, gestures, movements, architectural dimensions as expressive, significatory, revelatory.[10]

THE RITUAL PATTERN: THE SANCTIFICATION OF LIFE

Any society shapes and is shaped by certain rites which enact the myth of the community. To function within the society a person needs these rites (contrast the Englishman and the half-breed in the movie *A Man Called Horse*). Traditionally these rites center around certain crisis points in the life of the individual and the community.

Initiation—The community rite par excellence is initiation. When a child reaches an appropriate age, he passes ritually from childhood to adulthood. He is instructed in the myth of the community. He is tested for readiness. The rites are designed to make an indelible impression. Such liturgies are almost universally spoken of as new birth and as death and resurrection. Those who have been through the same rites are blood brothers, people who can be counted on to the death, people who bear their weight within the adult community.[11]

Penance—Certain offenses which seriously endanger or disrupt the community bring excommunication, separation from the community. After appropriate penalties, self-examination, testing, and re-education an excommunicate may be reinstated, reincorporated into the community.

Marriage—When persons approach marriage a series of rites separates them from their parents and from among the bachelors and spinsters of the community, prepares them for marriage, and integrates them into the life and responsibilities of the married couples of the community.[12]

Pregnancy—At some point an expectant mother is formally relieved of certain of her family and community responsibilities. After the birth of the child, regardless of whether the child lives or dies, she is reincorporated into the life of the community, resuming her normal responsibilities within the family and the community, or, if it is a first child and it lives, assuming a different place within the life of the community from that which she had occupied hitherto.

Childbirth—Within a period of days or weeks after a birth, the child is presented publicly to the community and recognized as a member of its family and of its community. Certain persons, in addition to the parents, are publicly recognized as having certain special responsibilities for that child.

Vocation—For certain vocations persons are separated from among the laity, instructed, tested, and finally integrated among those of the vocation and recognized publicly as belonging to this vocation.[13]

Sickness—In certain types of sickness a person is separated from the normal life and responsibilities of the community, and the community brings to this crisis appropriate rites which provide help and support.[14]

Death and Burial—Tightly scheduled days of texts and actions are made use of in connection with a death and burial. The rites are designed to make certain that the dead

stay dead and to carry the members of the community
through the grief process, re-align the family structure, and
redistribute the property and the community responsibilities
of the deceased, so that the family and the community can
move on.[15]

THE SANCTIFICATION OF TIME

In almost every society, certain components which are a
normal part of these crisis rites (repetitions of the myth,
sacrifices, and meals) are periodically repeated, normally in
some relationship to the cycles of nature. Through these cyclic rites the members of the community immerse themselves in the myth of the community, offer to the gods, receive strength from the gods, and thus bind themselves to
the other members of the community and celebrate with
them. Through these the community is re-created, reinforced, brought under the judgment of its myth.[16]

The Liturgical "Day" and Liturgies of the Word—Liturgies of the word develop from the repetitions of the myth by
the old seers of the community and by the singing of songs
and dancing of dances within which the myth is proclaimed
or acted out.

The Liturgical "Week" and Sacrifices and Meals—At certain intervals the community offers sacrifices and partici-
pates in community meals. The sacrifices and meals provide
for differentiation and cohesion. Those who eat together
tend to think alike, act alike, profess the same faith, share
the same values, and be loyal to one another. Sacrifices and
meals tend to center about three elements: *meat, bread,* and
alcohol. To eat *meat* is to gain the vitality of that from
which the meat comes. It is related to sacrifice. We identify
with animals killed. Blood binds together. *Bread* is basic to
existence. It is related to slaughter. Man puts something of
himself into producing bread. It is a symbol of fellowship (a
"com*pan*ion" is one with whom one shares bread). *Alcohol* is
associated with vitality, fellowship, joy, celebration, the

numbing of pain, the overcoming of fatigue, the liberating of inhibitions, the opening up of communication, the swearing of loyalty (the toast).

The Liturgical "Year" and Creation, Manifestation, and Initiation—The community is typically re-created or resurrected and members of the community recall their initiation into the community in rites which are repeated annually which recall the principal manifestations of the god. These rites are typically related to the agricultural cycles and to the initiation of new members into the community.

Most societies justify their crisis rites and their cyclic rites not in terms of producing "invisible grace" but by pointing to concrete results. The rites do not function as signs of what they are supposed to do; they *do* what they are supposed to do. Their liturgies are functional.

THE SANCTIFICATION OF SPACE

Sacred space is a point from which to acquire orientation, a "position." It is the "center of the world." It is the threshold, the place of passage, "the gate of heaven." It is the whole of creation on a microcosmic scale. It is the meeting-place, the home, of the community. It is a place of pilgrimage, the heavenly home. The sacred space speaks of the world, the community, the eschaton.[17]

Every community marks such events, times, and places. For example, "the American way of life" involves initiation consisting of naturalization for immigrants or such milestones as graduation, the attaining of a driver's license, and/or service in the armed forces for the native. Criminal offenses bring excommunication, and the whole process is replete with rites and ceremonies. Certain rites and ceremonies are expected in connection with marriage, childbirth, entering upon certain vocations, sickness, and death. The rhythm of the year (the school year, the fiscal year, the calendar year) is marked by certain ceremonies. Certain days (Thanksgiving Day, Independence Day, Washington's

Birthday, Labor Day) reinforce the myth. Certain activities, foods, and manners of dress are associated with certain periods of the day, of the week, or of the year. Certain places (Mount Vernon, the Capitol, the Statue of Liberty, state parks) partake of the nature of sacred space, reinforcing the myth; they are places of pilgrimage.[18]

CRITERIA FOR JUDGING RITES AND CEREMONIES

White gives three categories of questions for judging rites and ceremonies and for approaching liturgical revision and experimentation, *pastoral, theological,* and *historical:* (1) *pastoral*—does it communicate? does it function to meet the cultic needs of the community? (2) *theological*—is it expressive of the myth of the community *(lex orandi lex credendi,* that is, the law of prayer, the law of faith)? (3) *historical*—is it gimmickry, dilettantism, idiosyncratic, or antiquarian, or is it well-grounded?[19]

Schmemann provides a penetrating series of questions to be applied to any text, appurtenance, or ceremony: when, under what circumstances, did it appear? is it basic (that is, basic to man as a ritualistic animal and/or basic to the particular heritage), or did it stem from some peculiar set of circumstances? why did it appear, what did it say to the people of its day? can we say that, or do we want to say it? if so, how can we best say it in our day? what does this text, appurtenance, or ceremony say to the people of our day? can we say that, or do we want to say it? what changes, revisions, subtractions, or additions need to be made?[20]

SIGNS, SYMBOLS, AND SACRAMENTS

Distinctions must be drawn between *signs, symbols,* and *sacraments.* A *sign* (for example, a road sign or a cross) points to something beyond itself; it signifies. A *symbol* does more than signify: it reveals; it holds together apparently disparate elements (as when the Fathers spoke of Christ as Symbol—God and Man); it binds a community together; it has power over those for whom it is a symbol; it reminds or recalls; it extends frames of reference. Signs speak to the intellect, symbols speak to the whole man. Behind the word *sacrament* lies the Latin *sacramentum*, an oath of loyalty and/or a partial payment given as pledge of a full payment yet to be made (sacrifice and commitment), and the Greek *mysterion*, a religious rite, a "mystery," with a causal relationship to that which it symbolizes, a means as well as a sign or symbol.[21]

A religious sign, symbol, or sacrament has three frames of reference: the *world*, the *community*, the *eschaton*. For example:

> The setting apart of one day a week has reference to the *world*, for it represents the day of Creation, and it is a sign of all days, "to serve him truly all the days of my life" (Book of Common Prayer [1928 ed.], p. 288). It has reference to the *community*, the church, for it represents the day of the Resurrection, the day of the outpouring of the Spirit, "to worship God every Sunday in his Church" (Book of Common Prayer [1928 ed.], p. 291; see also the prayer for Sunday Morning, p. 595). It also represents the *eschaton*, the "eighth day," the eternal Sabbath rest, the "Day of the Lord."

> The text "Do this in remembrance of Me" has reference to the *world:* as I break my body and pour out my blood, you are to do the same with your body and blood "for the life of the world." It has reference to the *community:* perform this cultic action "in remembrance of Me." It has reference to the *eschaton*, the heavenly banquet, when all shall eat together in the Kingdom.

The whole of life, of time, of space is sanctified, made holy, by setting apart particular events, moments, and places.

Karl Jaspers has catalogued ways in which symbols degenerate: *superstition*, idolatry, a confusion of the symbol with the reality itself; *allegorization*, false meanings are found in or forced upon the symbol; *aestheticism*, the sym-

bol is made "the object of detached aesthetic contemplation
. . . the impetus for the enjoyment of random emotions, or
of unlimited possibilities"; *dogmatism* or *conceptualization*,
the symbol is made comprehensible, the reality is abandoned
"in favor of rationally accessible knowledge"; and *magic*, the
symbol is used for wrong ends ("I cannot control [symbols]
but can only be conquered by them").[22] Because of this tendency of symbols to degenerate, a certain amount of iconoclasm is always in order (compare the priestly and the
prophetic traditions).

RELIGIOUS CEREMONIAL

W. H. Frere divided religious ceremonials into four
types, the *utilitarian* or *practical*, the *interpretative*, the *significatory*, and the *allegorical*. (1) The *practical* are those
actions which must be done in some way or other for the
performance of the rite, and the best ceremonials are those
aimed at doing these things in the most efficient and effective manner (for example, facing the people for texts
addressed to them, standing to sing, etc.) (2) The *interpretative* are ceremonials which dramatize or bring out the meaning of the text (for example, the "Manual Acts," lifting the
Paten and Cup at "which we now offer," the raising of the
priest's hands at "Lift up your hearts," the sign of the cross
in Baptism, etc.). (3) The *significatory* are ceremonials
which typically need to be explained in order to make sense
(for example, the use of candles, colors, and vestments, facing East for the creed, etc.). (4) The *allegorical* or *mystical*
ceremonials are those which have no relationship to the text
or rationale of the rite (sometimes they are imported from a
rite within which they are significatory or interpretative or
practical) but are imposed upon it (for example, the use of
eight signs of the cross over the baptismal water, the use of
an invocatory gesture where there is no invocation in the
text, an interpretation of the Eucharist as analogous to the
life of Christ, etc.).[23]

The ceremonial actions required by the Book of Common

Prayer are all either practical or interpretative. Significatory ceremonials, adequately explained, can be meaningful. The use of allegorical ceremonials in our day (or any day) is highly questionable. Such ceremonial actions tend to trivialize the text, to mystify the congregation, and to encourage the congregation to view their role as spectators rather than as participants.

"Form follows function." "The medium is the message." The purpose of religious ceremonial is to bring out or play up the essential structure of a rite. What is basic to a rite can be lost either because of a lack of ceremonial in association with basic elements or because too much ceremonialism is associated with secondary elements within the rite.

Many persons defend their ceremonial usages with one or the other of two reasons, "I like it," or "That is what I am used to." Neither of these reasons is adequate. Persons should not be bound by a particular system; nor should they adopt or refuse to adopt a particular ceremonial action because it is Eastern, Roman, British, Liturgical Movement, what their favorite priest does, or what was done in their seminary chapel.

Ceremonial actions must be subjected to continuous questioning and modification: (1) Does this ceremonial have to be imposed upon this text or does it bring out this text? (2) Does this ceremonial play up basic elements and/or play down secondary elements? (3) What does this ceremonial say to this particular gathered group? (4) Is this ceremonial appropriate [a] to the size and architecture of the building, [b] to the size, the relative sophistication, and the manners of expression of the congregation, [c] to the relative importance of the day or occasion, and [d] to the traditions of the parish? (5) Can *I* perform this particular action with ease and conviction and provide a rational explanation for others?

CHAPTER II

THE PERIOD OF THE ORAL TRADITION

The history of the church's liturgy can be divided into periods according to the types of liturgical books in use. For the first several decades we have no explicitly liturgical documents. Early Christians apparently continued the ritual pattern (See pp. 7–10) of Judaism while re-interpreting and re-molding it in terms of the Christian myth and in terms of particular circumstances—geographical, linguistic, cultural, philosophical, etc. Liturgically, there was both a continuity and a discontinuity with first century Judaism.[1]

Our knowledge of Christian worship for the period of the oral tradition is based upon sources often open to widely varying interpretations: (1) explicit statements and liturgical forms in the New Testament ("Amen," "Maranatha," hymn texts, statements concerning reading, prayer, Eucharist, baptism, laying-on-of-hands, etc.) and the use of technical liturgical terms;[2] (2) knowledge of the liturgy of first-century Judaism;[3] (3) the liturgical construction and content of books or portions of books of the New Testament;[4] (4) some explicitly liturgical statements of the second and third centuries, which, applied with caution, seem to illumine New Testament passages; and (5) New Testament descriptions of such things as how Jesus was baptized, how the Eucharist was instituted, and the worship of heaven (Revelation), which may be molded by liturgical practices of New Testament times.

Yet each of these sources must be approached with caution. Terms later used in a technical liturgical sense may not have had that sense in New Testament times. Many changes came in Jewish liturgy with the fall of Jerusalem and the dispersion of the Jews. The construction of New Testament books may have influenced the liturgy, rather than vice versa.[5] New Testament descriptions of rites and ceremonies may have influenced the liturgical development, rather than described current liturgical practice.

The principal issue liturgically of the period of the oral tradition was the re-interpretation and re-molding of the Jewish liturgy in terms of the Christian myth.

THE SANCTIFICATION OF LIFE

Initiation—For a person not born into Judaism the rite of initiation involved circumcision and baptism. Presumably after a period as a "God-fearer," attending the synagogue services, a person was brought for examination for admission as a candidate or proselyte. At this time he was questioned as to why he would wish to become a Jew. If admitted, he entered into a period of intense instruction, dogmatic, ethical, and eschatological, and was brought to repentance and renunciation of his old life. Having been instructed in the Law and immersed in the Jewish heritage, he was brought to baptism, the male having first been circumcised. For the baptism, there were witnesses to vouch for the candidate. The baptism was in the nude in living water. At the point of the immersion there was some dialogue concerning the Law—an oath of loyalty or act of adherence. The newly-baptized was now a "son." Brought out of the water, he was branded as God's sheep, slave, and soldier by being marked on the forehead with a Taw (T), the last letter of the Hebrew alphabet, which signified the Name of God (compare the "mark" of Cain, of Ezekiel, of Paul, of Revelation). His baptism was for him his crossing of the Red Sea, entering into the Promised Land, accepting the heritage and hopes of the Jewish people as his heritage and hopes. One of the descriptions of early proselyte baptism which has survived is that of Yebamoth:

> One who comes to be made a proselyte in the present time is to be asked, "Why do you come to be made a proselyte? Do you not know that at this time Israel is afflicted, buffeted, humiliated and harried, and that sufferings and sore trials come upon them?" If he answers, "I know this, and I am not worthy," they are to accept him immediately.

> They are to instruct him in some of the lighter and some of the weightier commandments, and to inform him as to the sins in regard to the corner of the field, the forgotten sheaf, the gleaning, and the tithe for the poor. Then they are to teach him the penalties for transgressions: "Know that . . . from now on if you eat the forbidden fat of cattle you will be excommunicated, if you profane the Sabbath you will be stoned." In the same way they should teach him the rewards for observance of the commandments. . . . Yet one must not multiply words or go into too much detail.

> If he accepts the obligations he is to be circumcised immediately . . . and when healed he is to be brought to baptism immediately.

> Two men learned in the Law shall stand near him and instruct him in some of the lighter and some of the weightier commandments. He immerses himself, and when he comes up he is in all respects an Israelite.[6]

John the Baptist came preaching a baptism of repentance which signified a new beginning and incorporation into a new community, and which had eschatological significance (compare the ritual washings of various Jewish communities, as that at Qumran).[7]

Jesus ushered in His ministry by submitting to the baptism of John, and He referred to His death as a baptism. The New Testament accounts of the baptism of Jesus reflect Jewish rites of adoption. They were affected by and/or affected local rites and teachings concerning baptism.

The early Christian baptismal rite surely took its basic form from the Jewish initiation of converts. The practice of circumcision was not maintained, for it spoke of a nationalistic cult, ritual purity, exclusion of women from full membership, and the blood of the old covenant. The church proclaimed that the true circumcision is the circumcision of the heart (Jer. 4:4; Gen. 17:10ff.). The early Christians, however, retained the cultic act of baptism which spoke of repentance, cleansing, new birth, adoption, death and resurrection. The act was re-interpreted and re-molded in terms of the Christian myth: cleansing by the blood of Jesus; new birth in Christ; death and resurrection in Christ; incorporation into His Body; the "mark" or "seal" of the Lord Jesus. To be baptized was to be adopted by God, to share in His Sonship, His anointing (compare the anointings of kings and priests), to receive the Holy Spirit, to confess one's faith in Him, to swear one's loyalty to Him. We distinguish between baptism and repentance, between baptism and confession of faith; for New Testament writers to be baptized was to repent, to confess the faith.

For those converted from Judaism, their whole lives had been long candidacies. Matthew 28:19 was apparently not for centuries interpreted as a formula for use in baptizing but as a shorthand description of the faith into which one was baptized, for the early liturgical documents make use of credal statements rather than this formula. Acts 8:37, an interpolation for which Irenaeus is probably the earliest reliable witness, "I believe that Jesus Christ is the Son of

God," may be an early formula. Ephesians, I Peter, and Revelation may give some hints of early baptismal liturgies. The accounts of a laying-on-of-hands in Acts 8:17 and 19:6 both seem to deal with irregular situations and are probably irrelevant to a discussion of the normal initiatory rite.

The Bar Mitzvah celebration, as we know it, in connection with a boy's thirteenth birthday, at which time he comes under the obligation to observe the religious duties, does not date back beyond the Middle Ages, though some formal entrance into these obligations does seem to be attested in Luke 2:41-52 and in second-century Jewish sources. In New Testament times Christian baptisms were normally (probably exclusively) of adults, and there is no hint of anything corresponding to the Jewish entrance into the obligation to keep the law which later developed into the Bar Mitzvah.

Penance—Within Judaism certain offenses or states brought excommunication or a condition of ritual uncleanness. Rites and ceremonies analogous to uses associated with mourning and with baptism preceded or accompanied repentance, restoration, or cleansing (the Penitential Psalms, prayers of confession, ashes and sackcloth, fasting and weeping, rending of garments, kneeling and prostration, ritual washings). Possibly restoration was attested by a laying-on-of-hands, a sign of blessing, of identification, of transfer, in the Old Testament.

The New Testament contains evidences of discipline and excommunication for those who had brought scandal upon the church. Members of the church were subject to the discipline of the church. Excommunication was possibly a formal act which followed a solemn assembly of the congregation (See, for example, I Cor. 5; I Tim. 1:20; Titus 3:11-12). Reconciliation or restoration, also, was a formal act, probably attested by the laying-on-of-hands (See, for example, II Cor. 2:5-11; I Tim. 5:19-22).

Marriage—The rites of marriage among the Jews involved a ceremony of betrothal, at which the father of the bride gave his consent and the *mohar* was discussed and paid, some time prior to the wedding. The wedding itself was accompanied by the procession of the bridegroom (wearing a diadem) and friends to the bride's home. She was richly dressed, wearing a veil which would not be removed until entry into the bridal chamber. For the ceremony, which included vows and a written contract ("covenant") and a blessing over a cup of wine, the bride and groom stood under a canopy, surrounded by at least ten witnesses (the minimum for a synagogue service). The procession and entry into the groom's home was accompanied by love songs (See Psalm 45 and the Song of Songs), brandishing of a sword, dancing, and a feast which lasted from seven to fourteen days.

While the New Testament contains teaching concerning the duties of husbands and wives, of parents and children, it gives no hints concerning the marriage rite, possibly because that of Judaism was simply continued with little modification.

Pregnancy and Childbirth—After childbirth a Jewish woman was considered ritually unclean (that is, relieved from certain responsibilities) for forty days after the birth of a male or eighty days after the birth of a female. Leviticus 12 prescribes both the number of days and the burnt offering and the sin offering which were to be made at the conclusion of this period.

A newborn baby was washed, rubbed with salt, wrapped in swathing bands, suckled by the mother, named, and received by the father on his knees. In contrast to other societies which normally circumcised males upon entry into adulthood, a Jewish child was circumcised on the eighth day, a day symbolic of the covenant.

The early church did not insist upon the circumcision of Gentile converts, for fear that the external rite might obscure the meaning of the Gospel (See pp. 16, 18), and there is no explicit evidence of the continuation of the practice of Purification in the early decades or of any Christian significance attached to ceremonies associated with the birth of a child into a natural family, though such rites may have been continued with appropriate modifications and re-interpretations.

Ordination—Within Judaism, rites and ceremonies were associated with setting apart for certain vocations. Kings and priests were anointed. The High Priest was set apart with a rite which included purification, vesting, and anointing with a specially prepared chrism. Kings were anointed and given a "diadem" or "sign of consecration." Hands were laid on Levites (sign of identification, blessing, appointment, transfer, passing on of charismatic gifts).[8]

When ministry is spoken of in the New Testament it is difficult to separate offices and functions. Within the New Testament period, at least in some localities, bishops ("overseers" or "pastors and teachers") and deacons ("servants") must have occupied something of at least a semi-professional status. The term "presbyter" or "elder" is reminiscent of the elders or leading men of the community who within Judaic institutions constituted a collegiate ruling body. Associated in the New Testament with the setting apart of men for various ministries were such elements as popular election, recognition by authority, prayer and fasting, and the laying-on-of-hands.[9]

Sick Rites—Within Judaism prayer and anointing of the sick was practiced. Oil was a common medicine of the day. Though it has additional dimensions as well, the Law of Purity concerning lepers (Lev. 13-14) may provide something of a prototype for rites of the sick. It contains elements of cleansing and exorcism, an anointing, and the offering of sacrifice.

James 5:13–16 apparently indicates a continuation of the use of a sick rite which included confession of sins, prayer, and anointing with oil by the "presbyters of the church."

Burial—The rituals and ceremonies associated with Jewish burials included a preparation of the body; the tearing of garments, dressing in sackcloth, cutting of hair, and fasting on the part of the mourners; the bringing of bread and the "cup of consolation" on the part of neighbors; the offering of prayer and sacrifice for the dead; lamentations and funeral hymns; and the placing of offerings of bread and wine on the tombs.

Central to New Testament teaching is the proclamation

of the resurrection and exaltation of Jesus Christ and our assurance of resurrection in Him. Except for re-interpretation in terms of the Christian myth, the rites of burial in the New Testament period were probably not vastly different from those of the Jews.

THE SANCTIFICATION OF TIME

In Judaism certain components which were a normal part of crisis rites (repetitions of the myth, sacrifices, and meals) were periodically repeated in connection with the cycles of the day, the week, the month, and the year.

The Liturgical Day—Within Judaism the day was marked liturgically in the Temple at Jerusalem with morning and evening sacrifices, and with services which consisted of Psalms and prayers at 9 a.m. and 3 p.m.

Devout Jews also marked times of the day with private prayers, "in the evening, in the morning, and at noon" (Psalm 55:18). For these private prayers they faced toward Jerusalem and the Temple.

During the Exile, if not before, the institution of the synagogue came into being. The services of the synagogue were centered about the reading and exposition of the Scriptures. The lections (which consisted of readings from the Law and from the Prophets, and possibly also from Wisdom literature) were in different times and places probably chosen according to one or another of three systems: (1) the synagogue ruler's discretion; (2) "in course" readings *(lectio continua);* or (3) a fixed lectionary. The *shema*, Psalms, and prayers ("benedictions") also came to be included as a regular part of the synagogue service. By the first century the synagogue Liturgy of the Word was made use of on at least some week days as well as immediately prior to the Sabbath Meal.[10]

The early Christians rejected the Temple with its sacrificial worship, performed by a Levitical priesthood, for this had been fulfilled in Christ—the Temple, the one Priest, the one Sacrifice (See Hebrews).

They retained the practice of marking periods of the day with private prayer ("pray without ceasing").

The early Christians apparently attended or participated in the synagogue services so long as they were available, interpreting the Psalms and Scriptures as fulfilled in Christ. Where this was not possible, they apparently imitated the synagogue services, with Liturgies of the Word which included the reading of Christian writings in addition to the Old Testament lections, and with prayer in the Name of the Lord Jesus.[11]

The Liturgical Week—The basic unit of time in the Jewish ritual pattern was the seven-day week. Genesis 1 indicates a liturgical significance associated with each of the days. Mondays and Thursdays were days for private fasting, and sometimes for public fasts. Sundays, Wednesdays, and Fridays were days of particular liturgical significance, and in the Priestly documents these days seem to be associated with particular types of events. In the Temple liturgy particular Psalms were associated with particular days of the week. Basic to the liturgical week was the Sabbath. To be a Jew was to be a man who kept the Sabbath, the day of rest, the day which symbolized the covenant and circumcision.[12]

The high point of the Jewish week was the Sabbath Meal, the pattern of which was also followed in such other meals as the annual Passover Meal (which had certain peculiarities of its own) and *chabûrah* meals which were shared by groups bound together by special intentions or vows.

Having come into the home from the synagogue Liturgy of the Word, the group participants possibly performed ritual ablutions and then shared conversation over wine (over which sometimes a blessing was said), prior to being called to the table. Assembling at the table, God was blessed (or thanked) over the bread, "Blessed be God, King of the universe, who brings forth bread from the earth." The bread was then broken and distributed. This provided the utensil with which to eat, somewhat like the bread under a pizza. To break bread was to eat together, to share one loaf. Though at Passover unleavened bread was used, leavened bread was the norm for these religious meals. After the meal, which might have been accompanied with wine, the lamp was brought in and blessed, and then there came the blessing over the cup. The poor seldom had wine, but all made use of wine for such occasions. To participate in this was to express one's credo, to be bound together with those with whom the cup was shared, to symbolize one's heritage and hopes (*anamnesis* and *prolepsis*), to reaffirm one's commitment. The wine was blessed by blessing God. To *bless* in Hebrew thought equals to *thank*, to name the Name of God. The forms of the blessings (*berakoth*) varied with the different days of the Jewish Year. At the climax of the meal the *pater familias* called upon the group to stand ("Lift up your hearts"), and he asked permission to give thanks in their name ("Let us give thanks unto our Lord God"). He then proceeded to bless God, as Creator, Sustainer, Redeemer, in terms of the particular day or occasion. He then prayed for the community of Israel, typically in petitions which had an eschatological thrust. The third paragraph of the following typical form is thought to go back to the second century B.C., while the first two are possibly older still.

> Blessed be God, King of the universe, who feeds the world with goodness, with grace and mercy, who gives food to all flesh, for you nourish and sustain all beings and provide food for all your creatures. Blessed be God, who gives food unto all.

> We thank you, Lord our God, for a desirable, good and ample land which you were pleased to give to our fathers, and for your covenant which you marked in our flesh, and for the Torah which you have given us, and for life, grace, mercy and food which you have bestowed upon us in every season. For all this, Lord our God, we thank you and bless your name. Blessed be your name upon us continually and forever. Blessed be God for the land and for the food.

> Have mercy, Lord our God, upon your people Israel, upon your city Jerusalem, upon Zion, the abiding place of your glory, upon the kingdom of the house of David your anointed, and upon the great and holy house that was called by your name. Feed us, nourish us, sustain us, provide for us, relieve us speedily from our anxieties, and let us not stand in need of the gifts of mortals, for their gifts are small and their reproach

is great, for we have trusted in your holy, great and fearful name. And may Elijah and the Messiah, the son of David come in our lifetime, and may the kingdom of the house of David return to its place. And may you reign over us, you alone, and save us for your name's sake, and bring us up in it and gladden us in it and comfort us in Zion your city. [A *festal insertion:* Our God, the God of our fathers, may the remembrance of ourselves and of our fathers, and the remembrance of Jerusalem your city, and the remembrance of the Messiah, the son of David, your servant, and the remembrance of your people, the whole house of Israel, arise and come, come to pass, be seen and accepted and heard, be remembered and be mentioned before you for deliverance, for good, for grace, for loving kindness and for mercy on this . . . day. Remember us, Lord our God, on it for good, and visit us on it for blessing, and save us on it unto life. And a salutary word and compassion grant us, and have mercy on us and save us, for to you we look, for you are, God, a gracious and merciful king.] Blessed be God who rebuilds Jerusalem.[13]

The early Christians retained from the Jews, as the basic unit of time in the ritual pattern, the seven-day week. Though Jesus had given warnings concerning the possible abuse of fasting, He Himself fasted, and the practice was continued in the early Church. It was soon, apparently, to become dissociated from Mondays and Thursdays. As the Jewish week was organized about the Sabbath, the Christian week was organized about the first day of the week —the day of creation, the day of light, the day of Pentecost —which was also called the Lord's Day—a phrase with eschatological implications from Old Testament times, the day of the Resurrection of Jesus Christ and of the outpouring of the Holy Spirit. In the New Testament two things in particular are linked with the first day of the week: (1) the putting aside of money (which was not a matter of convenience, for early Christians were not paid according to a seven-day week pattern), and (2) the gathering of the community for their Sacred Meal.[14]

Undoubtedly Jesus had shared many sacred meals with His disciples. John 6 (the story of the feeding of the five thousand) contains some of the technical liturgical terms associated with such meals. One of the occasions on which Jesus and the disciples gathered for such a meal was immediately prior to the Arrest and the Crucifixion. (Was this a Passover Meal? Evidence is conflicting. The Synoptics say it was; the Johannine Gospel says that it was not. Efforts have been made to reconcile the two views by saying that it was an anticipated Passover or that it was a Passover celebrated according to the Calendar of the Book of Jubilees.) The procedure on that occasion was evidently that which would have been used by any good Jew in presiding over such a meal. The things that were new were the words of administration associated with the Bread and the Wine: "This is My Body" and "This is My Blood." What Jesus did was to add one more dimension to an old rite.[15]

The Resurrection appearances generally have connotations of sacred meals. The early disciples did continue to gather as a family for sacred meals, and when they broke bread together they did remember Jesus, He was present with them. They probably continued the Jewish ritual, using forms of prayer appropriate to the day or occasion. They did shift the time from the Sabbath (the day which spoke of the completion of Creation, of the old Covenant, of circumcision, of the bondage of the Law, of the approach of death) to the first day of the week, the Lord's Day (the day which spoke of Creation, of Light, of the Resurrection of Jesus Christ, of the new Covenant, of the outpouring of the Holy Spirit, of the freedom of the sons of God, of the eschaton). The day and the rite reinforced each other. Were the early gatherings for the Breaking of Bread a continuation of the Resurrection Meals or commemorations of the Last Supper? At a relatively early stage they certainly came to bear the weight of both interpretations, and whether the Last Supper was in fact a Passover Meal or not, it soon came to have Passover connotations for the early Christians.[16]

Before the end of the New Testament period, due to the practical difficulties of accommodating greater numbers of persons in a home, because of abuses which were sometimes associated with the meal, and because of a need for brevity in times of persecution, the seven-action shape of the sacred meal ([1] taking bread; [2] thanking God; [3] breaking the bread; and [4] giving the bread—prior to the meal; [5] taking wine; [6] thanking God; and [7] giving the wine—after the meal) was reduced to a four-action shape ([1] taking bread and wine; [2] thanking God over bread and wine; [3] breaking the bread; and [4] giving the bread and wine) apart from the meal, which in some places developed into an *agape*.[17]

The Liturgical Year—There is no doubt about the fact that within the New Testament we find the beginnings of the development of a weekly liturgical cycle. Some authors also find within the New Testament the beginnings of a yearly cycle.

Basic to the Jewish liturgical year were three Pilgrimage Feasts, the origins of which may have been agricultural: Passover (possibly associated with the new flock); Pentecost (the wheat harvest); and Tabernacles (the new wine).

The Passover commemorated the slaying of the first-born, the Exodus from Egypt, the entry into the Promised Land. High points of its celebration were the slaying and partaking of the Passover Lamb, the use of unleavened bread, and the special Passover Cup. The early Church found the fulfillment of the old feast in the event of Jesus Christ. (Hymns 89, 92, and 95 of *The Hymnal 1940* build upon this imagery.) In almost every language except English the same word is used for the Jewish Passover and the Christian Easter. Some authors find the feast (re-interpreted) being celebrated within New Testament times and associated with baptisms, with all of the imagery of the Jewish Passover being brought into play—Exodus, Passover, entrance into the Promised Land, etc.[18]

The offering of barley after the Passover celebration inaugurated the seven weeks of harvest which culminated in the feast of Pentecost, at which the giving of the Law and the Covenant with Israel were commemorated. Acts 2 associates with Pentecost the outpouring of the Holy Spirit, baptism, and the mission of the new community to all nations.

The third of the Pilgrimage Feasts was Tabernacles or Booths. It was associated with ingathering, the new wine, dwelling in booths or huts in the wilderness, choice of the House of David, choice of Jerusalem as God's dwelling place, and the dedication of the Temple. Dancing, palm branches, and torches were used in the celebration of this feast. Some commentators have found correspondences between this feast and the events of the early chapters of the Johannine Gospel and have seen a continuation of this feast (re-interpreted) in the Advent-Epiphany cycle of the Church Year. Certainly what the booths, the city of Jerusalem, the House of David, and the Temple meant in the life of Judaism was proclaimed as fulfilled in the Incarnation.

Music—The services of the Temple and of the synagogue contained musical elements, exclamations, responses, or refrains. In the Psalter we have the hymnbook of Judaism. Certain Psalms were associated with certain days and occasions. The Hallel (Psalms 113–118) was sung on the great feasts. The Songs of Ascent (Psalms 120–134) were sung by those who came up to Jerusalem for the Pilgrimage Feasts. Other Psalms were associated with particular lections in the worship of the Temple, the synagogue, or the home.[19]

New Testament writers refer to the use of Psalms, hymns, and spiritual songs. Responses, refrains, and exclamations such as those used in Jewish worship continued to be used, along with the Psalter. We have in the New Testament several examples of a Christian hymnody (for example, the Magnificat, Benedictus, and Nunc dimittis [Luke 1:46–55, 68–79; 2:29–32]; Rom. 8:37–39; 11: 33–36; Eph. 5:14; Phil. 2:6–11; I Tim. 3:16; 6:15–16; II Tim. 2:11–13; Titus 3:4–7; I Peter 3:18–20; Rev. 15:3–4 [The Song of the Redeemed]).

THE SANCTIFICATION OF SPACE

For the Jews, the Temple in Jerusalem was the sanctuary, the religious center of the nation. It was the place where sacrifice was offered by the priests. It was God's dwelling, the place of God's presence. It was the creation, the "center of the world." It was modeled after a heavenly original. It was a sign of God's election. It was a place of pilgrimage.[20]

The religious life of the neighborhood centered about the synagogue, the gathering place. These buildings, constructed for Liturgies of the Word, were oriented toward Jerusalem and the Temple. The courtyard apparently contained a place for ablutions. The building itself contained an Ark for the scrolls of the Torah at one end, toward which people turned when they prayed, and a *bema* or platform (with a stand for reading and a seat for preaching) in the center, toward which people turned for the reading and exposition of the Word.

The sacred meals were typically eaten within the home, about the family table. Certain utensils were typically reserved for use in connection with these particular meals.

The early church rejected the Temple, for Jesus had made the one sacrifice which fulfilled all that the Temple, with its priesthood and sacrifices, had represented within Judaism. They refused to sanctify *one* place because of their conviction that God could be found and worshiped everywhere (John 4:21–23; Rev. 21; Heb. 4:14–16; 10:19–25), and they accepted the sanctification of many places—meeting places in various towns, homes of believers, even places where some significant event had taken place, as Caesarea Philippi, Gethsemane, the Upper Room.

CHAPTER **III**

THE PERIOD OF THE CHURCH ORDERS

When the church moved further away from its Jewish roots and had to adapt itself to the languages, culture, and thought of the Gentile world, it developed a type of book which contained more explicit descriptions of the various liturgies and directions for their conduct, the *Church Orders*, which are the principal sources of knowledge of the liturgy from the second through the fourth centuries.

The Church Orders are manuals for the administration of a church, for teaching and discipline as well as for the conduct of public worship. The most important of the Church Orders are the *Didache*, an Eastern document probably of the early second century;[1] the *Apostolic Tradition* of Hippolytus, which probably originated in Rome c. 215 A.D.;[2] the *Didascalia*, a third century Syrian document;[3] and the *Apos-*

tolic Constitutions, a Syrian document of the late fourth century which used the first three of these Church Orders as sources.[4] The *Didache* is composed of a section of catechetical instruction (1–6) and directions concerning Baptism (7), fasting and daily prayer (8), the Eucharist (9–10), various ministries (11–13), the Lord's Day (14), bishops and deacons and penance (15), concluding with an eschatological section (16). The *Apostolic Tradition* gives instructions on the ministry and ordinations (2–15), initiation (16–23), fasting (25), the *agape* (26–27), the offering of first-fruits (28), fasting (29), visiting the sick (30), the daily services (33), the cemetery (34), and private devotions (35–37). The *Didascalia* and the *Apostolic Constitutions* are bulkier, but they are similar in outline and content.

Other sources of knowledge of the liturgies of the period include (1) the Apostolic Fathers, especially I Clement, Ignatius, Barnabas, the Shepherd of Hermas, and the Martyrdom of Polycarp;[5] (2) the New Testament Apocrypha, especially the Acts of John (2d century) and the Acts of Thomas (3d century);[6] (3) the Christian Apologists, especially the First Apology of Justin Martyr 61-67;[7] and (4) the early Fathers—Irenaeus, Tertullian, Clement, Origen, Cyprian.[8]

The principal issue of the period liturgically was the maintaining of the integrity of the Christian faith while reinterpreting and remolding the liturgy in terms of the languages, the cultural differences, the philosophies, and the religious backgrounds of the people of the Greco-Roman world.

THE SANCTIFICATION OF LIFE

Initiation—Typical of the initiations of the Mystery Religions of the period was that of one of the most popular, Mithraism. The initiate was admitted as a candidate, given instruction, subjected to trials (fasting, acts of humility, immersion, etc.), sealed on the forehead as a soldier of Mithras, given honey (the food of new babes), given the right hand of fellowship, and fed a meal of bread and of wine mixed with water.[9]

The fullest description of a Christian initiation of the period is that of the *Apostolic Tradition* 16–23. Converts who wished to be admitted as hearers (*catechumens*) were brought to the teachers for examination by persons who could vouch for them (sponsors). If the person was not judged sane, or if his occupation and his manner of life were not satisfactory, his admission was postponed.

> Let those who present themselves for the first time for the hearing of the word be first brought to the teachers before all the people enter, and let them be asked the reason why they accede to the faith. And those who bring them shall testify that they are capable of hearing the word. And they shall be questioned about their state of life: has he a wife or is he a slave? If he is a slave of one of the faithful, and his master permits him, let him hear the word. If his master does not give him a good testimony, let him be rejected.

> If his master is a pagan, let him be taught to please his master that there be no scandal. If a man has a wife or a woman a husband, let them be taught to content themselves, the man with his wife, the woman with her husband. If a man does not live with a wife, let him be taught not to fornicate, but to take a legal wife or remain as he is. If one is possessed of demons, he is not to hear the word of teaching until he is cleansed.

> Inquiry should be made about the trades and professions of those who present themselves for instruction. If one is a pimp who supports whores, let him cease or be rejected. If one is a sculptor or painter, he must be instructed not to make idols; if he will not cease, let him be rejected. If one is an actor or pantomimist, let him cease or be rejected. If one teaches small children, it is better that he cease; but if he has no other livelihood, he may be permitted to teach. A charioteer, or one who races or frequents races must either cease or be rejected. If one is a gladiator or if one teaches gladiators to fight, or if one is a huntsman in the wild beast shows, or a public official who is connected with the gladiatorial shows, let him cease or be rejected. A soldier with authority must not kill people. If he is commanded, he must refuse, and he must not take an oath. If he will not agree, he must be rejected. Those who have the

power of the sword, or a civil magistrate who wears the purple, must cease or be rejected. If a catechumen, or one of the faithful, wishes to become a soldier, let him be rejected, for he has despised God. A harlot or licentious man or sodomite, or one who does things which are not to be mentioned, are to be rejected, for they are impure. A magician is not to be brought for examination. One who does incantations or an astrologer or a diviner or an interpreter of dreams or a charlatan or a maker of amulets must cease or be rejected. A concubine may become a hearer if she is a slave and has reared her children and been faithful to her master alone; otherwise, let her be rejected. If a man has a concubine he must cease and marry legally; if he will not, let him be rejected.

Those admitted as hearers entered into a three-year period of instruction, attending services which consisted of readings, instruction, and prayers. These rites were concluded with a laying-on-of-hands by the teacher.

The catechumens remain three years as hearers of the word. However, if one is zealous and applies himself well to these things, it is not the time but the conduct alone which is decisive.

When the teacher has finished giving instruction the catechumens are to pray alone, separate from the faithful. . . . And when they have finished praying, they are not given the peace, for their kiss is not yet holy. Only the faithful kiss each other, men with men and women with women; the men do not kiss the women. . . .

After the prayers the teacher imposes a hand over the catechumens, and he prays and dismisses them. Whoever does the teaching is to do this, whether a clergyman or a layman.

If a catechumen is apprehended for the name of the Lord, let him not be of two minds about witnessing. If he is treated violently and killed before his sins have been forgiven, he shall yet be justified for he will have received baptism in his blood.

After three years, those who had proved themselves by their sober lives, their good works, and their appropriation of the Old Testament heritage were admitted several weeks before Easter as candidates (*competentes*, elect) and entered into a period of instruction in the Gospel and of daily exorcisms. The last of the exorcisms were performed by the bishop himself and partook of the nature of ordeals. The baptism of those whose reactions were not of the right sort was postponed.

> When those are chosen who are to be set apart for baptism, their lives are to be examined. Have they lived honestly during the time they were catechumens? Have they honored the widows, visited the sick, done all sorts of good things? If those who sponsor them testify that they have done these things, let them hear the Gospel.

> From the time that they are separated, let a hand be laid on them daily for exorcism. When the day approaches on which they are to be baptized, the bishop exorcises each one of them that he may know if he is pure. If any of them is not good or not pure, let him be put aside, for he did not hear the word in faith, for it is impossible that the alien always be hidden.

The candidates bathed on the Thursday and fasted on the Friday and Saturday immediately prior to the baptism. On Saturday the bishop performed the final exorcism and then breathed in the faces of the candidates and sealed the bodily openings so that the devil might not re-enter.

> Those who are to be baptized are to be instructed to wash and cleanse themselves on Thursday. If a woman is menstruating, she shall be put aside and baptized another day. Those who are receiving baptism are to fast on Friday; and on Saturday those who are receiving baptism are to be brought together in one place by the bishop. He shall bid them all to pray and bend the knee. And laying his hand on them, he shall exorcise every alien spirit that they flee from them and never return to them again. And when he has finished exorcising, he shall breathe in their faces, and when he has signed their foreheads, ears, and noses, he shall raise them up.

Saturday night was spent in vigil, listening to readings and instructions.

They shall spend all that night in vigil, in reading and instruction. Those being baptized shall not bring any other vessel than that which each will bring for the Eucharist. It is right that those deemed worthy offer an oblation at this time.

At cockcrow prayer was made over the water. (The Fathers compared the water of baptism to the primordial waters, the water of the grave, the Red Sea, the water from the Rock, that in which Naaman was immersed, the water of the womb of Mary, the River Jordan, the living water promised the woman at the well in Samaria, the Pool of Bethsaida, the water from the side of Christ, and the waters of Paradise.) The water was to be cold and to flow through the tank or to pour into it from above. The bishop also set apart two oils—exorcising the "oil of exorcism" and giving thanks over the "oil of thanksgiving." The candidates removed all clothing and jewelry. They individually renounced "Satan, all his servants, and all his works"—a renunciation not just of sins but of their former way of life. The presbyter then anointed the candidate all over with the oil of exorcism (compare the anointing which was the application of soap before a bath; the oiling of the fighter before he entered the arena), and said, "Let all spirits depart far from you."

At the time when the cock crows, prayer shall first be made over the water. The water should flow into the fountain or pour from above, unless there is a necessity (constant or sudden); in that case use what water can be found. They shall remove their clothes. And first baptize the small children. Let those who can, speak for themselves. If they are not able to speak for themselves, let their parents speak for them, or some others from their family. Next baptize the men, and last of all the women who shall have loosened their hair and removed all gold and silver ornaments which they were wearing; and let nothing alien go down into the water.

At the time set for the baptizing, the bishop shall give thanks over oil and put it in a vessel; this oil is called "the oil of thanksgiving." And he shall take other oil and exorcise it; this oil is called "the oil of exorcism." Let a deacon take the oil of exorcism and station himself at the left hand of a presbyter, and let another deacon take the oil of thanksgiving and station himself at the right hand of the presbyter. And when the presbyter takes hold of each of those receiving baptism, let him command him to renounce, saying, "I renounce you, Satan, and all your servants, and all your works." And after each one has renounced, he shall anoint him with the oil of exorcism, saying to him, "Let all spirits depart far from you."

A deacon then took the candidate into the water, where the baptizing was done by a presbyter (or bishop). The presbyter asked the candidate, "Do you believe in God, the Father Almighty?" The candidate answered, "I believe." The presbyter then, with his hands on the candidate's head, pushed him down into the water. The presbyter next asked, "Do you believe in Jesus Christ, the Son of God, who was born of the Holy Spirit from the Virgin Mary, and was crucified under Pontius Pilate, and was dead and buried, and rose again the third day, alive from the dead, and ascended into heaven, and sat at the right hand of the Father, and will come to judge the living and the dead?" The one being baptized answered, "I believe." The presbyter pushed him a second time into the water. The presbyter then asked, "Do you believe in the Holy Spirit, and the holy church, and the resurrection of the flesh?" The one being baptized answered, "I believe." (The Christian creeds grew out of such baptismal forms.) Having thus made his saving confession of faith, the person was pushed down into the water for the third time. Coming out of the water, he was anointed fully by the presbyter with the oil of thanksgiving (compare the perfumed oil used after a Roman bath; the first bath of a baby, which was with oil; the anointing of priests and kings), as the presbyter said, "I anoint you with holy oil in the name of Jesus the Anointed One." The newly-baptized then clothed themselves (possibly in new white robes) and were led back into the congregation where they were presented to the bishop (compare the Roman custom of the mid-wife taking the new-born child to the father who was seated at the family table for his public recognition of the child as a member of the family). The bishop then recognized publicly before the congregation the fact of the baptism by a token repetition of the laying-on-of-hands of the presbyter in the act of baptizing the candidate and of the anointing with the oil of thanksgiving (compare the giving of a diploma as the public recognition of something which had been completed more privately). The bishop then signed the newly-baptized person on the forehead (possibly with a *Taw* [compare the tattoo of sheep, slaves, and soldiers]).

> And each one, having dried himself, is clothed and then is led into the assembly. Then the bishop, imposing his hand, prays, saying, "Lord God, who made these worthy of the forgiveness of their sins through the laver of regeneration of the Holy Spirit, send into them your grace, that they may serve you according to your will; for to you is glory, Father and Son with the Holy Spirit, in the holy church, both now and unto the ages of ages. Amen." Then pouring the oil of thanksgiving from the hand and imposing it on the forehead, he shall say, "I anoint you with holy oil in the name of the Father Almighty and Jesus the Anointed One and the Holy Spirit." And signing [sealing] him on the forehead, he gives a kiss, and shall say, "The Lord be with you." And he who is signed shall say, "And with your spirit." This is done to each one.

The newly-baptized then for the first time joined in prayer with the faithful (possibly praying "Our Father" for the first time). This was followed by the Kiss of Peace—an opportunity for congratulations, for welcoming into the Christian family.

> And immediately afterwards they pray with all the people, but they do not pray with the faithful until all these things have been completed. And when they have prayed, they are given the Kiss of Peace.

The Kiss of Peace led into the offertory, for which those baptized brought oblations. At this first Eucharist, in addition to the Bread and the chalice of Wine mixed with water, over which thanks was given, the newly-baptized drank also from a cup of water (to get the baptism inside) and from a cup of milk and honey (the food of babes, the Promised Land).

> And then the offering is brought by the deacons to the bishop and he gives thanks over the bread for an *exemplum* [that is, *copy, that which illustrates*], or as the Greeks say, "antitype," of the body of Christ; the cup of mixed wine for an "antitype," or as the Greeks say, "similitude," of the Blood which was poured out for all who believe in him; and milk and honey mixed for the fulfillment of the promise which was made to the fathers when he spoke of a land flowing with milk and honey, in which way Christ gave also his flesh, by which those who believe are nourished like small children, the sweetness of the word making sweet bitterness of heart; and water into an offering indicating the washing, that also the interior of man, which is the soul, may receive the same effects as the body.

> The bishop shall give the reason for all these things to those who receive. When he breaks the Bread, in distributing to each a part he shall say, "The Bread of heaven in Christ Jesus." And he who receives shall respond, "Amen." And presbyters shall hold the cups—and if there are not enough of them, deacons also—and they shall stand by reverently and modestly; first he who holds the water, second the milk, third the wine. And those who receive shall drink from each three times. He who gives shall say, "In God the Father Almighty," and he who receives shall say, "Amen," "And the Lord Jesus Christ," [and he shall say, "Amen,"] "And the Holy Spirit and the holy church," and he shall say, "Amen." This shall be done to each one.

Because of the *disciplina arcani* (the discipline of secrecy), it was not until after participation in these rites that their meanings were explained to the initiates. The whole initiation experience was so traumatic that those who went through it felt that they had died and been raised up, that they had been reborn, that the ones with whom they had most in common were those who had gone through this same initiation. An old baptistry inscription reads, "Nothing can separate those who are reborn. They are one: one baptism, one Spirit, one faith, one God and Father."

The Hippolytan rite can be taken as typical of the period, though the different accounts vary in various details.[10] Some, for example, give no account of any action between the immersion and the praying with the congregation or the Eucharist. Having two anointings after the baptism seems to be a Roman peculiarity. Texts or writers, speaking homiletically, attribute various effects to various aspects of the rites, but these aspects do differ from rite to rite, and various texts point out that the use of water suffices when various other ceremonies are missing.[11]

Penance—The fullest descriptions we have of the rites of excommunication and reinstatement from this period are those of Tertullian (*De poenitentia* 9) and of the *Didascalia* 5–7. The liturgy of penance was divided into three stages: (1) the *excommunication* or *imposition of penance*, of which we may have a relic in Acts of John 84, where an anathema is set within the context of the Eucharist prior to the Liturgy of the Table; (2) the *exomologesis* or *acts of penitence*, which included sackcloth and ashes, fasting and prayer, intercession of the faithful, and dismissal from the public services (with prayer and laying-on-of-hands) prior to Communion; and (3) the *absolution* or *reinstatement*, over which the bishop normally presided and which normally consisted of prayer and the laying-on-of-hands and readmission to the Eucharist. Such readmissions presumably were normally associated with the Easter Vigil, though a dying penitent was not denied the Eucharist.[12]

Marriage—The rites of marriage among the pagan Romans began with a rite of *betrothal* at the home of the bride in which a contract was signed before witnesses. The man offered a betrothal present or *arrhae*, gave the woman a kiss and placed a ring on the fourth finger of her left hand, and then the hands of the two were joined. A banquet generally followed. Some time elapsed before the *wedding*. On the day of the wedding the bride dedicated the clothing and playthings of her youth to the gods and was arrayed in her wedding clothes, which included a girdle (symbol of virginity), a flame-colored veil, and a floral crown. The bride and groom made a solemn declaration before witnesses, after which the *pronuba* (representing Juno, the goddess of marriage) joined their hands. They offered sacrifice at the family altar. The *auspex nuptiarum* recited a prayer which was repeated by the couple as they processed around the altar. At some point in the rite a veil or pall was held over the couple. A banquet followed. At nightfall the bride was led to her new home, where she anointed the doorposts and was carried over the threshold by her husband. Together they lit the hearthfire, and she was sprinkled with water. The *pronuba* prepared the marriage bed, and the couple went through rites of loosening the girdle and praying to the gods of marriage. On the following day, the bride received her new relatives and sacrificed to the gods of her new home.[13]

The incidental references to marriage in the Church Fathers would indicate that the rites were not radically different among the Christians, except for indications of the consent of the bishop and possibly his attendance and participation in some marriages and the substitution of Christian prayers or blessings for pagan ones and of the Eucharist for pagan sacrifices.

Pregnancy and Childbirth—There is no documentation from this period concerning rites which might have been connected with pregnancies or childbirth. Probably local customs were continued with some adaptations.

Ordination—Out of the effort to maintain the tradition, combating various heresies, the pattern of special offices or ministries within the priestly body of the church became more clear-cut. Though various other orders—confessors, widows (or "presbyteresses"), readers, virgins (or "deaconesses"), subdeacons, and healers—were appointed or recognized for their gifts, three orders—bishops, presbyters, and deacons—were set apart by ordination.[14] The right to perform various functions became more and more limited to certain orders. Though, for example, the bishop was considered the normal officiant at the Eucharist, legislation of the fourth century forbade anyone below the rank of presbyter to substitute for the bishop in this function.

In the *Apostolic Tradition* 2–15 we have the prototype

for ordinations in the early church. The *bishop* was chosen by the people as the one among them who best personified the continuity, the succession, the tradition. On a Sunday, presumably after the Liturgy of the Word, the bishops who were present laid hands upon him while the presbyters stood around and all the people prayed in silence. One of the bishops then laid his hands upon him and said a prayer, in which the office of a bishop is depicted as that of a Christian patriarch and that of the high priest within the priestly body.

> God and Father of our Lord Jesus Christ, Father of mercies and God of all comforts, who dwellest in the heights and hast respect to the lowly, who knowest all things before they come to be, thou who hast set bounds within the Church through the word of thy grace, preordaining from the beginning the race of the just people of Abraham, establishing princes and priests and not leaving thy sanctuary without a ministry, thou since the beginning of the world hast had pleasure among those whom thou hast chosen to be given. Pour forth now that power which is from thee, the princely Spirit, which thou gavest to thy beloved Son, Jesus Christ, which he gave to the holy Apostles, who established in every place the Church, thy hallowing, to the glory and unceasing praise of thy name.
>
> Father who knowest the heart, grant to this thy servant, whom thou hast chosen for a bishopric, to feed thy holy flock; and to exercise high priesthood for thee without rebuke, serving night and day, to propitiate thy countenance unceasingly and to offer the holy gifts of thy Church; by the Spirit of high priesthood to have the power to remit sins according to thy commandment; to give lots according to thy direction; to loose also every bond according to the power which thou gavest to the Apostles; to please thee, too, by gentleness and a pure heart, offering to thee an odour of sweet savour, through thy Child [*or* Servant] Jesus Christ, through whom be glory and power and honour to thee, to Father and Son with the Holy Spirit, both now and world without end. Amen. (See note 14.)

After the prayer, all offered the new bishop the Kiss of Peace, and he then presided with his presbyters at the Liturgy of the Table. A *presbyter* was ordained in much the same manner, with hands being laid upon him by the bishop

and the other presbyters among whom he would be an asso-
ciate and with a prayer in which the office of the presbyters
is depicted as that of successors to the Jewish elders whose
collegial duty is to "sustain and govern" the people:

> God the Father of our Lord Jesus Christ, look down upon
> this thy servant and impart to him the Spirit of grace and
> counsel for presbyters, so that he may support and govern thy
> people with a pure heart, as thou didst look down upon the
> people of thy choice and didst command Moses that he select
> presbyters [i.e. elders] whom thou didst fill with thy Spirit
> which thou didst give to thy servant [i.e. to Moses].

> And now, O Lord, grant that the Spirit of thy grace may
> without fail be preserved among us, and make us worthy, in
> believing, to minister to thee, praising thee in simplicity of
> heart; through thy Child [or Servant] Christ Jesus, through
> whom be glory and power to thee, to Father and Son with the
> Holy Spirit in the holy Church, both now and world without
> end. Amen. (See note 14.)

At the ordination of a *deacon*, hands were to be laid
upon him only by the bishop, for the deacon is the assistant
or servant of the bishop, under his authority (compare the
"herald" of cultic rites), and the prayer depicts the deacon's
ministry in this manner:

> God who hast created all things and set them in order by
> thy Word, O Father of our Lord Jesus Christ, whom thou sent-
> est to minister thy will and to make known to us thy desire,
> give the Holy Spirit of grace and care and diligence to this thy
> servant, whom thou has chosen to minister to thy Church and
> to bring forward [in thy holy of holies the gifts which are of-
> fered to thee by thine appointed high priests, so that serving
> blamelessly and with a pure heart, he may be counted worthy
> of this high office and glorify thee through thy Servant Jesus
> Christ; through whom . . .] (See note 14.)

Sick Rites—The *Apostolic Tradition* 5 and 30 contains
two notes concerning ministry to the sick: the bishop is to
be informed of sickness so that he may visit, and a form is
provided for giving thanks when oil is offered at the Eucharist. This form is a prayer for health for those who "use" or

"partake of" the oil. The oil was possibly offered with the bread and wine, blessed at the Eucharistic Thanksgiving, and then returned to the offerer for his use. Similar forms of the period provided for the blessing of water or bread as well as oil. In these cases the substance was probably self-adminis-tered. There are also many accounts from this period of a clergyman or a layman with gifts of healing visiting a sick person, praying, and then anointing him with oil. In this period the Eucharistic Bread (and Wine?) were often carried from the service to those not able to be present.[15]

Burial—Pagan burial customs of the time included the *viaticum* (the last meal for the dead, or the coin for Charon, the ferryman, who was to carry the dead across the river Styx); the final kiss; the arranging, washing, anointing, and clothing of the body; the procession to the grave with torches, lamentations, dirges, and mourners dressed in black; the (cremation and) burial of the remains; the cere-mony of departure (*vale*) and the funeral oration; and commemorations at certain intervals. A wake was normal, though in some areas it preceded the burial, whereas in other areas the burial was normally on the day of death and the wake followed the burial and was held at the grave.[16]

The early Christians substituted Communion for the *via-ticum*. The use of torches in the procession was rejected because of their associations with the Emperor Cult. The singing of Psalms, hymns, and Alleluias was substituted for the lamentations and dirges. The Church Fathers inveighed against the use of black. Cremation was rejected. Psalms and hymns and prayers were substituted for the *vale*. The ceremonies at the grave were apparently in some places con-cluded with the Eucharist, and commemoration was made by offering the Eucharist at certain intervals.

THE SANCTIFICATION OF TIME

The Liturgical Day—At least in some places within this period the day was marked liturgically with morning and evening services. The *morning service* was a Liturgy of the

Word which consisted of readings, instruction, and prayers, and it possibly included the laying-on-of-hands and the Kiss of Peace. The clergy and those of the laity who could were expected to be present for this daily service. Those laity who could not be present were expected to study the Scriptures and to pray at this time at home.[17]

The *evening service*, which included Psalmody, prayers, and (at least on occasion) readings, was often introduced by a blessing of light (*lucernarium*) and was sometimes associated with an *agape*.

In addition to the public services (or private devotions at times corresponding to them), other times of the day were to be marked by private prayer. The *third*, *sixth*, and *ninth hours*, which had been associated with private prayer in Judaism and which marked divisions of the Roman day, were associated with events of the Passion. To these times two others were added—*midnight* and *cockcrow*. Midnight was associated with the praise of God by all creation and with the expectation of Christ's return; cockcrow, with the Jews' denial of Christ and with the hope of resurrection. Frequent devotional use was made of the sign of the cross on the forehead (reminiscent of baptism).[18]

The Liturgical Week—The liturgical week was organized around the day known as the First Day or the Lord's Day, and also known as "the Eighth Day." Eight is the number which transcends seven, which represents the breaking of the closed cycle symbolized by seven; the number which symbolizes redemption, baptism; which symbolizes the New Age, the *kairos*, the fulfillment of time, the Eschaton. The structure of the liturgical week was based upon looking back to the First Day (Creation, Light, Resurrection, Pentecost) and looking forward to the Eighth Day (*kairos*, redemption, the Eschaton).[19]

The Eucharist—The rite which expressed the meaning of Sunday, the rite toward which the week day Liturgies of the Word and private devotions, rites of *chronos*, pointed was the Sunday liturgy of *kairos*, the Eucharistic Feast. The week was organized around the Sunday Eucharist.[20]

Those who could not attend liturgies of the Word (*Pro-Anaphora, Synaxis*, Liturgy of the Catechumens) on week days came on Sundays. The liturgy began with Old Testament lections, sometimes apparently taken from the Jewish synagogue lectionary, or, in other places, apparently read "in course" or according to the choices of the presiding officer. The Old Testament lections were followed by Psalmody and then by readings from Christian writings. (Those lections which found a regular place in liturgical usage eventually became the New Testament Canon.) The lessons were read by a lector or reader from a reading stand, and they were followed by a sermon by the presiding officer, who was seated in his chair. After the sermon the catechumens were dismissed (apparently in some places with a special prayer or blessing). Next came the intercessory prayers or "Prayers of the Faithful," led by a deacon. The Liturgy of the Word was concluded with the Kiss of Peace. On week days the service normally ended at this point, and the congregation departed in an informal manner.

On Sundays the rite continued with the Liturgy of the Table (*Anaphora*, Liturgy of the Faithful). A cloth was spread over a small table, which in some places was apparently not brought into the room or moved into a prominent position until this point in the rite. The deacon then apparently moved among the faithful and received the offerings of bread and wine which they had brought with them. A sufficient quantity for the celebration was selected and placed upon the Table, and the remainder was put to one side for the use of the clergy and for distribution among the poor. The presiding officer and his assisting presbyters then gathered around the Table and laid their hands upon the bread and wine (an ancient sign of offering, of identification, of transfer) over which thanks was to be given while they and the people stood with hands raised (the "orans" position).

The presiding officer then led the Great Thanksgiving, the text of which was not fixed. We have several prayers or fragments of prayers which date back to this period.[21] Among them are prayers of thanksgiving, prayers for the communicants, prayers which name the Name of God over the elements, and prayers which call for the descent of the Spirit (*epiclesis*). Some are more reminiscent of Jewish blessings, while others seem to have taken in elements from prayers associated with the Mystery Religions. A prayer from the Acts of John 109 is made use of in the Ethiopian Anaphora of St. John the Evangelist, and one from the Acts of Thomas 49-50 is incorporated in a Eucharistic Prayer which is found in a seventh century Irish palimpsest. The prayer from this period which was to have the greatest influence upon later liturgies, however, is that associated with the ordination of bishops in the *Apostolic Tradition* 4. This prayer, after the Sursum corda (the opening dialogue), has a giving of thanks for Creation and Redemption, the Words of Institution (the only pre-Nicene text which includes them), an *anamnesis* and oblation, an *epiclesis* and prayer for the church, and a doxology:

> The Lord be with you.
> *Answer:* And also with you.
> Lift up your hearts.
> We lift them to the Lord.
> Let us give thanks to the Lord.
> It is meet and right.

> We give you thanks, O God, through your beloved Child Jesus Christ, whom in the last times you sent to us, a Savior and Redeemer and Messenger of your will, who is your Word, inseparable from you; through whom you made all things and whom, in your good pleasure, you sent from heaven into the womb of a virgin, and who, conceived within her, was made flesh, and was manifested as your Son, born of the Holy Spirit and a virgin; who, fulfilling your will, and winning for you a holy people, spread out his hands when he suffered, that by his passion he might set free those who believe in you; who, when he was given over to his voluntary suffering, that he might destroy death and break the bonds of the devil, and tread hell under foot, and enlighten the righteous, and set up a boundary post, and manifest the resurrection, taking bread and giving thanks to you said, Take, eat, this is my body, which is broken for you. In the same manner, also, the cup, saying, This is my blood, which is poured out for you. When you do this, you make *anamnesis* of me.

Therefore, remembering his death and resurrection, we offer to you this bread and cup, giving thanks to you because you have counted us worthy to stand before you and to minister as priests to you.

And we pray you to send your Holy Spirit upon the oblation of the holy church, gathering into one all who receive the holy [mysteries], that we may be filled with Holy Spirit, to the confirmation of faith in truth, that we may praise and glorify you, through your Child Jesus Christ, through whom be glory and honor to you, with the Holy Spirit in the holy church, both now and world without end. Amen.

The only ceremonial actions which might date back into the pre-Nicene period are possibly an extension of the hands over the oblations or a sign of the cross (or an extension of the hands crossed one over the other) at the invocation (*epiclesis*), and possibly an elevation of the Bread and Cup at the end of the prayer.

At the end of the Eucharistic Prayer the Bread was broken (the *fraction*) and then the presiding officer, the presbyters, and the deacons received in both kinds, and some of the ordained ministers (standing at the sides of the Table), administered to the people (who came forward and moved from one to another to receive). After all present had received, the deacons left to take Eucharistic Bread (and Wine?) to members of the congregation who had not been present. In some localities those present took Bread (and Wine?) home to receive privately during the week as reminders and foretastes of the Sunday Eucharist.

As early as the *Didache* 8, Wednesdays and Fridays became days for (voluntary?) fasting, *station days* (a military term for days of keeping watch). These days became associated with the Betrayal and the Crucifixion. Some places which did not have Liturgies of the Word daily did have them on these station days. In some places the end of the fast was marked by the receiving of Eucharistic Elements set apart the previous Sunday (compare the Eastern Liturgy of the Pre-Sanctified Gifts).

To be a Christian was to remember and to expect. The pattern of the Christian life was the pattern of the liturgical week, a rhythm of preparation and fulfillment, of Word and Sacrament, of *chronos* and *kairos*.

The Liturgical Year—Several elements entered into the development of the liturgical year. Jewish feasts and Jewish lectionaries certainly made some contributions to its development. In some sense the Church Year at an early stage in its development was a dramatization of the more basic weekly cycle; the Great Fifty Days ("The Great Sunday") (seven squared), a seventh of the year, of the Passover-Pentecost cycle were to the year what Sunday was to the week. The greatest influence upon the development of the liturgical year was the liturgy of initiation. The Great Fifty Days which began with the Baptismal Vigil were days for special celebration, days when kneeling and fasting were outlawed, days for teaching which had been withheld from the catechumens, days when the Eucharist could be celebrated on a week day. The candidates (and others who wished to fast with them) prepared for the Easter Vigil by a rigorous fast on the prior Friday and Saturday (or Saturday only) and, at a later stage, by a less intense fast from Monday through Thursday. Some degree of fasting also seems to have been associated with the several-week period of candidacy. It is probably from the combination of these two types of fasts that the Lenten fast of forty days, a tithe of the year, (which was counted differently in different places) developed.[22]

From the mid-second century the liturgical year began to be punctuated with annual celebrations in commemoration of local martyrs, often at the place of their burial. Martyrdom of Polycarp 18 gives the reasons for such commemorations: "both in memory of those who have already contested, and for the practice and training of those whose fate it shall be." In this period, such commemorations seem to have been confined to local witnesses for the faith.

Music—Psalms and hymns were a normal part of many of the services, and the musical and poetic forms of the pagan cultures were apparently made use of in the church. Among the hymns dating from this period are the *Gloria in excelsis* ("Glory to God in the highest"), which was used in some places in the daily morning service; *Phos hilaron* (*The Hymnal 1940* 173, 176), which was associated with the *lucernarium;* and a hymn by Clement of Alexandria for the newly-baptized, "Master of eager youth" (*The Hymnal 1940* 362).[23]

THE SANCTIFICATION OF SPACE

The early Christians typically met in homes of members of the congregation, but there are evidences from the third century of buildings owned by the congregation. Typically these were converted residences (house-churches). The best preserved example is from Dura-Europos, a house which was converted for church use c. 232 A.D. Opening off the central courtyard were three rooms. One (16½' x 43') had been created by joining together two smaller rooms. This room had a raised platform at one end (for the bishop's throne or for the Table) and a small room opening off it, which probably served as a sacristy or storeroom. Another room (13' x 23') possibly served as a lecture room or as a place for the *agape*. The third room (somewhat smaller) had been adapted as a baptistry by the addition of a large rectangular font under a canopy (reminiscent of a tomb) at one end and of frescoes depicting Biblical types of baptism.[24]

Rather than facing Jerusalem for prayers, as had the Jews, the early Christians faced the geographical East, the rising sun, the symbol of the Parousia, the heavenly Jerusalem, and their churches were oriented in this direction.

Another important aspect of early Christian worship was movement. The rites of passage (baptisms, marriages, burials, etc.) were accompanied by physical movement from one place to another. Within the normal Sunday liturgy the congregation gathered around and faced the reader for the Liturgy of the Word, turned to the East for the prayers, and then gathered about the Table for the Anaphora. The rites commemorative of the martyrs and of the dead were apparently celebrated at the graves or martyria.

The art associated with the buildings and their appurtenances was not primarily decorative or instructive but partook of the liturgical notes of *anamnesis* and *prolepsis*. Associated with the baptistry, for example, were Biblical types of baptism, original sin, salvation, and resurrection. Associated with the place of the Table were types of the Eucharist, the Last Supper, the Feeding of the Multitudes, Resurrection Meals, etc.[25]

CHAPTER IV

THE PERIOD OF THE SACRAMENTARIES

The toleration and establishment of the church in the early fourth century created situations which were radically to affect the liturgy. Aspects of the Emperor Cult, which in the pre-Constantinian period had been symbols of apostasy, came to be accepted by the church. Etiquette and ceremonial appropriate to and associated with the court were brought into the church. The great increase in numbers of converts and the lack of earnestness on the part of some of them was to affect the rites. As an established religion, the church had less to fear from the Mystery Religions, and many additional aspects of those cults came to be accepted by the church. The clergy stepped into certain vacuums in civic leadership, and they brought something of the mentality and some of the trappings asso-

ciated with civic office into the liturgy. These new trends
fostered a monastic reaction. Rites were revised and developed particularly for those under monastic discipline. The
church was racked by theological controversies—Trinitarian,
Christological, Donatist, and Pelagian—which affected the
rites as well as the theology of the rites. All of these movements tended toward the development within the liturgy of
greater formalism and elaboration, more theological definition within the rites, more stringent regulations in regard to
the functions of various orders of ministers, and greater fix-
ity of texts.[1]

Extemporaneity gave way to written forms. Over the
fourth and fifth centuries the Church Orders were replaced
by *libelli* which were gathered together and used in the creation of books for those responsible for the variable parts of
the rites. The book which contained the prayers read by the
officiant was the *sacramentary*. The reader's portion was
contained or indicated in a *lectionary*, which might have
been in any of three forms: (1) a table which indicated the
beginnings and endings of readings; (2) a marked Bible; or
(3) a collection of pericopes or selections. Another book evidently contained the litanies and other portions of rites for
which the deacon was responsible. The choir's portions were
found in the *antiphonary*, *Psalter*, *gradual*, or *hymnal*. The
fixed portions of the rites were known from memory. It
was, under this system, necessary to have a gathered congregation to celebrate a Eucharist, Daily Office, baptism,
marriage, or burial.

The liturgies which developed in the different areas took
on special characteristics. Eastern Liturgies tend to be conservative in regard to ancient practices and structures. Ceremonial and hymnody are highly developed. The texts are
rich in Biblical and homiletical content. In theory the liturgy
is always in the vernacular. The function of the deacon has
been retained. Litanies are prominent in the rites. Icons
have an important place in a piety which is more Resurrection or Eschaton centered and which retains more of the
tension between *chronos* and *kairos*. Readings about

Eastern Liturgies must be approached with caution for many of the lesser Eastern Churches have submitted to Rome (Uniates) and their liturgies have become highly Romanized, and most of what is available in English on Eastern rites is written by Uniates or other Romans or by Anglicans who impose Western interpretations and/or describe or picture Uniate rites.[2]

Eastern Liturgies can be broken down into two families: the "Coptic," "Alexandrian," or "East African" ("Monophysite") and the "Antiochene," "Syrian," or "Asian." The Coptic Family is composed of two rites: the Coptic or Egyptian and the Ethiopian or Abyssinian. The sacramentary of Sarapion (c. 350 A.D.) is an early witness to the liturgy of Egypt. The principal liturgy of the Coptic Rite is the liturgy of St. Mark, which dates, in part, from the fourth century.[3] None of the extant books or manuscripts of the Ethiopian Rite ante-dates the fifteenth century. It seems, at an early stage, to have incorporated many elements from the Coptic Rite and from that of West Syria.[4] The Syrian Family is composed of two rites: East Syrian and West Syrian. The East Syrian Rites are the rites of Persia, Mesopotamia, and India. The principal early sources of knowledge of this "Nestorian" liturgy are the writings of Theodore of Mopsuestia, the liturgical homilies of Narsai, and the Liturgy of Addai and Mari (Thomas and His Lord). The principal liturgy is that of Malabar (See *The Hymnal 1940* 201).[5] The West Syrian Rites were the rites of Palestine, Syria, Greece, Russia —Western and Northern Asia and Eastern Europe. The two principal centers were Jerusalem and Antioch. Our principal early sources of knowledge of the liturgy of Jerusalem are the catechetical lectures of Cyril of Jerusalem, the travel diary of Egeria (Aetheria, Etheria, Silvia) from c. 381–84 A.D., and an early fifth-century lectionary. The principal liturgy is that of St. James of Jerusalem (See *The Hymnal 1940* 197 and 492).[6] Our principal early sources of knowledge of the early liturgy of Antioch are the *Didascalia*, the Apostolic Constitutions, and the catechetical lectures of St. John Chrysostom. The Byzantine or Constantinopolitan Liturgy, which was to become through suppression and influence the leading Eastern Liturgy, was developed largely from the West Syrian Rites.[7]

Western Liturgies, also, can be broken down into two families: the Gallican and the Roman. The Gallican Liturgies tend toward elaboration, while remaining conservative in regard to the basic elements of the rites. A great deal of congregational participation is provided for through a more or less fixed framework of people's parts. Within this framework the parts for the clergy vary greatly with the day. The content is often heavily homiletical or exhortatory, and it is often highly poetic. The Gallican rites tended to be quite receptive to influences from the East.

The Gallican Family is made up of four rites: the Gallican, the Mozarabic, the Celtic, and the Ambrosian. The Gallican Rite was the rite of what is now France and Southern Germany until systematic efforts were made, principally under Charlemagne, to suppress it to give place for the Roman Rite.[8] The end result of these efforts was a Gallicanization of the Roman Rite. The Gallican Rite's most notable special characteristics were the multiplication of texts and the elaboration of ceremonials. Our principal sources of knowledge of the rite are the sixth century writings of Caesarius of Arles and Gregory of Tours and, from the seventh and eighth centuries, the *Exposition* of Pseudo-Germanus, the *Lectionary of Luxeuil*, the *Masses of Mone*, the *Missale Gothicum*, the *Missale Gallicanum vetus*, and the *Missale Francorum*.[9] The Mozarabic Rite was the rite of what is now Spain and Portugal until it was suppressed, except in a few places, under Pope Gregory VII in the eleventh century.[10] Some of its special characteristics are anti-Arian formulae, prayers punctuated by Amens, and prayers addressed to Jesus. It contributed a number of forms which were eventually accepted throughout the West (for example, the Trinity Sunday Preface). Our principal early sources of knowledge include canons of councils, the writings of Isidore of Seville and Ildephonsus of Toledo (seventh century), and *Liber commicus*, the *Antiphonary of León*, the *Visi-*

gothic Orational, Liber Ordinum, and *Liber Mozarabicus sacra sacramentorum.*[11] The Celtic Rite was the rite of the British Isles, prior to Augustine, and of missionary outposts on the continent.[12] It was not finally suppressed until the twelfth century. One of its principal characteristics was its eclecticism. A number of texts and ceremonials which originated in this rite came to be accepted throughout the West. Our principal early sources of knowledge are fragments of various rites, the *Bangor Antiphonary, Das Irische Palimpsestsakramentar Im CLM 14429,* the *Stowe Missal,* and (possibly) the *Bobbio Missal.*[13] The Ambrosian Rite was the rite of what is now northern Italy and Switzerland.[14] Eventually it was confined to the archdiocese of Milan, where it is still in use in a highly Romanized form. Our principal early sources of knowledge include the writings of Ambrose, the *Sacramentary of Biasca,* and the *Sacramentary of Bergamo.*[15]

The Roman Family of liturgies tends towards terseness, simple and direct formularies, a dearth of popular hymnody or vocal congregational participation, and a somberness not characteristic of other liturgies.[16]

The Roman Family is made up of two rites: the North African and the Roman. The North African Rite was the rite of Western North Africa until the death of the church there. The rite is principally known through the writings of Tertullian, Cyprian, and Augustine.[17] The Roman Rite[18] up to the late eighth century was the rite of the city of Rome, of a portion of Southern Italy, and of Roman missionary outposts (for example, Canterbury).[19] After that time it gradually superseded other rites throughout most of Western Europe. Its special characteristics include its terseness and simplicity, its reduction of readings, preaching, and intercessions, and its particular developments of Mariolatry and of the cult of the saints. Principal liturgical books of the Roman Rite are the so-called *Leonine (Verona), Gelasian,* and *Gregorian Sacramentaries,* the *Ordines romani* (directions for use in shifting from the Gallican to the Roman Rite), and the Gallicanized *Gelasians of the VIIIth Century.*[20]

THE SANCTIFICATION OF LIFE

Initiation—The loss of tension between the church and the world and a lack of zeal on the part of many of the new semi-converts and of the sparse professional clergy were to curtail the rites of initiation within the fourth century. A good picture of the rites of this period can be found in the catechetical instructions of St. John Chrysostom, of Ambrose, of Theodore of Mopsuestia, and of Cyril of Jerusalem (for which Egeria's diary and the Armenian lectionary provide supplementary information).[21] Out of the Donatist controversy came a definition of what constitutes a valid baptism (water and the Word), and out of the Pelagian controversy came an increased emphasis upon the doctrine of Original Sin, which, over a period of several centuries, brought an increase in the frequency of clinical baptisms and of infant baptisms.

Within the period of the sacramentaries the series of rites and instructions associated with initiation was normally confined to a period of several weeks. Adult baptism was still considered the norm, though apparently small children increasingly were carried through the rites and the instructions physically, or vicariously, by their parents or god-parents.[22]

At the beginning of Lent a person was made a catechumen. He was expected to attend a number of services during the following weeks, at which lections chosen because of their association with baptism would be read and expounded and instructions would be given. At these services the catechumens received Exorcisms, Insufflations, Laying-on-of-hands, and/or Anointing. In some rites the catechumens were also given salt ("Ye are the salt of the earth," "Remember Lot's wife," "the salt of wisdom").

Typically it was on the Sunday before Easter that the catechumen was made a candidate (*competentes*, elect). Sometimes associated with this were additional Exorcisms, Insufflations, Anointings, Laying-on-of-hands, and the Effeta. Within the Roman Rite there was also a ceremony of the Delivery of the Gospels. Typically this was the day for the Delivery of the Creed *(traditio symboli)*, which would be "returned" *(redditio symboli)* at or prior to the baptism.

The baptism itself was associated with the Paschal Vigil. The Vigil typically began with the *Exultet* and the blessing of (the new fire and) the Paschal Candle and proceeded to a series of from six to twelve Old Testament readings, interspersed with canticles and prayers. The readings typically included the stories of Creation, the Fall, the Sacrifice of Isaac, the Passover, the Crossing of the Red Sea, the Entry into the Promised Land, Isaiah 55 ("Come ye to the waters"), the Valley of Dry Bones, and Jonah. The water of the font was then exorcised and/or blessed with a form replete with Biblical typology, and in some places the people were sprinkled as a reminder of their baptism or allowed to take water from the font to their homes. The blessing of water was sometimes followed by a blessing of oil and an anointing, though in the West these tended to move up to earlier days. Typically the candidate was then called upon for a three-fold renunciation of Satan. He then confessed the faith in a three-fold form and was immersed in the water. The *neophyte* or *infante* was then anointed (chrismated, sealed) with *chrism* (perfumed oil, the "oil of thanksgiving" of Hippolytus [III 8]), typically by the *sacerdos* (priest) or *presbyteros* (presbyter), and in the Mozarabic Rite this was followed by a laying-on-of-hands by the *sacerdos*. A peculiarity of the Roman Rite was that this was followed by a second anointing or chrismation by the bishop. The neophytes were clothed in white garments *(in albis)*, which they would continue to wear for several days. In the Gallican rites, the feet of the neophytes were washed by the ranking clergyman. In the Celtic Rite, the right hand of the neophyte was signed with the sign of the cross. After these post-baptismal ceremonies, the Easter Eucharist was begun. The lections and prayers of this Eucharist, at which the neophytes made their first Communion, were filled with baptismal references, as were those of the Easter Octave, which the neophytes were expected to attend still dressed in their white robes.

In these rites the classical pattern of Christian Initiation had been retained, even though the three-year catechumenate had been reduced to a few weeks, the several week candidacy to a week, and the Great Fifty Days to an Octave (eight days).

It is within this period that we get the first uses of the word *confirmation* in any sense that could be said to be anticipatory of later uses of the word. The baptisms of persons who had been baptized within heretical or schismatic groups, of persons who had received clinical baptism, or of persons who had undergone public penance, were sometimes publicly attested by a laying-on-of-hands or an anointing (chrismation). Though within the Roman Rite the normal minister for such a rite was the bishop, it seems in other rites normally to have been the pastor, and at times it was performed by a deacon (witness the regulations against this being done by a deacon). Other uses of the word *confirmation* in this period refer to the receiving of Communion: one's initiation is confirmed, completed, attested by the public receiving of Communion.

Penance—During this period, also, the period of public penitential discipline was greatly reduced. In the fourth century, those undergoing discipline had gone through as many as four stages between their excommunication and their reinstatement: (1) *weepers*, who stood outside the church door, begging for the intercessions of the members of the congregation as they went in; (2) *hearers*, who were allowed into the church porch or narthex; (3) *kneelers*, who were allowed into the church but had to kneel among the standing congregation; and (4) *standers*, who were allowed to stand with the congregation but had to leave prior to the Communion. The Council of Nicea condemned apostates to two years as hearers, seven as kneelers, and two as standers. Basil condemned adulterers to four years as weepers, five as hearers, four as kneelers, and two as standers, and perjurers to two years as weepers, three as hearers, four as kneelers, and one as standers. During this period the penitent had, in effect, temporarily to become a monk, subject to such disciplines and humiliations as intense prayer and fasting and the wearing of sackcloth or a hair shirt.[23]

In the time of the sacramentaries public penitence was linked up with the season of Lent. At the beginning of Lent, or on the Wednesday prior to Lent, the penitents were placed under discipline. They were admonished and prayed for and received a laying-on-of-hands before being ejected from the church prior to the Eucharist. In the ninth century the Imposition of Ashes and the seven Penitential Psalms (6, 32, 38, 51, 102, 130, 143) were added to the rite of expulsion, and the day came to be known as Ash Wednesday. Lenten services contained readings, scrutinies, and prayers for the penitents, who were excluded from the Communion. Near the end of Lent (Maundy Thursday in the Roman Rite, Good Friday in Gallican Rites) was the time for reconciliation. The penitents were admonished and given warnings. They prostrated themselves, and the congregation cried out for pardon for them. Prayers were read over them, and then hands were laid upon them, and they were raised up and admitted to Communion. The books contained special forms for the reconciliation of dying penitents.[24]

It was within the Celtic Church, with its peculiar monastic organization and ideals, that the practice of private penance arose. From the sixth through the ninth centuries *Penitentials* (books which prescribed the penances for various offenses) appeared. The authority of these depended upon the prestige of their authors or editors. Whereas public penance was assigned for sins which brought scandal upon the church, private penance began to be expected for other matters of conscience. We have no forms from this period for the rites of private penance; those from the rites of public penance were probably adapted by the confessors, who were sometimes lay monks.[25]

Marriage—During the period of the sacramentaries, the rites of marriage were brought under the sway of the church. The setting for what was the equivalent of the old civil marriage was the church porch, and the liturgical books provided prayers. Proper lections, Psalms, responses, and prayers were provided for the Nuptial Eucharist, which typically included a blessing of the couple prior to their Communion. Forms for blessing the newlyweds in bed were also provided. Some books included propers for use at Daily Offices preceding the wedding, and the Gelasian sacramentary provided propers for the Eucharist at thirty days and at one year.[26]

Pregnancy and Childbirth—The Canons of Hippolytus consigned unchurched women to a place among the catechumens. The eighth century *Barberini Euchologion* contains prayers for infants, to be used upon the eighth day after birth (at the giving of the name) and upon the fortieth day, which are obviously to be used some time prior to the making of a catechumen.[27] Possibly similar rites for the birth of a child existed in other areas as well. It was apparently not rare for a child to be admitted as a catechumen, and within this period the practice of infant baptism became more common, so that the catechumenate or even baptism itself began to function as a rite of childbirth rather than as a rite of initiation.

Ordination—In the East during this period there was some elaboration of the ordination rites, but not such great changes as in the West. The practice of popular election was dropped, but the people were still given a chance within the rite to express their approval or disapproval of the man. Within the Roman Rite, the orders of deacon, presbyter, and bishop were conferred between the reading of the Epistle and the Gospel. The intercessions of the congregation were asked, a litany was sung, and the "consecration" (the ordination prayer) was said by a bishop. Apparently an open Gospel Book was at times held over the head of the ordinand in place of a laying-on-of-hands, and it is not clear that more than one bishop laid hands upon the head of one being ordained bishop or that presbyters joined in the laying-on-of-hands at the ordination of a presbyter. The "laying-on-of-hands with prayer" was no longer that which was associated with the silent prayers of the congregation. The consecration of bishops depicts the bishop as the successor of Aaron, as a high priest, and as the ruler of the church. The consecration of presbyters depicts presbyters as successors of the Levites, of the "seventy wise men" appointed by Moses, and of the sons of Aaron. They are to be companions and helpers of the bishop, teachers of the faith, and "virtuous colleagues." The consecration of deacons depicts the deacons as "sons of Levi," dedicated to ministry. The Gallican Rites are more reminiscent of those of Hippolytus, but the rites have been expanded with exhortations and additional prayers and ceremonial elaborations (vesting, giving of books, anointing of the hands—the precedents for which are found in earlier baptismal rites). The bishop is high priest, ruler, pastor, preacher, and teacher. The presbyter is an adviser to the bishop, a ruler and teacher, and a minister of the Eucharist and of blessings. The deacon is a successor of the Levites and of the seven deacons of Acts, who is to minister and to teach.[28]

Vestments—It is within this period that we find the first use of vestments by the clergy. The amice, alb, girdle, maniple, tunicle, dalmatic, and chasuble were simply the clothing of the middle class people of the day, which conservative clergy continued to wear after they had passed out of fashion. The alb was the basic garment; the amice, a neckpiece or collar; the girdle, a belt; the maniple, a handkerchief or napkin; the chasuble, tunicle, and dalmatic, types of coats. It is the stole (or its ancestor) which was the distinctive mark of office, analogous to marks of civic office.[29] Corresponding to the incense, candles, and mace which were carried before certain ranking civic officials on ceremonial occasions, incense, candles, cross or crozier (which later was to be interpreted as a shepherd's crook or pastoral staff) began to be carried before ranking clergy.[30]

Sick Rites—From within the period of the sacramentaries we have forms for the Visitation (and unction) of the Sick in Eastern and Gallican Rites. The Mozarabic rite consisted of a sprinkling with holy water, an anointing, Psalmody, a prayer for healing, and a blessing. The Celtic rite was longer and more elaborate. It began with a bidding, prayers for healing, and lections. In one version a short form of the Creed and in another version a blessing of water and "Blessing of the man" preceded the anointing with "the oil of gladness." The anointing was followed by the Lord's Prayer with Protocol ([variable] introduction) and Embolism (a [variable] petition drawn out from a phrase in the prayer). This was followed by a formula which may have been associated with the Peace but is more probably a short presbyter's blessing prior to Communion. The rite ended with post-communion prayers, anthems, and a blessing. It seems to be a reasonable assumption that the asperges (sprinkling with holy water) and the unction were later additions to older rites for Visitation or Communion of the Sick.[31]

Burials—Books of this period contain proper lections and prayers for use in connection with burials. Prayers are provided for use at the time of death and (apparently at the conclusion of a wake) before the body was carried from the house. The procession was accompanied by the singing of Psalms such as Psalms 23, 32, 115, and 116. Prayers and lections were provided for use at (Matins and Vespers and) a Eucharist, and prayers were also provided for use in connection with the interment and at anniversary celebrations on the seventh and the thirtieth days.[32]

THE SANCTIFICATION OF TIME

The Liturgical Day—The day was marked liturgically by morning and evening services (Matins and Vespers). These congregational rites (or "cathedral offices") typically began with (the *lucernarium* in the evening and) selected Psalms (Psalms 51, 95, 148–50 being typical for the beginning of Matins). The lection(s) (and instruction) followed. The people responded with canticles (often the Te Deum) or hymns. The office was concluded by the use of the Kyrie (relic of an earlier use of intercessions?), a variable prayer, and/or the Lord's Prayer (and a blessing). The *agape* dropped out of use, but it is possible that we have a relic of the *agape* in the blessed bread *(eulogia* or *antidoron)* which was in some instances given to the faithful after various rites.[33]

The monks based their devotional life upon praying the whole of the Psalter. Possibly a contributing factor was that anchorites who lacked books could memorize the Psalter. More or less "in course" use of the Psalms became attached to the traditional times for public and private daily worship. Some Eastern monks prayed the Psalter daily, Roman monks weekly, Gallican monks fortnightly. Such offices for the various times of the day were rounded off with hymnody and prayers. Offices said "in choir" (that is, in the chapel or church) were Matins (the midnight and/or cockcrow devotions), Lauds (the public morning service or time for private devotions and reading of Scripture), Terce (the third hour), Sext (the sixth hour), None (the ninth hour), and Vespers (the public evening service). In addition to these offices which corresponded to the old times for public services and private devotions, two more offices were added to the daily regimen: Prime (the first hour), which was said in the chapter house at the commencement of the daily duties, and Compline, which was said in the dormitories at bed time. Important early witnesses to the development of the monastic offices are John Cassian (*Institutes*) and Benedict of Nursia (*Rule*).[34]

Within this period the two systems of daily offices, the congregational and the monastic, coexisted or were combined in situations where the monks made use of the church or where the clergy (monastic or "secular") were bound by rule to the use of monastic-type offices. The monastic-type office became prefixed to the congregational morning and evening services. Typically the first things to be cut in order to shorten the elongated offices were the lections and instruction, which earlier writers (for example, Gregory of Tours) had considered the heart of the offices.

The Liturgical Week—The liturgical week was still organized around the Sunday Eucharist. Sunday was made a day of rest by Constantine in 321 A.D. (In Eastern areas Saturday was also a feast day and a day for the Eucharist.)

The Eucharist—In Eastern liturgies the people apparently brought their offerings to the sacristy upon their arrival at church. The Liturgy of the Word began with a Little Entrance (the bringing in of the Scriptures) and with Psalms or hymns of praise, which typically included the Trisagion ("Holy God, Holy Mighty, Holy Immortal One, have mercy upon us"). There was a tendency to cut back upon the readings, of which there had been four or five in the Apostolic Constitutions and the Liturgy of St. James (the Law, the Prophets, the Epistles and/or the Acts of the Apostles, and the Gospels). Typically Old Testament lections were separated from New Testament lections by Psalmody (the Gradual). The Gospel began to be surrounded by expressions of praise or Christian hymnody. After the Dismissal of the Catechumens and the Litany or intercessions came the transfer to the table of the gifts of bread and wine which had been presented and prepared in the sacristy. This transfer of the gifts eventually assumed a ceremonial significance and came to be known as "the Great Entrance." It was accompanied by hymnody (See *The Hymnal 1940* 197). Typically the Pax was moved to a position after the Great Entrance, and as early as the sixth century the Nicene Creed came to be associated with it. The Eucharistic Prayer was introduced by an ascription of praise and thanksgiving to God (the "Preface") which began with the Sursum corda and ended with the Sanctus ("Holy, holy, holy Lord, God of power and might, heaven and earth are full of your glory"). Eventually, in places, the Benedictus qui venit ("Blessed is he who comes in the name of the Lord. Hosanna in the highest") was added to the Sanctus. The Post-sanctus, in which the principal events of salvation history were recalled, reached its climax in (the "preliminary *epiclesis*" in Coptic rites and) the recitation of the Words of Institution, typically ending with a kergymatic reference. Next came the *anamnesis* and oblation, and often an Acclamation of the people (for example, "Christ has died, Christ is risen, Christ will come again"). This was followed by the *epiclesis*, which came to take the form of a prayer that the bread and wine might be transformed into the Body and Blood of Christ, and prayer for the fruits of Communion. As early as the time of Cyril intercessions came to be included in the Eucharistic Prayer—after the *epiclesis* in Antiochene rites, prior to the preliminary *epiclesis* in Coptic rites. A prayer noted for its antiquity, its wide-spread use, and its ecumenical significance which exhibits these characteristics is the Alexandrian version of the Anaphora of St. Basil:

> The Lord be with you all.
> *Answer:* And also with you.
> Lift up your hearts.
> *Answer:* We lift them to the Lord.
> Let us give thanks to the Lord.
> *Answer:* It is meet and right.
>
> It is meet and right, meet and right, truly meet and right.
>
> Lord of Lords, You are God of truth, existing before all ages and reigning unto eternity, inhabiting the heavens and watching over the humble. You made the heavens and the earth and the sea and all that is in them; Father of our Lord and God and Savior Jesus Christ, through whom you made all things seen and unseen, who reigns with you seated upon the throne of your holy glory. You are worshiped by all the holy powers, assisted by angels and archangels, principalities and powers, thrones, dominions and virtues. Around you are the many-eyed cherubim and the six-winged seraphim, always praising, acclaiming, and saying,
>
> Holy, holy, holy Lord, God of power and might, heaven and earth are full of your glory.
>
> You are truly holy, holy, holy Lord, our God, who made us and placed us in the paradise of delight. But we transgressed your commandments, through the deception of the serpent, and we fell from eternal life, and were cast out of the paradise of delight; but you did not cast us out unto eternity but continued teaching us through your holy prophets, and in the last days you appeared to us who were seated in darkness and the shadow of death through your only-begotten Son our Lord and

God and Savior Jesus Christ. From the Holy Spirit and from our holy mistress and Godbearer and ever virgin Mary, he took flesh and was made man, showed us the ways of salvation, gave to us the supernatural rebirth by water and Spirit, and made us a redeemed people, sanctifying us by his Holy Spirit.

He loved his own who are in this world and gave himself for our redemption from the death which reigned over us, unto which we were bound and given over because of our sins. Through the cross he descended into hades. He was raised from the dead the third day. He ascended into heaven, and is seated at the right hand of the Father. He appointed a day in which he will judge the world in equity and render to each according to his works.

He left us this great mystery of piety. For when he was to hand himself over to death for the life of the world, he took bread, blessed, sanctified, broke, and gave it to his holy disciples and apostles, saying, Take and eat from this all of you. This is my body which is given for you and for many for the forgiveness of your sins. Do this in *anamnesis* of me. In the same way also the cup, mixed of wine and water, after they had eaten supper. He blessed and sanctified, gave thanks over it, and gave it to them, saying, Take and drink from this all of you. This my blood which is poured out for you and for many for the forgiveness of your sins. Do this in *anamnesis* of me. As often as you eat this bread and drink this cup, you proclaim my death until I come.

Recalling, therefore, his passion and his resurrection from the dead and his ascension into heaven and sitting at the right hand of the Father, and his glorious and awe-inspiring coming again, we offer to you and before you from what you have given us, this bread and this cup, and we your sinful and unworthy and sorrowful servants, worshiping you, pray you, our God, that through the benevolence of your goodness your Holy Spirit may descend upon us and upon these gifts placed here and sanctify them to be the holy of holies.

Make us worthy of sharing in them for the sanctification of soul and body, that we be made one body and one spirit, and that we come to have a part with all the saints who have been pleasing to you throughout all ages.

Remember also, Lord, your one, holy, catholic Church, and give it the peace which you have bought with the precious blood of your Christ, and remember all the orthodox bishops in it.

In the first place, remember your servant the Archbishop Benjamin, and his ally in ministry, the holy bishop Colluthos, and those who with them dispense the word of truth. Grant that they may shepherd the holy church, your orthodox flock, in peace.

Remember, Lord, the presbyters and all deacons who minister in virginity and purity, and all your faithful people, and be merciful to them all.

Remember also, Lord, this place and those in the faith of God who inhabit it.

And good weather, remember, Lord, and the fruits of the earth.

And remember, Lord, those who offered gifts to you and those for whom they were offered, and give them all the riches of heaven.

Since, Lord, it is the commandment of your only-begotten Son that we share in the memory of your saints, remember our fathers who from eternity have been pleasing to you: patriarchs, prophets, apostles, martyrs, confessors, teachers, evangelists, and all the righteous who in faith have been made perfect; chiefly, the holy and glorious Theotokos and ever-virgin Mary, and have mercy upon us all through her prayers and save us according to your holy name invoked over us.

In the same way remember all in the priesthood and all in the order of the laity who have fallen asleep, and give them rest in the bosom of Abraham, Isaac and Jacob, in a place of green pastures and restful waters, from which has fled all sadness, sorrow and sighing. (*The names are recited.*) Give them rest with you.

Keep us the living in your faith, and lead us to your kingdom, and grant us at all times your peace, through Jesus Christ and the Holy Spirit, Father in Son, Son in Father, with the Holy Spirit in your one, holy, catholic and apostolic Church.[35]

Communion devotions to prepare the people for worthy receiving came to be associated with the Fraction and Commixture (putting the Bread into the Chalice, from which both Elements were administered by spoon or straw). Typically these Communion devotions included the Lord's Prayer, Benedictus qui venit, and "Holy (set apart) things for holy (set apart) people." Psalms or hymns were sung at the time of the administration of Communion. Typical selections were Psalms 23, 34, 145, and 150. The rite was normally concluded with prayers or hymns (See *The Hymnal 1940* 201 and 492). Communicants were no longer given consecrated Elements to take home for reservation and consumption, but the Elements were reserved in the sacristy for Communion of the Sick.[36]

Among the Eastern Rites, there were few, if any, variables within a particular Anaphora, but special days were marked by the use of different Anaphoras.

Within the Gallican Rites, also, the offerings of bread and wine were presented by the people prior to the Entrance Chant. The entrance was followed by songs of praise (typically the Kyrie, Trisagion, and Benedictus in the Gallican rite; the Gloria in excelsis in Mozarabic, Celtic, and Ambrosian rites), which were typically followed by a (variable) prayer which built upon a phrase from the canticle. The Liturgy of the Word normally consisted of an Old Testament lection (or Revelation during the Great Fifty Days), a Psalm, an Epistle (or Acts during the Great Fifty Days), a song of praise (typically the Benedicite), and a Gospel. Marks of honor (candles, etc.) which had begun to mark the entrance and exit of the clergy also began to surround the Gospel Book, which was seen as a symbol of Christ's presence in His Word. Short exclamations of praise, such as Gloria tibi ("Glory to you, Lord"), also began to surround the reading. The homily was followed by a deacon's litany (a prayer form imported from the East, which had precedents in Eastern Mystery Religions), which was concluded with a (variable) prayer said by the officiant. The dismissal of the catechumens preceded the Great Entrance, which was accompanied by hymnody and ceremonials such as those which had clustered about the entrance of the clergy (See p. 61) and about the Gospel Book. The Great Entrance was followed in the Gallican Rite by a Preface (a bidding which set forth the reasons for celebrating the particular day) and the variable prayer of the day. This was followed by the reading (of a variable prayer and) of the Diptychs (the names of those who had offered and of the dead for whom prayers were asked) and a variable prayer for those whose names had been read. Next came the Pax, which was accompanied by hymnody and followed by a variable prayer. Major portions of the Eucharistic Prayer itself varied with the day. The Sursum corda led into a variable preface which introduced the Sanctus. A variable Post-sanctus then led into the Words of Institution, which ended with a kerygmatic reference. The prayer was then concluded with another variable section. The three variable sections stressed the reasons for commemoration of the particular day, largely in terms of praise and thanksgiving. Explicit notes of *anamnesis*, oblation, *epiclesis*, and prayer for the communicants were not necessarily present in the prayers for a particular day, though all of these notes did show up over the course of several celebrations. Typical of Gallican Eucharistic Prayers is that for Christmas Day of the *Missale Gothicum*, with the missing Words of Institution filled in from another Gallican book, a seventh century Irish palimpsest:

> It is meet and right, it is our duty and healthful for us to give thanks to you, Lord, Holy Father, Almighty, Everlasting God, who this day stooped to visit the world in our Lord Jesus Christ, proceeding from the temple by the body of a virgin. The angels sang Gloria in excelsis when salvation was declared unto men. All the hosts of the angels shouted exultantly when earth received the eternal King. The Blessed Mary was made a precious temple bearing the Lord of Lords. A brilliant life was born for us sinners who would have been seduced by bitter death. The sins which man is not able to cleanse, God came to carry away. Jesus Christ, your Son, our Lord, who always lives and reigns in heaven is born on earth. Therefore with angels and archangels, and with all the company of heaven, we

laud and magnify your glorious Name; evermore praising you, and saying,

Holy, holy, holy Lord, God of power and might, heaven and earth are full of your glory. Hosanna in the highest. Blessed is he who comes in the name of the Lord. Hosanna in the highest.

Glory to God in the highest, and on earth peace to men of good will, for our redemption has drawn nigh, the expectation of the nations has come, the promise of the resurrection of the dead is here, the expectation of the blessed has shown forth through Christ our Lord,

Who the day before he suffered for the salvation of us all, standing in the midst of his disciples and apostles, took bread into his holy hands, looked to heaven to you, God the Father Almighty; giving thanks, he blessed and broke and gave to his apostles, saying, Take, eat from this, all of you. This is my body which is broken for the life of the world. In the same way, after supper, taking the cup into his hands, he looked to heaven to you, God the Father Almighty; giving thanks, he blessed and gave to his apostles, saying, Take, drink from this, all of you, for this is the cup of my holy blood of the new and eternal testament, which is poured out for you and for many for the remission of sins. In addition to this saying, you have also said, As often as you eat of this bread and drink of this cup you make memorial of me, you proclaim my passion, you hope for my advent until I come again.

We believe, Lord, your advent, We recall your passion. Your body was broken for the remission of our sins. Your holy blood was poured out as the price of our redemption, who with the Father and the Holy Spirit lives and reigns unto eternity.

Communion devotions came to be associated with the Fraction and the Commixture. These included the Lord's Prayer with variable Protocol and Embolism (See p. 61) and a (variable) blessing upon the people. The Nicene Creed came to be included at this point in the Mozarabic rite (Council of Toledo 589 A.D.). Communion was accompanied by Psalms or hymns (See *The Hymnal 1940* 202). The rite ended with a variable bidding and a variable prayer (and a formal dismissal).[37]

While we see great elaboration upon the basic structure

within the Gallican rites, the changes within the Roman Rite were more drastic. Churches which had choirs added Psalmody to dignify the entrance of the clergy (Introit), to set the Gospel off from the Epistle (the Tract which was sometimes used at this point in place of the Alleluia), at the Offertory, and at the Communion. Variable prayers in collect form (a form, which possibly derives from Western Mystery Religions, consisting ideally of (1) an address, (2) an attribution, (3) a petition, (4) the reason for making the petition, and (5) a doxology [See the Book of Common Prayer [1928 ed.], p. 17, for two examples]) came into use prior to the first lection (Collect of the Day), at the spreading of the tablecloth (Prayer of the Veil), at the presentation of the bread and wine (Prayer over the Offering, *super oblata*, Secret), after the Communion (Post-communion), and as a sort of final blessing "over the people" *(super populum)*. After receiving the gifts of the people (among which may have been root vegetables and animals) and selecting sufficient bread and wine for presentation, the clergy washed their hands *(lavabo)*. A fixed Eucharistic Prayer, within which a Proper Preface was inserted for each occasion, came into use. The oldest known form of the Roman Canon (Eucharistic Prayer) is that found in *De sacramentis* IV. After the Sursum corda and Preface (and Sanctus?) there is a short petition that "this oblation, which is the figure of the Body and Blood of our Lord Jesus Christ," might be made "for us right, spiritual, and worthy." This petition is followed by the Words of Institution, an *anamnesis*, an oblation of "this holy Bread and Cup of eternal life," and a petition that this oblation might be accepted on God's "altar on high":

> Make for us right, spiritual, worthy this oblation, which is the figure of the body and blood of our Lord Jesus Christ, who the day before he suffered, took bread into his holy hands, looked up to heaven, to you, holy Father, almighty, eternal God; giving thanks, he blessed, broke, and having broken, gave it to his apostles and disciples, saying, Take and eat of this, all of you, for this is my body which shall be broken for many. In the same way, after supper, on the day before he suffered, he took the cup, looked up to heaven to you, holy

Father, almighty, eternal God; giving thanks, he blessed, and gave it to his apostles and disciples, saying, Take and drink of this, all of you, for this is my blood. As often as you do this, you make memorial of me, until I come again. Therefore, calling to mind his glorious passion, resurrection from the dead, and ascension into heaven, we offer you this immaculate sacrifice, this reasonable sacrifice, this bloodless sacrifice, this holy bread and cup of eternal life, and we pray and beseech you to take up this offering by the hands of your angels to your altar on high, as you deigned to receive the gifts of your just servant Abel and the sacrifice of our father Abraham, and that offered to you by Melchisedech the high priest.

The prayer in this form lacks an *epiclesis* or prayer for the communicants, and, in comparison to other Eucharistic Prayers, it is particularly sparse in the giving of thanks.[38]

Revisions of the Roman rite are associated with Popes Gelasius (492–96) and Gregory the Great (590–604). Under Gelasius the Prayers of the Faithful (or Solemn Prayers) which consisted of a series of biddings each of which was followed by a period of silence and by a collect said by the president of the assembly (of which a relic remains in the Good Friday rites) were replaced by an introductory litany after Eastern models. Under Gregory this was dropped, except for the responses (Kyrie eleison). The Lord's Prayer (with a fixed Protocol and Embolism) apparently had been brought into the rite as a Communion devotion prior to the time of Pope Gregory, but it was moved up by him to form a conclusion or extended Amen after the Canon. Well prior to Gregory the reading of the Gospel had become a duty of the Deacon, and the procession to the ambo with the Gospel Book was accompanied by incense and candles. The lections had been reduced to two (except for extraordinary occasions), and preaching had become infrequent. The Pax had been moved from its traditional association with the Offertory and placed between the Fraction and the Communion.

Within the seventh and eighth centuries other changes were made in the Roman Rite. The Gloria in excelsis came into use on special occasions. The lectionary became more fixed, with lections which were shorter than those typical of other rites and with a particular dearth of Old Testament readings. The variable collect which had been associated with the spreading of the tablecloth was dropped, and the *super populum* was dropped from normal usage. The variable presentation prayer began to be said silently by the priest. Many of the Proper Prefaces were dropped, leaving the Canon even poorer in terms of the giving of thanks. The portion of the Eucharistic Prayer which followed the Sanctus was greatly expanded with paragraphs reminiscent of (or found among) the variable prayers associated with the Diptychs or the presentation of the gifts in other rites.

Therefore, most merciful Father, we humbly pray and implore you, through Jesus Christ our Lord, to accept and bless these gifts, these presents, these holy unblemished offerings.

In the first place, we offer them to you for your holy catholic church throughout the whole world, that you deign to keep it in peace, to preserve, to unite, and to govern it; and also for your servants our pope, *N.*, and our bishop, *N.*, and all who are orthodox and hold the catholic and apostolic faith.

Remember, Lord, your servants and handmaids, *N.* and *N.*, and all here present, whose faith and devotion are known to you, who offer to you this sacrifice of praise for themselves and all their own, for the redemption of their souls, for the hope of their preservation and health who render their prayers to you the eternal, living, and true God.

Joining in communion, and reverently commemorating first the glorious Mary, ever-Virgin, Mother of our God and Lord Jesus Christ, as also your blessed apostles and martyrs Peter, Paul, Andrew, James, John, Thomas, James, Philip, Bartholomew, Matthew, Simon and Thaddeus, Linus, Cletus, Clement, Sixtus, Cornelius, Cyprian, Lawrence, Chrysogonus, John and Paul, Cosmas and Damian, and all your saints; grant that in all things we may, through their merits and prayers, be defended by the help of your protection; through the same Christ our Lord.

This, then, is the oblation of us and of your whole family which we offer to you. We beseech you, Lord, to receive it with favor, and order our days in your peace, deliver us from eternal damnation, and judge us to be numbered in the flock of your elect; through Christ our Lord.

Deign, O God, in all respects, we beseech you, to make blessed, approved, ratified, reasonable and acceptable this oblation, that it may become for us the body and blood of your dearly beloved Son, our Lord God, Jesus Christ.

Who the day before he suffered took bread in his holy and venerable hands, and with his eyes lifted to heaven to you, God, his almighty Father, giving thanks to you, blessed, broke and gave to his disciples, saying, Take and eat from this all of you, for this is my body. In the same way, after supper, he took also this glorious chalice in his holy and venerable hands, and giving thanks to you, blessed, gave to his disciples saying, Take and drink from this all of you, this is the cup of my holy blood of the new and eternal testament, the mystery of faith, which for you and for many shall be poured out unto remission of sins. As often as you do this you make my *anamnesis*.

Wherefore, Lord, in memory of the blessed passion of the same Christ, your Son, our Lord, of his resurrection from among the dead and of his ascension to heavenly glory, we your servants and with us all your holy people offer to your sovereign majesty, from among your gifts bestowed upon us, a pure victim, a holy victim, a spotless victim, the holy bread of everlasting life and the chalice of everlasting salvation.

Deign to look upon these offerings with a favorable and gracious countenance, and accept them as you deigned to accept the offerings of your servant Abel the righteous, the sacrifice of our father Abraham, and that of Melchisedech, your high priest, a holy sacrifice, a spotless victim.

We humbly pray you, almighty God, to bid these things to be carried by the hands of your holy angel to your altar on high, in the sight of your divine majesty, that all who shall by the participation from this holy altar receive the most holy body and blood of your Son may be filled with all heavenly benediction and grace; through Christ our Lord.

[*An occasional insertion:* Remember also, O Lord, the names of those who have preceded us with the sign of faith and rest in the sleep of peace, *N*. To them, O Lord, and to all that rest in Christ we pray that you grant a place of refreshment, light, and peace; through Christ our Lord.]

To us, also, your sinful servants who hope in the multitude of your mercies, deign to grant some part and fellowship with your holy apostles and martyrs, with John, Stephen, Matthias,

Barnabas, Ignatius, Alexander, Marcellinus, Peter, Felicity, Perpetua, Agatha, Lucy, Agnes, Cecilia, Anastasia, and with all your saints, into whose company we beseech you to admit us, not weighing merits but bestowing pardon; through Christ our Lord.

Through him, O Lord, you ever create, sanctify, quicken, bless, and bestow upon us good things.

By him, and with him, and in him, be unto you, God the Father Almighty, in the unity of the Holy Spirit, all honor and glory, world without end. Amen.

An Eastern chant, Agnus Dei ("Lamb of God, you take away the sins of the world, have mercy on us"), began to be repeated as long as was necessary to cover the Breaking of the Bread. In some situations, at the Commixture, a portion of consecrated Bread from a prior Eucharist (*sancta*) or from the bishop's Eucharist (*fermentum*) was added to the Chalice.[39]

The loss of tension between the world and the church and the growing influence of the monks led to a diminishing of the tension between *chronos* and *kairos*, between feast and fast, week day and Sunday, public and private. At an early stage the monks came to the church to participate in the Sunday Eucharist. Later they had a priest come out to them or they had their own priest, so that they could celebrate the Eucharist apart from the Sunday Eucharist of the Christian community. The life of the monk was a life of fasting—even on feast days, and fasting began to be understood less as keeping watch, or as preparation (or identification with those undergoing a special fast in preparation) for baptism, and more as a matter of self-denial or self-discipline. Fasting for the faithful lost its initial voluntary character. The Eucharist began to be celebrated more frequently, and in the West it was even celebrated on fast days, though at this stage it was not normally until the end of the day, the end of the fast.

The Liturgical Year—The liturgical year was greatly affected by the changes which came with the toleration and establishment of Christianity and the influx of those only semi-converted from paganism. The feasts of Christmas and Epiphany arose from efforts to offset or Christianize popular pagan festivals. December 25 was celebrated in Rome as the winter solstice, the birthday of the Unconquerable Sun (*dies natalis Solis Invicti*), and probably by 336 A.D. Christians had appropriated this as the day for the celebration of the Incarnation, making use of figures and ceremonials associated with the pagan feast. In Egypt January 6 was celebrated as the winter solstice, as the appearance (*epiphany*) of the sun-god among men. It was a celebration of light, of water, and of wine. The Christians appropriated this as a feast of the Incarnation and connected with it the Gospel stories of the Magi, the Baptism of Jesus, and the Wedding Feast at Cana, the first miracle. It was not long before both feasts were celebrated throughout most of the Christian world. Over the next centuries in Ambrosian and Roman territory an anticipatory note came into the rites of the weeks immediately prior to Christmas. In Gallican territory, as in the East, Epiphany became a time for baptisms, and it began to be preceded by a forty-day season of preparation, a sort of Lent ("St. Martin's Lent," for it began at St. Martin's Day, November 11). The season of Advent came out of a wedding of these two traditions, which fact explains its mixed notes of penitence and joy.[40]

This period also saw a great multiplication of Saints' Days, probably in part to offset the celebration of the days of pagan gods, protectors, or heroes. Churches which had no local martyrs to commemorate began to seek relics (of saints or of the so-called True Cross) and to institute commemorative days. The days of some saints also began to be celebrated in churches where the commemoration had not originated and that had no relic. In Celtic books (as in some Eastern ones) Old Testament worthies were commemorated. Eventually, in various areas, a day began to be celebrated as a day of All Martyrs or of All Saints. The saints came to be understood less as witnesses to the faith and more as intercessors or protectors. Within the Roman Rite a "Litany of the Saints" was developed.[41]

Constantine was responsible for the building of churches

in Jerusalem at sites traditionally associated with events in the life of Christ. These became places for pilgrimage, and by the time of Egeria's travels (c. 381–84 A.D.) it had become customary to commemorate principal events of the last week of our Lord's life with services in the appropriate churches. These services were less a celebration of the Mighty Acts of God, as had been true of the primitive Sunday and the primitive Easter-Pentecost, and more the recalling of particular historical events. The rites of Jerusalem provided the prototype for an historical treatment of Holy Week which gradually spread throughout the church, with rites such as a procession on Palm Sunday, an evening Eucharist (and washing of feet) on Maundy Thursday, and devotions (with veneration of the cross) and the Liturgy of the Pre-Sanctified Gifts on Good Friday. With this breakdown in the understanding of the Easter Vigil, practices which had at an earlier time been associated with it (the blessing of oils, the reconciliation of penitents, the return of the creed) were also pushed back earlier into the week.[42]

After liturgies for Holy Week had evolved from such an historical approach, this same approach was also applied to the Great Fifty Days (the Pentecost), and the fiftieth day came to be understood not as the climax of a season but as a day for the recalling of the event of the outpouring of the Spirit. Thus understood, Pentecost became a secondary day for baptisms, and it was given a Vigil modeled after the Easter Vigil. The Ascension began to be commemorated on the fortieth day after Easter. The Great Fifty Days were in some sense reduced to an Easter Octave.[43] Other days also were given over to the commemoration of particular events in the life of our Lord, such as the Annunciation (March 25), the Presentation (February 2), and the Birth of John the Baptist (June 24). When these feasts were imported to Rome from the East, the first two (along with two others imported with them, the days of Mary's Birth [September 8] and of her Dormition [August 15]) began to be understood as Marian Feasts rather than as feasts of our Lord. In Gallican territory, January 1 began to be celebrated as the Circumcision, and the three days prior to Ascension were set apart for special prayer for the crops (the Rogation Days). In Rome there grew up a pre-penitential season of Pre-Lent, and the seasonal Ember Days (the observances of which were modeled upon the Pascha), which probably began as quarterly periods for spiritual renewal, gathered to themselves agricultural associations and became the times for ordinations. In the sacramentaries the Propers tended to be separated into two groups—days which hinged around the dates of Easter and Christmas (the Temporale), and those independent of those dates, chiefly Saints' Days (the Sanctorale).[44]

Music—With the move to larger congregations and buildings more music was brought into use to add dignity to the entrances and exits of the clergy, to the Offertory, and to the Communion. The struggle over Arianism gave hymn singing an added impetus. The Arians used hymns to propagate their teachings, and they were met by rival compositions. Hymns came to find a place in the Eastern and Gallican Rites more than in the Roman, which tended to restrict music to Psalmody. A number of hymns from this period are currently in use (See *The Hymnal 1940 Companion*, p. xii). Greek modes were used as the basis for plainsong melodies (Ambrosian and Gregorian chant), the purpose of which was to enhance and to project the words. Ambrose and Gregory the Great are credited with reforms of the music, and Gregory is credited with founding the *schola cantorum*, after which time choirs tended to come into more prominence, and the music tended to become more complicated, especially within the Roman Rite. An impetus was given to antiphonal Psalmody, which sometimes displaced the older responsorial Psalmody.[45]

THE SANCTIFICATION OF SPACE

Buildings—The increase in numbers led to a different type of church building from the house-churches of the early centuries. From the time of Constantine the typical church-house was the basilica, the precedents for which were in public meeting places for people rather than in pagan temples. A typical basilica contained a wide *aisle* with clerestory, and side aisles which were half the width of the main aisle. Opposite the entrance to the main aisle was an *apse* which functioned to set off the *cathedra* (the bishop's throne), around which were seats for the other clergy. The bishop officiated through much of the services and preached from the *cathedra*. Nearer the people was the small Table (typically almost cubic in dimensions), which was sometimes given prominence by being placed under a *ciborium*. The lections were read from a pulpit-like *ambo*, which was well-placed for seeing and hearing, sometimes being incorporated into the *cancelli* (rails surrounding the Table).[46]

Martyria, which took their forms from the mausoleums of the area (round, square, octagonal, or cruciform, and typically domed), were also built to house the tombs of saints and to provide a setting for commemorations (or to provide for the commemoration of particular events, as those erected in Jerusalem [See p. 77]). A modified form of the *martyria* gained popularity for church building in the East.[47]

As the martyria took their form from the mausoleums of the locale, so typically did the *baptistries*, within which the font occupied the place of the tomb or grave.[48]

The Consecration of Churches—The essential element for the dedication or consecration of a church in the Roman Rite was to celebrate the Eucharist there. In some cases relics were deposited in the altar (which led eventually to the designating of church buildings by the names of saints), and when the building had served as a pagan temple there was apparently a preliminary sprinkling with holy water. The Gallican rites, which were more reminiscent of the Eastern rites, were much more elaborate. The bishop and clergy entered during the singing of a litany. The bishop then consecrated a mixture of wine and water, asperged the church, and then (after another litany) asperged the altar. He then anointed the altar with chrism at the center and at each of the four corners, after which he circuited the church, anointing it. He then blessed the altar linens and vessels. The altar was then vested, and the Eucharist celebrated. The Roman rite has been said to be analogous to burial, and the Gallican to baptism. Later a tracing of the alphabet in Latin and Greek on the floor of the church (possibly Celtic in origin, and possibly a remnant from a ceremony at the laying of the foundations, which signified the claiming of territory) was added as the first act of the bishop upon entering the church, and the Roman disposition of relics was incorporated into the rite. As early as the fourth century the dedication was commemorated annually in some places.[49]

CHAPTER **V**

THE PERIOD OF THE
MANUSCRIPT
MISSALS

The alliance of the Papacy with the
Holy Roman Empire provided the stimulus for a concerted
effort to suppress the Gallican Rite, using the Roman Rite
as a symbol of unity. The ninth century was a time of great
illiteracy and superstition, when fewer and fewer of the people were able to understand the Latin of the rites, when
monks (bringing their monastic piety with them) were beginning to occupy more prominent positions in the church, and
when the people were particularly susceptible to a "mysteriological piety," and it was the time of the growth of the parochial system when bishops were no longer able to function
as *pater familias* to their people. The eleventh century was
a period of massive reorganization and revision of liturgical
books and of further concerted efforts, particularly under

Gregory VII, to suppress Gallican Rites. In the thirteenth century further revisions and moves toward uniformity were fostered by the Fourth Lateran Council (1215), the Papal Court, and the Franciscan Order.[1]

The process of the *Romanization of Gallican Rites* had extended back for quite some time (for example, the Synod of Whitby). Various Roman commemorations or texts had been picked up, replacing or supplementing Gallican forms. The *Bobbio Missal*, for example, contains a Eucharistic rite which is Gallican through the Sanctus but Roman from there to the end. The *Stowe Missal* contains the Roman Canon in its Eucharistic rite which still retains all of the elements of a Gallican Eucharistic Prayer. Some evidences of the *Gallicanization of the Roman Rite* are found in the Gelasian Sacramentaries, but the process was greatly accelerated with the efforts to suppress the Gallican Rites. A Gallican supplement (long associated with Alcuin but now thought more probably to have been the work of Benedict of Aniane) was provided for the Gregorian Sacramentary.[2] This supplement contained additional Propers, rites, and ceremonies which were important in the liturgical life of the Gallican people. The manner in which these were incorporated into the Roman Rite was sometimes incongruous. Many such Gallicanizations eventually affected the books used in Rome itself (for example, in the eleventh century the Gloria in excelsis came into normal use, and the Nicene Creed came to have a place in the Eucharistic rite) and were then promulgated from Rome.

With the exception of the area around Milan and some places in Spain, the Roman Rite was essentially the rite of Western Europe from the eleventh century. Various late medieval *uses* are sometimes mistakenly referred to as *rites*. The medieval uses were variants of the Roman Rite which were characteristic of a particular locality or monastic order. The uses were distinguished by Gallicanizations and innovations, or by resistance to particular revisions or innovations.[3] In England, on the eve of the Reformation, the most popular uses were those of Sarum, York, and Hereford. By far the most popular of these was that of Sarum, the use of the Salisbury Cathedral, the codification of which was probably begun with the founding of the new cathedral at Salisbury when Richard la Poore was bishop (1217–28).[4]

Dating back into the ninth and tenth centuries, but chiefly in the eleventh century, the liturgical books were reorganized in the West. All that was necessary to conduct the Eucharistic rite was gathered from the different books into one book, the *Missal*. The material needed for the conduct of the Daily Offices was gathered into the *Breviary;* litanies into the *Processional;* occasional offices needed by a presbyter into the *Manuale (Agenda, Rituale);* rites conducted by a bishop into the *Pontifical (Benedictional)*. Rules for the conduct of the rites were written up in an *Ordinale (Customary, Pie)*. In this reorganization the services were so arranged that a participating group was no longer necessary for the conduct of a rite: one man could now celebrate the Eucharist, say the Daily Offices, baptize, marry, or bury. Rules could now be made, and did begin to be made, which made the saying of the Eucharist and the Offices the individual duty of men in orders. For those on journeys there grew up the abbreviated *Missale itinerarium* and the *Portiforium* (a portable Breviary). The services could now be conducted for the people rather than by the people. A person could now be identified who could be paid to perform a rite for someone, and a system of stipends came into being. This reorganization arose partly out of the necessity imposed by the fact that few could read Latin, partly out of the imposition of a new rite (the Roman Rite) in formerly Gallican territory, and partly as a result of the spread of a new non-participatory, individualistic, mysteriological piety which was fostered by the language barrier. The liturgy became a spectator sport, or the rites became the private devotions of the priest and the setting for non-liturgical private devotions of the people. Theologians, as Peter Lombard, Hugh of St. Victor, and Thomas Aquinas, were put into the situation of having to provide definitions (for example, seven sacraments), justifications, rationales, and allegorical interpretations for the rites, whereas theologians of earlier periods had found in the rites the foundations and sources of theology *(lex orandi lex credendi).*[5] (See p. 5)

THE SANCTIFICATION OF LIFE

Initiation—In the West as early as the eleventh century we begin to find manuscripts which provide for the baptism of infants within one short rite. That of the Sarum Manuale, which was typical of those of the late Middle Ages, retains elements from various rites which had been parts of the process of Christian Initiation in earlier periods. At the door of the church the child was signed on the forehead and breast, and hands were laid upon his head. Salt was exorcised and placed in his mouth. This was all that remained of the old catechumenate. These rites and ceremonies were followed by remnants of the period of candidacy. The child was exorcised and signed with a prayer for "the light of understanding." Following this were forms reminiscent of the old Holy Saturday morning rite: the reading of the Matthean version of the blessing of the children and the *Effeta* (now as an opening of the ears to hear and the mouth to confess) performed with spittle. Taking the place of the *redditio symboli* was the repetition by the godparents of the Lord's Prayer, the Ave Maria, and the Apostles' Creed. The child was then signed on the right hand (relic of the Celtic post-baptismal signation?), blessed, and carried into the church. If the water in the font was to be renewed, the Blessing of the Font was inserted at this point. The order for the Blessing of the Font was made up of a Litany of the Saints, a collect, and the Gelasian Blessing, which was rich in Biblical imagery and was accompanied by an elaborate ceremonial. The rubrics made clear that contact with water so blessed constituted rebaptism. A three-fold renunciation, an anointing of the infant between the shoulders with "the oil of salvation," a three-fold interrogation concerning the Creed, and an expression of desire for baptism followed. The child was then immersed three times in the Name of the Trinity. He was then anointed with chrism on the back of the head, clothed in a white garment (actually a remnant of this, the *chrysom*), given a lighted candle, and "If a bishop is present he must immediately be confirmed and next communicated, if his age require it." The godparents were admonished to teach him the Creed, the Ave Maria, the Lord's Prayer, and how to cross himself, and to see that he is confirmed "as soon as the bishop comes within a distance of seven miles." The priest (to protect the child against epilepsy) then read Mark 9:17–29 and ended the rite by reading John 1:1–14.[6]

From the thirteenth century, only those born within eight days of Easter or Pentecost were to be saved for baptism at the Vigil. The priest was to instruct his people about how to baptize in emergencies. The fear of limbo had caused baptism to precede catechetical instruction and to lose its integral connection with the Church Year, with the bishop, and with the local congregation. Baptism no longer was the time of repentance, confession of faith, death and resurrection, the conferring of the Holy Spirit, manumission, the binding together of blood brothers (and much of this imagery had been lost from the rite) but a bath to wash away the taint of original sin.

The imposition of the Roman Rite upon former Gallican territory led to duplications within several of the rites (See p. 82, 88, 96), and the supplying of the peculiar second post-baptismal anointing of the Roman Rite, which was unknown to other initiatory rites—Eastern or Western—led to the emergence of a rite and a theology of confirmation. Something of the peculiarity of its development can be illustrated from liturgical books of the medieval period. Printed with clinical baptism in the *Gelasian Sacramentary* (after the baptism, the chrismation, and the Communion, possibly for use as a public reception of a person who had survived) is a form for use in connection with a signation by the bishop:

> Almighty God, Father of our Lord Jesus Christ, you have made your servant to be born again of water and the Holy

Spirit, and have given him remission of all his sins; pour upon him, Lord, your Holy Spirit the Paraclete, and give him the spirit of wisdom and understanding, the spirit of counsel and might, the spirit of knowledge and godliness, and fill him with the spirit of fear of God and of our Lord Jesus Christ; and grant him to be sealed unto life eternal by the sign of the cross; through your Son Jesus Christ our Lord, who lives and reigns with you in the unity of the Holy Spirit.

The person is then signed on the forehead with chrism by the bishop as he says, "The sign of Christ unto life eternal." In the later *Leofric Missal*, in a section devoted to miscellaneous episcopal blessings, under the title "At the imposition of hands," there is included (*sans* rubrics) a version of this prayer for the "sevenfold Spirit," followed by "Accept the sign of the cross, the chrism of salvation, in Christ Jesus, unto eternal life. Amen," and an antiphon (Psalm 128:1a and 6). In some of the Pontificals of the twelfth and thirteenth centuries a rite "For confirmation of infants" is found. It consists of prayer for the "sevenfold Spirit," chrismation on the forehead with the text, "I confirm [and sign] you in the name of the Father and Son and Holy Spirit," the Pax, a prayer that those confirmed may be "temples of glory," [the Antiphon,] and a blessing. By the time of the printed Sarum priest's Manuales, in the rite for the "Confirmation of children" "by bishops or deputies," the form which accompanied the chrismation had been expanded to read, "I sign thee *N*. with the sign of the cross ✠ and I confirm thee with the chrism of salvation, in the name of the Father ✠ and of the Son ✠ and of the Holy Ghost. ✠ Amen." Medieval theologians began to explain this new rite as a strengthening for spiritual combat which would come with adolescence. Thomas Aquinas defines confirmation as a signing with the sign of the cross that the one confirmed may not be ashamed to confess the faith of Christ crucified and manfully to fight under his banner (*Summa Theologica*, Part III, Question 72, Article 9). The rationale which was used throughout this period for this peculiar second anointing of the Roman rite which came to be called "confirmation" has been aptly and succinctly summarized in these words:

> We . . . do sign *him* with the sign of the Cross, in token that hereafter *he* shall not be ashamed to confess the faith of Christ crucified, and manfully to fight under his banner, against sin, the world, and the devil; and to continue Christ's faithful soldier and servant unto *his* life's end.[7]

Equation of this rite of "confirmation" and of this rationale with earlier practice in Rome, with Eastern chrismations, or with the post-immersion ceremonies of Gallican Rites is highly questionable.[8]

The practice of infant baptism and the new mysteriological Eucharistic piety worked together to separate First Communion from baptism. Though remnants of earlier practice prevailed into the sixteenth century, legislation of the thirteenth century forbade Communion prior to "confirmation" and linked "confirmation" with the "years of discretion."

Penance—By the eleventh century there were very few remnants of the discipline of public penitence. The old texts were, however, retained in use, and Lent was given a new dimension as a time in which, in a sense, all received ashes and underwent penitence.[9]

Within this period general confessions and absolutions came into use, largely as preparations for participation in the Eucharistic rite or the Daily Offices.

Several changes came in the Western rites of private penance. The order of the three stages (confession, acts of penitence, and reconciliation) came to be reversed: confession, then reconciliation, then acts of penitence. The outward sign of the laying-on-of-hands was dropped. Declaratory absolutions tended to displace or supplement precatory absolutions. Confessors were limited to priests, and a penitent was normally required to confess to his own parish priest. Confession became obligatory prior to Communion and at least yearly.[10]

Marriage—The rites associated with marriage were telescoped. Banns were posted. The equivalent of the old civil marriage was held on the church porch immediately before the marriage, and the giving of blessed bread and wine was often substituted for Communion.[11]

Pregnancy and Childbirth—The rite for the Churching of Women of the Sarum Manuale, which was fairly typical of late medieval Western rites, consists of Psalms 121 and 128, the Lord's Prayer, some Versicles and Responses, and a prayer—all of which were to be said on the church porch. The woman was then asperged, and then she was led into the church by the priest as he said the form which was also used when carrying an unbaptized child into the church. Other Psalms were often used (for example, Psalm 24, 51, 86, or 122) and/or the Magnificat or the Nunc dimittis, and Luke's account of the Presentation of Christ was sometimes read.[12]

Ordination—Within the tenth and eleventh centuries the Roman and the Gallican rites of ordination were combined in a manner which substantially retained the texts and ceremonies of both rites. In effect a man was ordained twice, once in a Roman manner and once in a Gallican manner. In the late Middle Ages, additional prayers and blessings (including a second imposition of hands with the words, "Receive the Holy Spirit; whose sins you remit . . . ," at the ordination of presbyters), the *Veni Creator* (See *The Hymnal 1940* 108, 217, 218, and 371 for various translations), the delivery of instruments of office (chalice and paten for presbyters; crozier, ring, and mitre for bishops), and an anointing (of the hands of presbyters; of the head of bishops) were added to the rites. The use of the word "priest" was extended to include those in presbyteral orders, and when three orders were spoken of the reference was often to priests, deacons, and sub-deacons. What was the essential matter of the sacrament of ordination came to be highly debatable.[13]

Vestments—During this period allegorical interpretations of vestments grew up, and additional vestments and insignia came into use: a stylized open-fronted version of the chasu-

ble, the cope; fuller forms of the alb, the rochet and surplice; the chimere (a doctor's habit), the tippet and the hood
(which are really academic insignia rather than clerical insignia); and the mitre (a pointed headdress worn by a bishop or
an abbot).[14]

Sick Rites—The Visitation of the Sick underwent great
changes during this period. There was an effort to revive
the practice of unction in the ninth century, for remission of
sins. When Communions became quite infrequent and confession prior to Communion became obligatory, prayers for
healing tended to drop out of the Visitation rites, and penitential elements were multiplied. The rite tended to be reserved for use with the dying. The Sarum Manuale still distinguished between "The Visitation of the Sick" and "Extreme Unction," however. The Visitation rite consists of the
Seven Penitential Psalms with Antiphon, the Pax, Adoration
of a crucifix, asperges, nine collects, an exhortation to faith
and love, the confession, and seven absolutions (one of
which is an old form for the reconciliation of public penitents). Extreme Unction consists of Psalm 71 with Antiphon
("O Saviour of the world"), the anointing of seven parts of
the body as eight Psalms are said, a prayer, Communion
from the Reserved Sacrament, and additional Psalmody,
prayers, and blessings. At the point of death the Nicene
Creed, the Seven Penitential Psalms, and a Litany of the
Saints are to be said.[15]

Burial—The changes in the burial rites were not so
much in the pattern (which still consisted of Commendation,
Vespers [Placebo], Matins [Dirge], Eucharist, Committal,
and anniversary commemorations) as in the texts and the
ceremonies associated with the rites. Black replaced white
as the color. The processions with Alleluias, Psalms of
praise, and the waving of palm branches were replaced by
mournful corteges with the Penitential Psalms. The hopeful
commendatory prayers were supplemented or displaced by
absolutions of the body and such prayers as "Deliver him
from the hand of hell, from the deep pit, from the lion's
mouth," and such hymns as the *Dies irae* (*The Hymnal 1940*

468). Other evidences of the changes in the piety are the addition of the daily Office of the Dead, the regular inclusion of a commemoration of the dead in the Eucharistic Prayer (See the bracketed paragraph on page 72), Votive Masses for the Dead, and the institution of All Souls' Day (November 2). The growing fear of purgatory had effected drastic changes in the liturgy.[16]

THE SANCTIFICATION OF TIME

The Liturgical Day—The daily services, having become the individual or collective duty of monks and those in orders, tended to become further removed from the people. A revision of the early twelfth century for the Papal Court and a revision of the thirteenth century by Haymo of Faversham for the Franciscans, which was adopted by the Papal Court and promulgated through much of Europe, resulted in a tremendous increase in the commemorations of Saints' Days and their Octaves and the introduction of many readings from the legends of the saints. The Lord's Prayer and the Ave Maria were prefixed to some Offices, and a creed, collects, and a confession were added to some. To make room for these additions and commemorations, the Psalmody and lections were reduced. "O Lord, open thou our lips," for example, remained as a relic of Psalm 51. The Sarum Offices for Advent, for example, were so affected that only two days were immune from commemorations, and less than two chapters were left of the old course reading of the Book of Isaiah. Offices tended to be grouped so that Matins, Lauds, and Prime were often said as one service, and Vespers and Compline were said together as another. The Office of Our Lady and the Office of the Dead were added to the Daily Offices. In the late Middle Ages a simplified breviary for the literate laity called a *Primer* or *Book of Hours*, based upon these Offices arranged for a daily or weekly cycle, came into being.[17]

The Liturgical Week—In the Eastern Rites the liturgical

week continued to center around the Sunday Eucharist. In the West this was still true in theory, but the multiplication of Saints' Days, the innovation of the Votive Mass, the increased frequency (and finally the obligation upon the priest) of a daily Mass obscured the structure of the liturgical week, the distinction between feast and fast, and the integral connection of Sunday and the Eucharist.

The Eucharist—In the Eastern Rites the mysteriological piety of the period affected the Eucharistic rites through an increase in penitential and preparatory elements, including the development of the *Prothesis* (Service of Preparation of the Elements). Portions of the rite began to be said silently by the priest, and a screen of icons, the *iconostasis*, was erected, separating the people from the sanctuary. A veil began to be drawn over the doors at the time of certain preparations and devotions of the priest. Communions of the people began to decline. Allegorical interpretations of the rite began to grow up. The Byzantine or Constantinopolitan Liturgy extended its sphere of influence more and more. Within the Byzantine Rite the Liturgy in normal use is that of St. John Chrysostom, but on the Sundays of Lent (except Palm Sunday), and on Christmas, Easter, and St. Basil's Day (January 1), the fuller Liturgy of St. Basil (which differs in the prayers said by the priest) is used instead.[18]

In the West a new type of Eucharistic piety (witness the Eucharistic controversies of the ninth century) began to affect the rite. The heading "The Canon" began to appear in the books after the Sanctus rather than prior to the Sursum corda, which in effect separated that note of thanksgiving which was retained from the Canon. In the commemoration of the living of the Canon, "Remember your servants who offer to You" became "Remember your servants for whom we offer or who offer to You." The Canon began to be said silently while the choir completed an elaborate Sanctus. Screens or veils were erected between the people and the altar in some places. Votive Masses, Masses for the Dead (as distinct from the older commemorative Eucharists), and regulations requiring priests individually to say Mass came into being, so the Low Mass which necessitated the presence of no one but a priest and a server was born. The old Patristic principle of One Altar was broken down, and side altars began to be erected for the multiplication of Masses. To economize on space, these side altars were placed against the wall, and the officiant typically had no congregation and no ambo, so lections were simply read at the altar. Since there were seldom offerers, the paten and chalice were prepared beforehand or by the server. The kissing of a Pax board was eventually substituted for the Kiss of Peace. Since there was no choir, Psalms began to be entered by title. Customs or ceremonials which were practical or appropriate to a Low Mass then began to affect the High Mass. The Offertory Procession, for example, dropped out of normal use. The awesome mysteriological piety of the period fostered a concern about even the tiniest fragments, and wafers began to be substituted for leavened bread. As further protective measures, the consecrated Wafer began to be placed in the communicant's mouth by the priest, houseling cloths came into use, the ciborium was substituted for the more significatory paten, receiving Communion in both kinds began to die out, Communion began to be withheld from infants, and ablutions began to be systematized. Private prayers of confession and preparation for the priest began to work their way into the rite. The rite became more and more the prerogative of the priest, and the Communions of the people began to be administered outside the rite after confession. Allegorical meanings began to be attached to ceremonies and appurtenances and to foster an increase in ceremonial (compare, for example, the restrained use of signs of the cross in the Canon in early books and the thirty-three of some late Missals). The rite itself began to be explained in allegorical terms. One system, for example, based upon the life of Christ, likens the Introit to the Prophets, the Kyrie to Zacharias, the Gloria in excelsis to the song of the Angels, the Collect to the visit to the Temple at the age of twelve, the Epistle to the preaching of John the Baptist, etc. Other systems were based upon Old

Testament typology, the forty works of Christ's life, the thirty-three years, etc.[19]

The Fourth Lateran Council (1215) accepted the doctrine of Transubstantiation, and this had a profound effect upon ceremonial and piety. Between 1215 and the turn of the century accounts of Eucharistic miracles appeared. People began to kneel within the rite. The Bread began to be elevated at the Words of Institution, and the sanctus bell came into use. Evidences of reverences to the Sacrament appeared. The Feast of Corpus Christi was instituted. In the fourteenth and fifteenth centuries people began to be directed to kneel when the Sacrament was carried to the sick. Processions of the Sacrament appeared. The place of reservation was moved from the sacristy to the church itself, where the Sacrament was reserved in an aumbry, dove, or ' tower, or, on occasion, exposed in a monstrance. Priests began to hold thumb and forefinger together from the Words of Institution until the ablutions, which began to be done publicly prior to the final prayers. On the Continent genuflections to the Sacrament began to appear. The Cup began to be elevated after the Words of Institution. Altars were elongated, made more tomblike in appearance, and equipped with retables and crosses (sometimes crucifixes), so that they provided a more impressive background for the Elevations. Pews having come into use, lawsuits appeared for seats that provided the best views for the Elevations. Seeing had been substituted for participating and receiving. By the end of the Middle Ages people had almost ceased receiving altogether (witness the frequency of legislation requiring a yearly Communion). An extant sixteenth century exposition explains to the layman that the reason some prayers in the Mass are in the plural is that in the first days of the church sometimes some others received Communion with the priest at Mass.

Preaching fell into disuse. Attempts to revive it were made through legislation (requiring sermons from one to four times a year) and by Friars. The *Prone* came into being as a setting for the sermon (sometimes after the Gospel, but

often outside the rite). The Prone typically contained biddings or intercessions, a general confession and absolution,
the Ave Maria, the Lord's Prayer, and the Creed.

With the loss of tension between fast and feast, between
Sunday and weekday, two movements tended to provide pattern to the week. One was a growing sabbatarianism in
some areas. The other was a linking of particular Votives to
particular days of the week (for example, Sunday as commemorative of the Trinity, Monday of the Birth, Tuesday
the Baptism, Wednesday the Betrayal, Thursday the Institution of the Eucharist, Friday the Passion, and Saturday the
Virgin Mary).[20]

The Liturgical Year—During this period the liturgical
year was affected in several ways. Lent became a time of
penance for all. Advent became a semi-penitential period of
preparation for Christ's coming again as Judge. The late medieval Missals contain commemorations of well over twice as
many Saints' Days as the old Gregorian Sacramentary, several times as many as the old Gallican books. Not only were
Saints' Days multiplied by the appropriation of Propers from
other congregations or areas where the feast had originated,
but additional feasts of Christ (for example, Transfiguration,
the Name of Jesus) and of Mary (for example, the Visitation) and of New Testament Saints who had not previously
been given a day (for example, Matthias) were also added to
the calendar. Probably the most significant of the other new
feasts were Trinity (and in England and northern Europe
the remaining Sundays of the year began to be numbered
from Trinity Sunday), Corpus Christi, and All Souls' Day.
Unfortunately the Vigils of Easter, Pentecost, and Epiphany tended no longer to be the times for baptisms. The
lections were reduced and shortened, and the celebration
was pushed up into the prior day.[21]

Music—During this period the repertoire of music was
increased by new hymns for the Offices, and by Sequences
(a hymn used between the Epistle and the Gospel), which
were quite frequent in some uses (particularly in uses such
as Sarum which at High Mass had something reminiscent of

a Great Entrance at this point). Many of the texts of the period were highly subjective, pietistic, or otherworldly. The organ and polyphony began to come into use before the period was over. Plainsong continued as the basic music of the rites, though there was a tendency toward elaboration in the music in order to cover those parts of the rites which were said silently. Settings for only certain parts of the Mass have survived, for after the beginning of musical notation these were the only parts of a High Mass which were heard: the Introit, Kyrie (often farced [a trope]), Gloria in excelsis, Salutation and Collect, Epistle, Gradual, Alleluia or Tract, Sequence, Gospel, Creed, Offertory Verses, Sursum corda, Preface, Sanctus, Benedictus qui venit, "world without end. Amen," Protocol and Lord's Prayer, Pax, Agnus Dei, Communion Verse(s), Post-communion, *super populum*, and Dismissal. Under the cover of the elaborate settings, the priest would apparently have proceeded to his initial private devotions, the preparation of the chalice and paten and the offertory prayers, the Canon, his Communion, and the closing prayers.[22]

THE SANCTIFICATION OF SPACE

Buildings—The medieval church building was developed as a functional setting for the worship of the period. The Daily Offices were the duty of the clergy, so a *choir* to provide an adequate accommodation for the clergy staff was protected from drafts by a rood screen. Since the late medieval Offices consisted primarily of Psalmody said or sung antiphonally, half the group faced the other half. Many altars were needed for each priest to say Mass daily, so they were provided in the bays, often with protective screening. Since the baptisms were normally private baptisms of infants, a screened bay near the door equipped with a font (typically about two feet across and one foot deep) sufficed. Since the part of the congregation was to be present rather than to hear and to participate, the nave served admirably for that purpose as well as for other parish functions (fairs, dances, courts, etc.). Some naves included pulpits, so placed that the people could best see and hear. A porch provided the setting for portions of certain rites and for the posting of notices (and theses). The art was designed to stimulate devotion and to provide teaching for those present while Masses were being said. The aim of the architect was not to create beauty or atmosphere but to provide a building which was functional in terms of the uses to which it was put.[23]

The Consecration of Churches—The late medieval rite for the Consecration of Churches represents a fusion of the Gallican and the Roman rites.[24]

Colors—Except for the use of white for baptisms and burials, and among the Gallican clergy for Eucharistic vestments, we have few indications of the deliberate use of particular colors before the late Middle Ages. Medieval paintings show differing colors on and about the altar and on the several clergy participating within a service. Where vestments were more limited, the best (regardless of its color) seems to have been reserved for the big feasts, the next best for other festal occasions. In more affluent situations, during the late Middle Ages various uses did begin to appear. Rather typically, light colors (white) were associated with the most joyous occasions, dark (black, dark blue, dark red) with occasions of penitence and sorrow, and bright (red) with occasions which evoked mixed or ambivalent reactions. The whole life of a group is typically symbolized in color by the use of red, white, and black or blue (for example, in flags). Such reactions to colors seem to be typical of all men, and the roots have been found in the reactions to bodily emissions.[25]

CHAPTER VI

THE PERIOD OF
PRINTED BOOKS

The invention of the printing press coincided with the New Learning of the Renaissance, a rising tide of nationalism, and a growing dissatisfaction with the church. The printing press was soon brought into use to foster greater uniformity within the Roman Rite, for the preservation of the Mozarabic Rite (Ximenes' edition of the *Missale Mixtum* and of the Breviary), and to spread the writings of Humanists and reformers. The principal issue liturgically was the remolding of the liturgy so that it would not be inconsistent with the teaching of the Scriptures, especially on the cardinal question of Justification.[1]

In Luther's *Babylonian Captivity* he attacked certain sacramental teachings and practices of the Roman Church. Impatient reformers (for example, Carlstadt) soon began to revise the liturgy. Luther's own efforts date from 1523. He

eventually provided forms or instructions for the revision of
the Mass, the Daily Offices, Baptism, Marriage, Ordination,
and the Litany. He also wrote Catechisms and a number of
hymns. A flood of German Church Orders, which treated of
doctrine, discipline, and worship, began to appear. Generally they adhered less to medieval forms than had Luther's.
Especially important are the Order of Brenz and Osiander
(with whom Cranmer boarded in 1532, and whose niece he
married) for Brandenburg-Nuremberg (1533), the Orders for
Cassel (1539), Saxony [Justus Jonas] (1539), Electoral Bran-
denberg (1540), Calenberg and Göttingen [Rabe] (1542),
Pfalz-Newberg [Osiander] (1543), and the *Consultation* of
Archbishop Hermann von Wied of Cologne (1543), which
was published in English in 1547, and again in a revised
version, in 1548.[2]

In 1524 German services were put into use at Strassburg. Martin Bucer soon made his influence felt there, and
his liturgical abilities came to be valued so that he began to
be consulted in the formulation of Church Orders. He was
primarily responsible for the liturgical portions (and Melancthon for the doctrinal portions) of Hermann's *Consultation*.[3]

At Zurich, after a more conservative attempt at revision
had not been satisfactory to radical reformers, Zwingli in
1525 proposed a German liturgy which was more didactic,
rationalistic, and subjective than the Lutheran liturgies. Calvin found at Geneva rites similar to those in use at Zurich,
but from his exile in Strassburg he brought back rites influenced by the liturgy which he found there. His stated
principle was that rites should be based upon the warrant of
Scripture and the custom of the early church. Calvin's rites
were put into use in England by exiles, and they were published by Pullain in 1551. During the reign of Mary, English
exiles in Geneva put into use a Service Book based upon
Calvin's rites, which formed the basis for the Scottish *Book
of Common Order* 1562).[4]

Other more radical reformers (Anabaptists, *et al.*)
stressed the principal that the congregation should be made
up of the converted, the Spirit-filled, and they feared stated

liturgies as quenching the Spirit. Eventually, principally through the Free Churches, they were to affect other traditions.[5]

In the first decades of the sixteenth century there were also efforts at liturgical reform among the Romans (for example, the revisions of the Breviary by Quiñones). Reaction, however, set in, and the Council of Trent ordered a revision. The revision seems to have taken the liturgy of the city of Rome during the pontificate of Gregory VII as its basis. A Congregation of Rites was established, and a stricter uniformity was enforced. Old rites and uses were allowed to be continued only in those places which could substantiate for them a tradition of two hundred years.[6]

Even Eastern Rites did not remain unaffected at this time. The printing press and renewed communications between the East and the West fostered standardization and Westernization. Some smaller Eastern groups submitted to Rome (Uniates), and their rites and their explanations of them have become highly Romanized.[7]

Typical twentieth century American Protestant worship has been influenced by many factors in addition to the Reformation. Puritanism, the rise of the Free Churches, reaction against establishmentarianism, pietism, pioneer conditions, pluralism, revivalism, rationalism, Romanticism, and (for immigrants from the Continent) the lack of vernacular liturgies have all had an effect.[8]

THE SANCTIFICATION OF LIFE

Initiation—Luther attempted to restore an emphasis upon baptism as death and resurrection and as the anointing of kings and priests. In 1523 he published a much abbreviated rite, but the one element of the medieval rite which is essentially missing is the Blessing of the Water. The one new element is a prayer (the "Flood Prayer") which is built upon the Flood and the Exodus as types of baptism and the Baptism of Jesus as the sanctification of water for baptism:

Almighty everlasting God, you of your justice did destroy by the flood the unfaithful world, and of your mercy did save faithful Noah, even his family of eight persons, and did drown in the Red Sea hard-hearted Pharaoh with all his army, and did lead your people Israel safely through it; thereby you did figure the washing of your holy baptism. And by the baptism of your dear Son, our Lord Jesus Christ, you did sanctify the Jordan and all waters for a saving flood and an ample washing away of sins. We beseech you, for your infinite mercy, that you will mercifully look upon this *N.*, and bless him with true faith in the spirit, that by this wholesome laver all that was born in him from Adam and which he himself has added unto it may be drowned and submerged, and that he may be separated from the unfaithful and preserved in the holy ark of Christendom dry and safe, and being fervent in spirit and joyful through hope may ever serve thy name so that he may attain everlasting life with all the faithful, through Jesus Christ our Lord. Amen.

In 1526 Luther brought out a simplified version of the baptismal rite which omitted all breathings, the use of oil, and the giving of the candle. Other German Orders (including Hermann's) tended to depart more from the Roman rite, separating in time the admission to the catechumenate from the baptism, inserting lengthy exhortations and prayers, linking the Naming of the child with the application of water, insisting that the rite be performed at the Sunday Eucharist, and setting new regulations for godparents and requiring that they make promises for themselves. The Reformed Churches rejected the doctrine of the damnation of unbaptized infants and the practice of baptism by lay persons, and they allowed private baptisms only in extreme circumstances. They rejected all of the ceremonies (exorcisms, signations, Blessing of the Font, anointings, vesting, giving of the candle) except the baptism itself, which among them was typically administered by pouring (affusion), which before the Reformation had become normal in their area. While not necessarily rejected at first by the Reformed Churches, the practice of godparents fell out of use among them. Their rites typically retained the rehearsal of the Apostles' Creed and the Lord's Prayer and the use of the

Trinitarian formula, and they were provided with new prayers and exhortations. The Anabaptists insisted that baptism must represent an adult commitment and rebaptized (typically by immersion) those who had been baptized in infancy. From the sixteenth century pouring has been the normal practice within the Roman tradition.[9]

Wycliffe had spoken of confirmation as "a frivolous rite," and the Bohemian Brethren had substituted instruction culminated by examination, an expression of a desire to renew the baptismal covenant, a renunciation of Satan, a confession of faith, prayer for the strength of the Holy Spirit, admission to Communion, and a laying-on-of-hands with an invocation "for strengthening their hope of heavenly grace." Erasmus expressed approval and made similar recommendations, suggesting that such a rite would have greater authority if performed by the bishops. Luther rejected the late medieval rite of confirmation as "mumbo-jumbo" which could add nothing to baptism. He devised catechisms which explained the Creed, the Decalogue, the Lord's Prayer, and the Sacraments (an outline for catechetical content which became classic among German Church Orders), and he stated that children should give an account before being admitted to Communion. Although he devised no rite for graduation from catechetical instruction, he stated that he did not find fault if a pastor examined the faith of the children and confirmed them by the laying-on-of-hands. Various German Orders provided such a rite. Bucer, in reaction to Anabaptist criticism, devised a rite for graduation from catechism, renewal of baptismal vows, and admission to Communion (which was to be administered publicly on the three great feasts) with an examination, laying-on-of-hands, and prayer. By the time of the Cologne Order he had come to feel that this rite should be administered by a bishop (or at least by a visitor) in order to get the bishops out into the parishes, so that the examination would be conducted by an outsider, to add dignity or impressiveness to the occasion, and as a sign of the catholicity of the church. Calvin denounced confirmation, particularly the use of chrism, but he (along with many

others of the period) believed that confirmation had once existed in a pure form, in which, after instruction, children
openly professed their faith, were catechized, and received
an imposition of hands as a "benediction." Eventually rites
of this sort emerged within the Reformed tradition. Among
the Moravians there grew up a periodic covenant rite, which
was picked up by the Methodists. Among the Romans several practices which had some medieval precedent came to
be accepted as normal. Seven became the recommended age
for confirmation. First Communion often precedes confirmation. As in the late Middle Ages, the power to confirm can
be delegated to presbyters. The officiant is to place his right
hand upon the head of the confirmand at the chrismation.
An initial blessing and a tap on the cheek (which are found
in some medieval uses) have become a part of the rite. The
tap on the cheek has been interpreted as the making of a
soldier of Christ, but it is possibly a relic of the Kiss of
Peace.[10]

Penance—In the Lutheran and Reformed Churches efforts were made to restore the ancient public penitence
through the institution of church discipline and the "fencing
of the Table." The Roman form for the reconciliation of excommunicates (which is used at the receiving of converts as
well) includes an amplified creed, Psalm 51 or Psalm 130,
and a form of absolution.

General confessions (and often absolutions) are typically
found in Lutheran and Reformed rites.

Private confession was for a time considered a sacrament
by Luther, and he and many of the German Orders provided
forms with declaratory absolutions. The principle of acts of
penance ("satisfaction") was rejected. The practice of private confession was not to be imposed on anyone (though
many of the Orders considered it normal in preparation for
Communion), and confession to a layman was again allowed.
Calvin denied the sacramental nature of private confession,
though he admitted absolution as a ceremony to confirm
faith in the forgiveness of sins. The Council of Trent reiter-
ated the teaching of the Scholastics, and the *Rituale Ro-
manum* provided a standardized form.[11]

Marriage—Luther looked upon marriage as a vocation rather than as a concession to human weakness. He greatly abbreviated the marriage rite. He retained the Publication of Banns. On the church porch the questions of betrothal were to be asked, followed by "Those whom God hath joined together," and a Proclamation of the Marriage (two items not found in the Sarum Use but which had medieval German precedents). The couple were then carried before the altar for the reading of Gen. 2:18, 21–24, an exhortation (consisting mostly of Scriptural quotations), and a prayer. The rites of the German Church Orders, however, tended to be fuller. That of Cologne, for example, requires an examination of the couple (and their parents), and the publication of banns on three Holy Days. The rite is to be performed within the Sunday Service. It begins with an exhortation which includes several Scriptural quotations. This is followed by silent prayer of the congregation, the betrothal questions, exchange of rings, the Proclamation of the Marriage, the singing of Psalms 127 and 128, and prayer. The Blessing of the Ring was typically omitted from German Orders. The Reformed rites were also to be conducted within the Sunday Service, banns having been published beforehand. Within the Reformed tradition the blessing or the giving of rings within the rite was typically rejected.[12]

Pregnancy and Childbirth—The churching of women is not usually found in the Lutheran or Reformed books. That of the Roman Rituale has been changed so that the woman is brought into the church prior to the prayer.

Ordination—Luther's ordination rite consisted of *Veni Sancte Spiritus* (see *The Hymnal 1940* 109), the Collect for Pentecost, I Tim. 3:1–7, Acts 20:28–31, an exhortation, a laying-on-of-hands by the presbyters during which the Lord's Prayer (and another prayer) were said, I Peter 5:2–4, and a blessing—within the Eucharistic rite. As a result of controversy with the Anabaptists in Strassburg, Bucer developed a stronger feeling for Church Order. He proposed a rite for ordination (which would be adapted for the different orders of bishops, presbyters, and deacons). The names of the ordinands were to be read out the Sunday prior to the ordination. The rite consisted of a sermon on the ministry and the duty of the people to the ministers, prayers, *Veni Sancte Spiritus*, Psalms, an Epistle (Acts 20: 17–35 or I Tim. 3), a Gospel (Matt. 28:18–20, John 10:1–16, or 20:19–23), an exhortation and examination, congregational silent prayer, prayer, the imposition of hands with a formula, and the Eucharistic rite beginning with the Creed. In the Reformed tradition, ordination was by election, examination, exhortation, and prayer of the congregation and the presbytery. Sometimes it was not accompanied by a laying-on-of-hands. At times the rite was repeated when a clergyman moved to a different congregation. The Romans continued the medieval rites with only minor changes.[13]

Vestments—Typically the German Orders retained the use of the surplice and of Eucharistic Vestments (except for the stole [which was correctly interpreted as the clerical insignia] and the maniple). Apparently first at Zurich, and then throughout the Reformed Churches, the academic gown (symbol of the aristocracy of the New Learning) was substituted for the medieval vestments. A distinctive vesture for the clergy was rejected altogether in the Free Church tradition. Within Romanism, the use of the chasuble became normally restricted to priests, and the shapes of the vestments were greatly modified during the Baroque Period —surplices became shorter, mitres became taller, and chasubles assumed a "fiddle-back" shape.[14]

Sick Rites—Both German Orders and Reformed books typically omitted the anointing from rites for the Visitation of the Sick. Typically the German Orders provided for exhortations, absolution, Psalmody, lections, and a celebration of the Eucharist. That of Electoral Brandenburg provided for Communion from the Reserved Sacrament on days of the public Eucharist. Reformed books typically left the order at the Visitation of the Sick to the minister's discretion. Among those of the Reformed tradition, some favored Communion of the Sick from the public rite, some a celebration for the sick, and some so violently opposed private Communions that they objected to either method. Within the Roman tradition the Communion was moved up to precede the anointings, and the anointing of the loins was dropped.[15]

Burial—The reformers were all violently opposed to the doctrine of purgatory and to Masses for the Dead. The burial rites of Cologne were fairly typical of the German Orders. During the procession to the grave, "In the midst of life we are in death," Psalm 130, or hymns were to be sung. At the grave a lection (from I Cor. 15, Phil. 3:20ff., or Romans 6:8–11) was read. A short office was also provided for use in the church. This office consisted of a lesson, an exhortation, the Lord's Prayer, and two collects. Typically the German Orders contained no formal Committal of the body. Within the Reformed tradition often the burial itself was "without any ceremony," but it was often followed by a service of readings, Psalms, sermon, and prayers in the church.[16]

THE SANCTIFICATION OF TIME

The Liturgical Day—Carlstadt discontinued daily Masses in Wittenberg and closed the churches on weekdays, but Luther reopened them for daily Matins and Vespers. The pattern which he arrived at consisted of several Psalms (in course, with antiphon and hymn, if available), a lesson and interpretation, the Te Deum or Benedictus in the morning or the Magnificat in the evening and/or a German hymn, the Lord's Prayer, Collect(s), and a Dismissal. Other Orders retained or added other elements such as "O Lord, open thou our lips," the Venite, a second lection, the Nunc dimittis, a Creed, and Fixed Collects. Among the Reformed Churches weekday services centering in a lecture, preaching, or prophesying and prayers were common. Within the Roman tradition, Quiñones produced a revised Breviary (1535) which in its second edition (1536) went through more than one hundred printings. Each Office had three Psalms, Saints' Days were curtailed, course readings were restored, the Te Deum was to be said daily except in Advent and

Lent, the Office of the Virgin was restricted to Saturdays, and the Office of the Dead was retained only on All Souls' Day. This Breviary was suppressed in 1568, but an official revised Breviary was published in 1570 in which the chief change from the medieval Roman Breviary was the reduction of commemorations of saints. Over the years, however, a number of new commemorations were added.[17]

The Liturgical Week—The Reformers attempted to restore the primacy of Sunday in the liturgical week, often building upon the sabbatarianism found in some areas in the late medieval period. Luther, Bucer, Zwingli, and Calvin all initially attempted to restore the Eucharist with Communions as the primary Sunday Service, but they all found that people accustomed to receiving Communion but once a year were not ready for such a restoration, and the reformers were all opposed to a non-communicating celebration. At Zurich the pattern of a quarterly Communion was established. Some other churches successfully established a monthly Communion. In most places the Pro-Anaphora was the regular Sunday Service, though in Zurich it was modeled upon the Prone (See p. 93).

The German Church Orders set apart Wednesdays and Fridays as days for the Litany. Among the Reformed Churches, though the principle of fasting was not rejected (witness the called days of fasting and humiliation), that of regular weekly fast days was abandoned or rejected.

Among those of both the Lutheran and the Reformed traditions, Sunday afternoons became a time for catechizing. Among the Romans extra-liturgical devotions in the form of Stations of the Cross and Benediction of the Blessed Sacrament typically became a part of the pattern of the week.

The German Church Orders and the Reformed Churches provided a Service of Preparation for receiving the Sacrament. The Cologne order, for example, consisted of Psalms with antiphons or hymns, the Magnificat, a German Psalm, a lection (I Cor. 10–11 or John 6), a sermon or exhortation, intercessory prayers (especially for those who were to communicate), silent prayer, a collect, and "private instruction of all, one by one" (which is elsewhere spoken of as confession and absolution). Within some traditions Communion Tokens were given to those who qualified to receive.[18]

The Eucharist—Luther did not provide a new Eucharistic rite but attempted to purify the existing rite by the omission of what he considered the later additions: the private prayers of the priest at the Introit, the Offertory, and Communion; the Sequences; the variable Offertory chants and prayers; the Canon; and the variable Postcommunion prayers. He inserted the Words of Institution in the place of the Proper Preface. He expressed a preference for the use of the whole of those Psalms from which verses had been taken. A sermon or homily was to be a part of every Mass. The communicants were to come up into the chancel for the Liturgy of the Table. The rite could be supplemented with vernacular hymns after the Gradual, the Sanctus, and the Agnus Dei. Private Confession before Communion was "not necessary but useful." Two years later (1525) he instituted a German Mass for those unable to understand Latin. German hymns or Psalms or metrical paraphrases were substituted for the Introit, the Gradual, the Creed, the Sanctus, and the Agnus Dei. A seven-action shape was restored (See p. 26), and an exhortation was added after the sermon. Various German Church Orders based their rites upon one of Luther's models or the other. Some instituted "in course" readings in place of the old Epistles and Gospels, a number added Intercessions, and some preceded the Introit with a General Confession, Comfortable Words, and an Absolution.[19]

At Strassburg Diebold Schwarz in 1524 had begun the use of the vernacular and had preceded the rite with a General Confession, Comfortable Words, and an Absolution. He struck the Offertory prayers and substituted an exhortation. When Bucer began to make his influence felt, "Table" replaced "Altar," lections "in course" began to be read from the pulpit, preaching was emphasized, the number of Holy Days was reduced, congregational singing of German hymns was brought into use, exhortations were inserted in the rite, a pattern of weekday Liturgies of the Word and Sunday Eucharists was established (with Ante-Communion being used on Sundays if there were no communicants), the Decalogue and Intercessions were brought into the rite, and a "Peace of God" Blessing was added at the end.

At Zurich, "for the sake of the weaker brethren," Zwingli's reformed rite of 1523 was quite conservative. The lections and sermon were to be in the vernacular, commemoration of Saints' Days was done away, the lectionary was simplified, and a new Canon (which consisted of four paragraphs—a thanksgiving, a sort of *epiclesis* upon the communicants, an *anamnesis*, and a prayer for worthy reception) was provided, but ceremonies, vestments, music, even the Ave Maria were retained in use. This revision was not sufficient to satisfy the iconoclastic radicals for long, however, and in 1525 Zwingli proposed a rite (without any music) in which he attempted to eliminate all that he did not deem scriptural. The model for the regular Sunday Service seems to have been the medieval Prone. It was to consist of Intercessions, the Lord's Prayer, the Ave Maria, reading(s) and sermon, notices of deaths and a prayer of thanksgiving for the departed, a general confession and an absolution. At the four annual Communions (Easter, Pentecost, autumn, and Christmas), this was to be followed by a preparatory prayer, a fixed Epistle (I Cor. 11:20–29), the Gloria in excelsis said antiphonally, a fixed Gospel (John 6:47–63), the Apostles' Creed said antiphonally, an exhortation, the Lord's Prayer, a prayer that the communicants may hereby give thanks faithfully and that they may live as becomes members of His Body, the Words of Institution, administration to the people in their seats from wooden trays and cups, Psalm 113:1–9 read antiphonally, a post-communion thanksgiving, and a dismissal. The Council would not countenance the antiphonal reading, so the only congregational participation was the receiving of Communion and an occasional Amen.

Calvin had found in Geneva a rite close to that of Zurich. While in exile in Strassburg, however, he instituted with his congregation there a rite which more closely approximated that of the German congregation. (One unique feature of his rite was a metrical version of the Decalogue in which each verse ended with the Kyrie.) When Calvin was recalled to Geneva he put into use a simplified version of his Strassburg rite. Typically within the Reformed tradition Communion was received standing or seated at tables rather than being administered to the people seated in the pews as at Zurich.

Within the Moravian tradition a supplementary rite, a sort of *agape*, the Love Feast, was established, which was later to be picked up by the Methodists.

In the Roman Tridentine reform the private prayers of the priest, which had varied from use to use, were standardized. The Proper Prefaces and Sequences were greatly reduced in number, and the Tropes were eliminated. During this period the Sacrament began to be reserved on the Altar in a Tabernacle, and the extra-liturgical devotions of Benediction of the Blessed Sacrament and the Forty Hours Devotion attained popularity.

The Liturgical Year—The German Church Orders typically retained the general structure of the Church Year, but they reduced the Holy Days to Feasts of our Lord (restoring Annunciation and Purification as Feasts of our Lord rather than of Mary), Apostles and Evangelists, St. Stephen the protomartyr, the Holy Innocents, St. John the Baptist, St. Michael and All Angels, and All Saints' Day. The last Sunday in October eventually came to be celebrated as Reformation Sunday. The Reformed Churches typically rejected Holy Days. Some even went so far as to reject the celebration of Easter, Pentecost, and Christmas. Among Moravians and Methodists the New Year became a time for a Covenant Service. At the Counter Reformation the Romans reduced the number of Saints' Days (especially those which had fallen in Lent), but over the next centuries the calendar was filled back up. Reformation Sunday was offset with a Feast of Christ the King on the last Sunday in October. During the Baroque Period there grew up among the Romans a Three Hour Good Friday Service based upon the Seven

Words from the Cross. A devotional based upon the Stations of the Cross also became a popular way of marking Lent (or Fridays).[20]

Music—A popular folk hymnody had been in existence during the Middle Ages. Luther brought it into the service of the liturgy. Among some of the Reformed Churches the use of music in the church was rejected, but Calvin copied the metrical psalmody in use at Strassburg and established its use at Geneva. The same sort of textual puritanism was also part of the Counter Reformation reaction. The use of hymns (Sequences, Tropes, etc.) was drastically curtailed within the Roman Rite. In the eighteenth century Christianized paraphrases of the Psalms (Isaac Watts) and hymns (Watts and the Wesleys) gained acceptance within the Reformed Churches. The use of the organ in church was readily accepted among the Lutherans, but it met with resistance among those of the Reformed tradition. Typically the metrical psalms were lined out. Sometimes village instrumentalists provided a lead or accompaniment. In the eighteenth century the use of organs or choirs for leadership began to come into use, and the presentation of organ voluntaries or of anthems. Among the Romans the Mass settings of the Baroque period seem to have been designed as challenges for choirs and entertainment for congregations, making no allowance for congregational participation. With the rise of Romanticism, choirs (or paid quartets) tended often to usurp the congregational parts of the Services within Lutheran and Reformed Churches, and organs imitative of the orchestra displaced earlier organs which had functioned better for giving a lead to the congregation. In the nineteenth century, hymnody pretty much displaced metrical psalmody. Those from within the Reformed tradition began to borrow from Lutheran sources and to recover the use of plainsong. In America on the frontiers a native folk hymnody (the camp-meeting hymns) arose (which has been said to be America's one native contribution to the arts) (See *The Hymnal 1940* 81, 117, 156, 443). During the later part of the nineteenth century this hymnody was largely displaced by "Gospel hymns" which grew out of the revivalism of the period.[21]

THE SANCTIFICATION OF SPACE

Buildings—In adapting medieval church buildings to reformed rites, the Lutherans were typically conservative. A pulpit was often placed on the side of the nave in the best position for hearing and seeing, and the chancel was treated as a separate room where the communicants could gather about the Table. The font was brought into the nave or chancel so that the congregation could see and hear at the time of baptisms. In new church buildings one room served all three liturgical centers, and the pulpit was sometimes placed above the Table, and the font nearby. Among the Reformed Churches, too, the chancel was sometimes used as a separate room for the Eucharist, but in other cases tables were set up in the nave at the times of celebrations. Reformed Churches which administered to people seated in their pews also began to place the pulpit above the Table. Rather than moving the font out into view, the Reformed Churches typically rejected the use of a font and substituted a basin. Roman architecture of the period tended to be influenced by the throne rooms, the audience chambers, of the time. The center was the new Tabernacle on the Altar with the Reserved Sacrament. No longer did screens or distances separate the people from the Eucharistic Action. But the "dim religious atmosphere" and the long vistas of Gothic seized the imaginations of both Romans and Protestants during the Romantic Period. Out of this fascination, for the first time in liturgical history, buildings began to be built which would determine the liturgy rather than serving the liturgy. The action at the altar was again removed from the people, as was the action at the font. A view even of the altar was often blocked by screens or by lecterns or pulpits, which were so placed that many in the congregation would find it difficult to see or to hear the reader or preacher. The effectiveness of the choir and organ in giving the congregation a lead was reduced by placing them up front and sideways. Access to the Communion rail was made more difficult.[22]

The ejection of community functions from the church

building was pretty much completed during the nineteenth century. The medieval nave had functioned as the community center. The buildings of the seventeenth and eighteenth centuries had typically served for the town meetings and other community affairs. The nineteenth century buildings were not themselves well adapted to serve such needs. Subsidiary buildings began to be built to provide for them, and the church building began to be considered too "holy" to accommodate them.[23]

A rebirth of iconoclasm at the Reformation was to be expected. It showed itself among the Reformed Churches rather than among the Lutherans. It expressed itself in an assertion that the building is the house of the church for the accommodation of its basic functions (the Scottish "bell, Book, basin, and Table") rather than a residence for the god, and in an aversion to images.

Colors—Among the Romans of the Post-Tridentine period the use of colors for vestments, etc., was standardized: purple for Advent, Pre-Lent, Lent, Rogation Days, and Ember Days; White for Christmastide, Epiphany and its Octave, Easter to Pentecost, Trinity Sunday, and the days of saints who were not martyred; red for Pentecost and martyrs; black for Good Friday; green for other days. The Lutheran use has been similar. The Reformed Churches typically did not pick up the use of a color sequence, though generous use of white has tended to be associated with baptism and with the Eucharist, and red has been the typical color for hangings used on the pulpit and Table on other occasions.

CHAPTER VII

THE BOOK OF COMMON PRAYER (ENGLISH)

Efforts toward liturgical reform in England gained momentum soon after Henry's break with the Papacy. "Marshall's Primer," the Ten Articles, the Royal Injunctions, the Bishops' Book, the Thirteen Articles, Hilsey's Primer, the Six Articles, the King's Book, the Rationale of Ceremonial, the reform of the Sarum Breviary, Cranmer's drafts for the Daily Offices, the English Litany, Henry's Primer, the Book of Homilies, the Edwardian Injunctions, the editions in English of Hermann's *Consultation* (See p. 98), the *Order of the Communion*, "Cranmer's Catechism" —each in one way or another paved the way for the Act of Uniformity which required that exclusive use be given to the Book of Common Prayer by Whitsunday 1549.[1]

The writings of the Fathers, English Reformation formularies, German Church Orders, Quiñones' revised Breviary,

Eastern liturgies, Gallican rites, and various uses of the medieval Roman Rite all made contributions to the first Book of Common Prayer.

In two writings dated 1549 Cranmer outlined the principles behind the book: (1) "grounded upon the holy Scripture"; (2) "agreeable to the order of the primitive church"; (3) unifying to the realm; and (4) "edifying" to the people.

The 1549 book was not well received. It was too radical for the Devonshire rebels, for such bishops as Bonner, Thirlby, and Gardiner, and for priests who continued the use of old Service Books or who "counterfeited Masses." On the other hand, it did not go far enough in its revisions to satisfy the Norfolk rebels, or Continental reformers who had come to England and had been given positions of prominence (such as Bucer and Peter Martyr), or the Anabaptists, or some of the clergy and bishops (such as Hooper and Knox).

The Second Act of Uniformity, which enforced the use of a new Prayer Book on All Saints' Day 1552, spoke of the old book as a "godly order" which needed reform only because of misinterpretations and because of doubts as to the manner of ministrations. The 1552 book tightened rubrics and teachings (for example, asserting baptismal regeneration explicitly), restored some medieval elements (for example, the individual obligation of clergy to say the Daily Offices; some Black Letter Days; a relic of the Octaves), and went further in reforming (generally by making explicit what was implicit in 1549, but possibly in some instances it was influenced by Calvinistic liturgies). In 1553 a reformed Primer was issued.

Mary restored the use of the Roman Rite. Some refugees to the Continent during her reign continued the use of the 1552 book; those at Frankfurt revised it; those at Geneva substituted a liturgy based upon that of Calvin.

In 1559, after Elizabeth had come to the throne, the 1552 book was again imposed in England with some changes. That same year the first Elizabethan Primer, modeled after that of Henry VIII rather than that of Edward, was published, and the Edwardian Injunctions were reissued with additions. In 1560 a Latin version of the Prayer Book was published for use in the universities. In 1562 the *Book of Common Order*, based upon Knox's Genevan Service Book, was established in Scotland. During Elizabeth's reign Puritan versions or revisions of the Book of Common Prayer were published surreptitiously. Toward the end of her reign Hooker provided the first systematic defense of the Prayer Book against the Puritans (*Ecclesiastical Polity*, Bk. V).[2]

When James I came to England he was immediately confronted with the Millenary Petition. The resultant Hampton Court Conference authorized the production of the King James Version of the Scriptures and a slightly revised edition of the Prayer Book (1604) which made few concessions to the Puritans. During the reigns of James I and Charles I a group of clergy came into positions of prominence (for example, Overall, Andrewes, Laud, and Cosin) who were anti-Calvinistic, concerned for "decency and order" in worship, and less negative than the Puritans in their reactions toward certain aspects of Roman, Lutheran, or Eastern theology and practice. During the reign of James I episcopacy was established in Scotland, and efforts were begun to bring Scottish liturgy more into line with the Book of Common Prayer. An attempt under Charles I and Archbishop Laud to enforce the use of the Prayer Book of 1637 (which incorporated some elements from Scottish traditions and some of the principles of the "Laudians" and which reverted at some points to the 1549 book) hastened a temporary end to episcopacy in Scotland.[3]

The Canons of 1640 legislated matters previously left to the individual conscience and furthered reaction. A Committee of the House of Lords in 1641 was critical of some Laudian innovations and recommended some conciliatory concessions to the Puritans, but it was too little too late. The use of the Book of Common Prayer was outlawed and *A Directory for the Publique Worship of God* was adopted in 1645. The Directory (the result of a compromise between several groups—Scotsmen and Englishmen of presbyterian persuasion, men of Free Church principles, and men of moderate episcopal principles) was not made up of fixed texts but of rubrics and models. It was fleshed out differently by different people: extemporary prayers, forms from the Scottish Calvinistic tradition, forms "in Scripture words," forms taken largely from or based upon those of the Book of Common Prayer (for example, those of Sanderson), or even forms based upon Eastern liturgies (for example, those of Taylor). In certain remote areas, the private chaplaincies, and among exiles abroad, the Book of Common Prayer continued in use throughout the period. The first systematic commentaries upon the Prayer Book (those of Sparrow and of L'Estrange) were published during the interregnum.[4]

At the Restoration certain revisions and freedoms were promised. At the Savoy Conference the Puritans presented their Exceptions and Baxter's alternative liturgy, but by this time the Laudians were in power in Convocation and Parliament. Cosin drew up a draft for the revision of the Prayer Book *(The Durham Book)* which made some concessions to the Puritans but was largely based upon notes he and Wren had made earlier. Though not all of the recommendations of *The Durham Book* were accepted, Convocation's revision included relatively few concessions to the Puritans, and with the Act of Uniformity over seventeen hundred clergy were ejected from their livings. The 1662 Restoration Book of Common Prayer is still the official liturgy of the Church of England.[5]

THE SANCTIFICATION OF LIFE

Initiation—The 1662 rite for the public baptism of infants, after an exhortation setting forth the necessity and meaning of baptism, proceeds to two prayers. The first is Luther's "Flood Prayer" (See p. 99); the second, though found in the Sarum Manuale, is apparently translated from Lutheran versions of the prayer. This is followed by a Gospel, an exhortation, and a prayer, all of which come in whole or in part from Hermann's *Consultation* (See pp. 98, 99–102).

Promises are made by the sponsors for the infants that they will renounce the devil, the world, and the flesh (contrast the old trilogy), believe the faith expressed in the Apostles' Creed (modified by Hermann's amplified version), and "obediently keep Gods will and commandments." After petitions (Mozarabic in origin, variants of which are extant in the blessing of the Font of the Mozarabic *Missale Mixtum* and of the Gallican *Missale Gallicanum vetus*), the infant is baptized and signed on the forehead with the sign of the cross. This is analogous not to the old post-baptismal anointing of the Sarum baptismal rite, where it is an anointing upon the crown of the head, but to the signation upon the forehead (derived from the problematical second post-baptismal anointing of the Roman baptismal rite) about which the medieval rite of confirmation was centered. In the Prayer Book the signation is accompanied by a text which has affinities with medieval definitions of confirmation (See p. 85). This is followed by a bidding to give thanks that this child "is regenerate," the Lord's Prayer, a prayer of thanksgiving, and a charge to the godparents. The last of the Promises, and the petition for the sanctification of the water in the last petition, had been added in 1662, but basically the rite is that of 1552. The 1549 rite had lacked the bidding and the thanksgiving (the two clearest statements of the doctrine of baptismal regeneration). That rite had, in the order of its components, resembled more closely that of Sarum, and it had contained additional petitions, an exorcism, a vesting, and an anointing. The baptismal anointing of the 1549 rite (which was replaced in 1552 by the form which encapsulates medieval definitions of confirmation) followed the vesting, whereas that of the medieval baptismal rites had preceded the vesting. That fact, together with a change in the text which accompanies the baptismal anointing and the absence of an anointing in the 1549 confirmation rite, indicates that the anointing was intended to perpetuate the medieval confirmation anointing rather than (or as well as) the anointing associated with baptism.[6]

The rite for "Private Baptism of Children in Houses" had

been reworked in 1604. The Puritans had wished to do away with private baptisms altogether. The Hampton Court Conference did not abolish the practice but sought to regulate it. In emergencies people were no longer to baptize children themselves but to "procure" a "lawful Minister." The rite originally had been derived from the public rite and from Hermann's *Consultation* or other German Church Orders.

New to the 1662 Prayer Book was a rite for the baptism of those able to answer for themselves, which was basically the public rite with appropriate substitutions for the Gospel (John 3:1-8) and in the exhortation and promises.

Prior to the 1662 revision (when it was given its own heading) a catechism had been included under the heading "Confirmation," as in Hermann's and other German Church Orders. The initial section of the catechism, which contains questions and answers concerning baptism, the Apostles' Creed, the Decalogue, and the Lord's Prayer, dates basically from 1549. The sources were principally English Reformation formularies. In 1604 a new section (the work of Dean Overall, based upon a catechism by his predecessor, Dean Nowell) had been added at the end, which deals with the sacraments of baptism and the Lord's Supper.

The "confirmation" rite begins with a preface and a renewal of baptismal vows. These are followed by a prayer for the strengthening gifts of the Holy Spirit, a 1552 revision of a 1549 prayer which had been shaped from a form in the confirmation rite of the Sarum Manuale. After this prayer comes the laying-on-of-hands with prayer, the Lord's Prayer, a "Collect" based upon a prayer from Hermann's *Consultation*, the "Decalogue Collect," and a blessing. The preface (framed from the old initial rubric), the renewal of vows (which takes the place of an examination on the catechism within the rite), the Lord's Prayer, and the Decalogue Collect had been added in 1662. Otherwise the rite dates from 1552. In 1552 the initial prayer of the 1549 rite had been revised, the prayer associated with the laying-on-of-hands had been added, and a signation and Pax deleted. Within the Book of Common Prayer three things—catechetical instruction, a laying-on-of-hands with prayer, and first Communion—have been linked together at the age of discretion. The precedent for this procedure is to be found in the German Church Orders. The administration of this rite is more tightly limited to the bishop than the rites of those orders or the medieval Roman rite of confirmation which the new rite superseded. The medieval teaching in regard to confirmation and the signation upon the forehead (which had been thought by some to be the essential action of the medieval confirmation rite) had, in a sense, been incorporated into the 1549 baptismal rite, but some remnants of the medieval confirmation rite had been retained in 1549 within a new rite of "confirmation" based upon the Reformation rationale of catechetical instruction, public renewal of vows, and admission to Communion.

Penance—The 1662 book included a Commination Office (little changed from 1549) for use on the first day of Lent and other occasions. An initial exhortation reminded the congregation of the public discipline of the early church and expressed a hope for its restoration. After "sentences of God cursing" are read to instill "earnest and true repentance," there is a homily proclaiming forgiveness to the repentant, Psalm 51, the Kyrie, the Lord's Prayer, Preces, two prayers, and an anthem which had in the Sarum use been associated with the distribution of ashes. The rite is largely abbreviated from the Ash Wednesday rite of Sarum.[7]

The use of a general confession and absolution was retained in the *Order of the Communion* of 1548 in a form largely based upon that of Hermann's *Consultation,* which had precedent in prones and medieval orders for receiving Communion outside the Mass. The 1548 texts were revised somewhat in the 1549 Prayer Book. The 1552 book also preceded the Daily Offices with Opening Sentences, an exhortation, a general confession, and an absolution, a practice which had precedents in both medieval and reformation rites.

The Eucharistic rite of the 1549 Prayer Book contained an apologia for non-compulsory private confession for those whose consciences were not quieted by "their humble confession to God, and the generall confession to the churche," and though the exhortation had been revised in 1552 the principle of non-compulsory private confession had been maintained. Within the Visitation Office those with troubled consciences are urged to make a "speciall Confession," and a form for absolution (constructed from texts in the Sarum Manuale and the *Consultation*) is provided.

Marriage—The marriage rite is to be preceded by the publication of banns on three Sundays or Holy Days. Marriages are to take place in the church. An exhortation lists three reasons for which marriage was instituted: (1) the procreation of children; (2) "a remedy against sin, and to avoid fornication"; and (3) "mutual society, help, and comfort." The couple is charged to disclose any known impediment. The charge is followed by the betrothal, the giving of the bride, the vows, and the giving of the ring (which is not blessed). When the ring is placed upon the priest's book it is to be accompanied with "the accustomed duty to the Priest and Clerk." The text associated with the giving of the ring begins, "With this Ring I thee wed, with my body I thee worship, and with all my worldly goods I thee endow." A prayer for grace to keep the vow and to live according to God's law, a proclamation of the marriage, and a blessing follow. The priest and the couple then move to the Table during the singing of Psalm 128 or Psalm 67. There the couple kneel for the Kyrie, the Lord's Prayer, Preces, prayers for the gift of children and for graces requisite to marriage, and the ancient priestly blessing. A homily is provided for use "if there be no Sermon declaring the duties of man and wife." In books prior to 1662 the rite was to precede the (Sunday) Eucharist, and the couple were required to receive Communion. The 1662 book urges Communion at the marriage or at the first opportunity thereafter. This was a concession to Puritans who, because of the festivities typically associated with weddings, objected to having them on Sundays or at the Eucharist. The sources behind the marriage rite are the uses of Sarum and York, the *Consultation* and some other German Church Order(s), probably that of Brandenburg, and the exposition of marriage from the King's Book.[8]

Pregnancy and Childbirth—The text (except for the addition of a reference to the vocation of women in the prayer) of the churching rite of the 1549 Prayer Book had been taken basically from the Sarum Manuale: an exhortation, Psalm 121, the Lord's Prayer, Preces, and a prayer. The rite had been moved into the church within the context of the Eucharist, and the Asperges and the leading into the church of the woman after she had been churched (with its text) had, however, been dropped. In 1552 the title had been changed from "Purification of Women" to "The Thanksgiving of Women after Childbirth, commonly called the Churching of Women," and in 1662 Psalm 116:1–12 or Psalm 127 had been substituted for Psalm 121, and the reference to vocation had been excised from the prayer.

Ordination—The model for the ordination rites was Bucer's proposed form modified for three orders (bishops, presbyters, and deacons), principally by the inclusion of materials from the Sarum Pontifical. The laying-on-of-hands with prayer was set forth as the essential action, but the imposition of hands was linked with late medieval formulae rather than with prayer. In 1662 the rites were somewhat tightened against presbyterian interpretations. The first English ordination rites of 1550 had contained some directions concerning vestments and also a delivery of a chalice to a presbyter and of a pastoral staff to a bishop, but these directions had been dropped in the 1552 revision. None of the minor orders was retained, but some of their functions were, until the nineteenth century, performed by a semiprofessional parish clerk.[9]

Vestments—The 1549 Prayer Book had specified as vestments for a priest officiating at the Eucharist a plain white alb with "vestment" (chasuble) or cope, and for the assisting clergy "albs with tunicles." The 1550 Ordinal prescribed albs for those to be ordained deacon or presbyter and surplice and cope for those to be ordained bishop. On the heels of

the vestments controversy, the 1552 book prescribed surplices only for deacons and presbyters in their ministrations,
and rochets for bishops. The Elizabethan book introduced an
"Ornaments Rubric," subject to varying interpretations,
which restored the vestments of "the Second Year of the
Reign of King Edward the Sixth." In actual practice, from
the reign of Elizabeth, the normal usage was surplices (full
and down to the ankles until the late nineteenth century) for
the services, gowns for preaching, copes for some important
occasions in some chapels and cathedrals, and rochets (and
chimeres) for bishops.[10]

Sick Rites—The rite for the Visitation of the Sick had
been constructed from the Sarum Manuale, Hermann's *Consultation*, and the Homily "Against the Fear of Death." The
Aaronic Benediction and an appendix of additional prayers
had been added in 1662, but the basic rite (the Pax, an Antiphon, the Kyrie, the Lord's Prayer, Preces, two collects, a
model for exhortation, the special confession, a prayer [from
the old Maundy Thursday reconciliation of public penitents],
Psalm 71, an anthem, and a blessing) dates from 1552. The
1549 rite had also retained one of the Penitential Psalms
(143) at the beginning and had provided a new form for use
with an anointing "upon the forehead or breast only." The
anointing is subject to the desire of the sick person. Though
the Visitation rite is grim, it is not primarily a "last rite" or
"extreme unction."[11]

All editions of the Prayer Book have included special
Propers for use at the Communion of the Sick. The 1549
book also made provisions (based upon those of the Brandenburg Church Order) for Communion of the Sick from the
Reserved Sacrament on the day of a public Communion, and
it allowed for an abbreviation of the Eucharistic rite when
used for Communion of the Sick.

Burial—The burial rite of the 1552, 1559, and 1604 books
had included Scripture Sentences to be said in procession
into the church or toward the grave, anthems to be said
while the body was being placed in the grave, a Committal
to be said while the grave was being filled, an anthem (Rev.

14:13), a lesson (I Cor. 15:20–58), the Kyrie, the Lord's Prayer, and two prayers to the effect that all the faithful departed may enter into everlasting glory. In 1662 a rubric was added which forbade the use of this office for unbaptized persons, excommunicates, or suicides. Immediately after the processional sentences the 1662 book prints Psalms 39 and 90 and the lesson from I Cor. 15 for use in the church, apparently as Propers for use at a Service of Morning or Evening Prayer, a use which continued into the nineteenth century. The first prayer was also revised somewhat and the Grace was added at the end of the service at the grave. The 1549 book had provided for Psalms 116, 139, and 146, the I Cor. lection, and a prayer, followed by the Eucharist (for which Propers were provided) to be said in the church before or after the burial. A Eucharist had continued in use in some places at least (witness the burial of Edward VI), presumably with the Propers of the Day, in connection with the 1552 rite. Elizabeth's Latin Prayer Book had provided some Propers for use at a Eucharist in conjunction with a burial. None of the Prayer Books retained provisions for anniversary or votive Eucharists, nor for absolutions of the body, nor for the use of the Penitential Psalms. The sources of the burial rites included the Sarum Manuale, German Church Orders, and the Diriges of English Reformation Primers.[12]

THE SANCTIFICATION OF TIME

The Liturgical Day—The core of the Daily Offices— the Lord's Prayer, Versicles and Responses, (Venite in the morning), Psalms, Old Testament lection, Te Deum or Benedicite (Magnificat in the evening), New Testament lection, Benedictus (Nunc dimittis in the evening), creed (normally the Apostles' Creed), the Kyrie, the Lord's Prayer, Preces, the Collect for the Day, and two Fixed Collects—goes back to the 1549 Prayer Book, which had derived these elements from the Hours of Matins, Lauds, and Prime for Matins

(Morning Prayer) and from Vespers and Compline for Evensong (Evening Prayer). The retention of these particular elements and the restoration of substantial lections "in course" has affinities with the revisions of Quiñones and of the German Church Orders, the first of which had provided the pattern for one and the second for another of two early drafts by Cranmer for Daily Offices. In the Offices, the Psalter is read monthly (in the translation of the Great Bible), "the most part" of the Old Testament and Apocrypha yearly, and the New Testament (except for Revelation) thrice yearly. The reading of Scripture was restored as the basic element of the Offices. Some Proper lections were provided for certain Sundays and Holy Days, and Proper Psalms for four principal days.[13]

In 1552 an order to ring a bell to call the people together for the Daily Offices was added. A penitential order was prefixed to the Offices (as in some medieval uses). Psalm 100 (Jubilate Deo) was provided as an alternative for the Benedictus, Psalm 98 (Cantate Domino) for the Magnificat, and Psalm 67 (Deus misereatur) for the Nunc dimittis. The saying of the Daily Offices also became binding upon all clergy, not (as 1549) just those serving congregations. In 1662 permission was given to sing an anthem after the Fixed Collects. Prayers for those in authority and for the clergy, "A Prayer of St. Chrysostom," and the Grace were also printed after the Offices, "to be read here, except when the Litany is read."

The 1549 Prayer Book included the *Quicunque vult* ("Athanasian Creed") for use on the six principal feasts. In 1552 its use was extended to thirteen days, apparently chosen in order to assure its use approximately once a month.

The 1549 book contained two Occasional Prayers (for rain and for fair weather). Each revision had added additional prayers (or, beginning in 1604, thanksgivings). A prayer "for all conditions of men" (which was to be said when the Litany is not said) and a "general Thanksgiving" were among those added in 1662.

The 1662 book provided adaptations of the Daily Offices

for use on ships (and special short offices for times of distress or of thanksgiving). These "Sea Forms" are generally credited to Sanderson.

Primers for private use had been issued in the reigns of Henry VIII, Edward VI, and Elizabeth. The 1559 and 1604 editions of the Prayer Book typically had bound with them a series of "Godly Prayers" for private or family use.[14]

The Liturgical Week—The Book of Common Prayer restored the primacy of Sunday in the liturgical week. On Sundays the Eucharist with Communions is to follow Morning Prayer, and since 1552 collegiate clergy have been expected to receive every Sunday and all confirmed persons at least three times a year (the 1549 book had prescribed a minimum of once a year). When a representative number of communicants is not available, the Sunday Service is yet to include Ante-Communion (that is, the Eucharistic rite through the Prayer for the Whole State of Christ's Church, concluded with a collect[s] and Blessing). People accustomed to receiving yearly did not move quickly to weekly Communions, and the typical pattern seems to have been a Eucharist about once a month according to a plan of rotation so that it was available each Sunday (for example, Boston in the 1750s, with three parishes, had Communion in each of them every third Sunday). In village and country areas, it was less frequently available, sometimes being celebrated only at the three great feasts and in the autumn. From at least as early as the 1690s some town churches provided an early Service to make the Communion available weekly for servants. The Sunday Evening Prayer was the time for catechizing.

Wednesdays and Fridays were marked by the use of the Litany after Morning Prayer. The 1549 book had also ordered the use of Ante-Communion on these days. A Table of Fasts, which designated Fridays as days of fasting, was included in the 1662 book. The Litany (which had been the first rite authorized in English [1544]) was largely drawn from the Sarum Processional and Luther's litany, a revision of which had been included in English Reformation Primers. The 1549 revision of the Litany had eliminated the invocation of saints, and that of 1559 deleted the petition for deliverance "from the tyranny of the Bishop of Rome and all his detestable enormities." Petitions for deliverance from "rebellion" and from "schism" had been added at the Restoration.[15]

The Book of Common Prayer did not provide a service for preparation for Communion as had Reformed and German Orders, nor did it require a private confession beforehand as did Rome. Rather it recommended self-examination, with private confession for those who could not quiet their own consciences, and it specified that those intending to communicate inform the clergyman in charge the day before (prior to 1662, before or after Morning Prayer on the day itself).

The 1549 book had provided some proper lections for the Daily Offices on some Sundays and Holy Days. In Elizabeth's reign proper Old Testament lections were appointed for each Sunday.

The Eucharist—The "Lord's Supper, or Holy Communion" in the 1662 book begins with the Lord's Prayer, the Collect for Purity, the Decalogue, a collect for the King, and the Collect for the Day. The "Priest" then reads the Epistle and the Gospel (in the King James Version from 1662), after which the Nicene Creed is said. If there is no sermon, an authorized homily is to follow. The form of this Pro-Anaphora dates basically from 1552. The 1549 order for "The Supper of the Lord, and the Holy Communion, commonly called the Masse" had included a Psalm for an Introit, during which the priest said the Lord's Prayer and the Collect for Purity as his private preparation. In place of the Decalogue of later books, the 1549 book had a ninefold Kyrie and the Gloria in excelsis. The Epistle could be read by him "that is appointed," the Gospel by a priest or deacon. The Gospel had in that book been preceded by the Gloria tibi, and the Exhortation had come immediately after the sermon. Most of the elements in the Pro-Anaphora had been retained from the Sarum use. Whole Psalms had been substituted for snippets as Introits. The exhortation and the re-

quirement of a sermon or homily had been added. Some new
Collects had been supplied in 1549 (for example, Advent I
and II, Christmas, Quinquagesima, the First Day of Lent,
Lent I, the second Communion of Easter [used also on Easter I], Easter II, the Sunday after Ascension, and most of
the Saints' Days). Many of the others had been translated
from German revisions or reworked to eliminate the intercession of saints and to stress the doctrine of justification by
grace (for example, "that we may deserve to praise thy holy
name" becomes "that we may worthily praise thy holy
name"). At the 1662 revision, Propers for a Sixth Sunday
after the Epiphany and a Collect for Easter Eve were provided, and a new Collect was substituted for that of the
Third Sunday in Advent. The use of the Decalogue within
the Pro-Anaphora had precedents in various medieval tropes
and prones and in the rites of Bucer, Calvin, and Pullain.
The use of any psalmody or hymnody between the Epistle
and Gospel had been eliminated in 1549 probably not only as
a rejection of some of the texts but also because, in the
Sarum use, some of the preparations associated with the offertory had been made at this point.[16]

The priest initiates the offering with one or more Scriptural Sentences. The receiving of the alms of the parishioners
is given a place at this point within the rite, following the
precedents of German Church Orders. The priest is then to
"place upon the Table so much Bread and Wine, as he shall
think convenient" and then to say a prayer "for the whole
state of Christs Church militant here in earth." The order of
these elements is that of the books of 1552, 1559, and 1604,
except that these books had not specified when the elements
were to be placed upon the Table. In many places it had
apparently been done by the clerk prior to the service, in
many at the place specified by the 1662 book, and in others
(for example, the chapel of Lancelot Andrewes) immediately
prior to the Sursum corda. A thanksgiving for the departed,
based upon a passage in the Bidding Prayer of the Canons
of 1604, had been added to the prayer in 1662. The 1549
book had required that the chalice be mixed, and in that

book the prayer did not come until later in the rite (though
there are reasons for believing that Cranmer had planned it
for a position prior to the offering). The 1549 book specified
that the wafers be larger and thicker than before and that
each was to be broken into two or more pieces. The later
books specified that the best wheat bread was sufficient. Typically, until the nineteenth century, a substantial quantity
of wine was consumed at the Eucharist (witness the bills for
the wine and the size of the flagons in proportion to the
number of communicants).

Three exhortations are printed within the 1662 rite, one
for use when giving notice of a celebration, one for use if
the people are "negligent to come," and a third for use at
each celebration. The first and third of these are 1552 revisions of 1549 Exhortations. The second, which came into the
book in 1552, comes from writings of Peter Martyr. The Exhortations are followed by the Invitation, General Confession, Absolution, and Comfortable Words. The texts of
these are basically those of the 1549 revision of the 1548
Order of the Communion, which was principally derived
from Hermann's *Consultation*.

Immediately after the Comfortable Words in the later
books, but immediately after the offering in the 1549 book,
is the Sursum corda, the Preface (with Proper Preface on
five principal feasts [1549] and throughout the Octaves
[1552ff.]), and the Sanctus. Beginning with the 1552 book,
the Prayer of Humble Access follows the Sanctus. The
Prayer of Consecration consists of a petition (which contains some overtones of thanksgiving for the One Sacrifice)
that the communicants "may be partakers of his most
blessed body and blood," and the Words of Institution:

> Almighty God, our heavenly Father, who of thy tender
> mercy didst give thine only Son Jesus Christ to suffer death
> upon the cross for our redemption; who made there (by his one
> oblation of himself once offered) a full, perfect, and sufficient
> sacrifice, oblation, and satisfaction, for the sins of the whole
> world; and did institute, and in his holy Gospel command us to
> continue, a perpetual memory of that his precious death, until

his coming again; Hear us, O merciful Father, we most humbly beseech thee; and grant that we receiving these thy creatures of bread and wine, according to thy Son our Saviour Jesus Christ's holy institution, in remembrance of his death and passion, may be partakers of his most blessed Body and Blood: who, in the same night that he was betrayed, [*Here the Priest is to take the Paten into his hands*] took Bread; and, when he had given thanks, [*And here to break the Bread*] he brake it, and gave it to his disciples, saying, Take, eat, [*And here to lay his hand upon all the Bread*] this is my Body which is given for you: Do this in remembrance of me. Likewise after supper he [*Here he is to take the Cup into his hand*] took the Cup; and, when he had given thanks, he gave it to them, saying, Drink ye all of this; for this [*And here to lay his hand upon every vessel (be it Chalice or Flagon) in which there is any Wine to be consecrated*] is my Blood of the New Testament, which is shed for you and for many for the remission of sins: Do this, as oft as ye shall drink it, in remembrance of me. *Amen.*

Since 1552 there has been no *anamnesis* or *epiclesis* (though both Puritans and Laudians had desired their restoration), and no oblation in any of the Prayer Books. The Words of Administration for the Bread are "The Body of our Lord Jesus Christ, which was given for thee, preserve thy body and soul unto everlasting life: take and eat this in remembrance that Christ died for thee, and feed on him in thy heart by faith with thanksgiving," and a similar Sentence is provided for the Wine. The first half (an expansion of a medieval form typical of German Church Orders) had been provided in the 1549 book. The 1552 book substituted the second half. The two halves were combined at the time of the Elizabethan Settlement. Until well into the seventeenth century the priest moved about among the people administering to them as they knelt in their places (where they were gathered around the Table in the chancel). The Administration of the Communion is followed by the Lord's Prayer, one or the other of two prayers, the Gloria in excelsis (in a place typically occupied by a Psalm in Reformed rites), and the blessing. The "Manual Acts" associated with the Prayer of Consecration, the titles for the various

prayers, the provisions for the consecration of additional Elements, and the regulations concerning ablutions had been
added in 1662. The "Black Rubric," which, over Cranmer's
protest, had been inserted in the 1552 book and then struck
in Elizabeth's reign, had been restored in 1662 in a revised
form which denies not "anye reall and essenciall presence"
but "any Corporal Presence of Christs naturall Flesh, and
Bloud."

In the 1549 book, the Sursum corda, Preface, and Sanctus had come immediately after the offering, and the Benedictus qui venit had been retained after the Sanctus. This
was followed by the Prayer for the Whole State of Christ's
Church, which in its 1549 form contained a commemoration
of the departed. The prayer owed some phrases to the Roman Canon and a great deal to intercessory prayers of German Church Orders. The Eucharistic Prayer which followed
opened with a passage which owed something to the King's
Book and possibly something to the *Antididagma*, the Cologne Chapter's answer to the *Consultation* (this section
was retained in the succeeding Prayer Books). Next came
an *epiclesis*, along Eastern lines. The Words of Institution
were in a form constructed from the Scriptural accounts, as
was typical of German and Reformed Orders. The Institution narrative was followed by an *anamnesis* and a self-obla-
tion (a revision of which was retained as the first of the
post-communion prayers of later Prayer Books), which are
dependent upon the Roman Canon and the *Consultation*.

O God, heavenly Father, which of thy tender mercy didst
give thine only son Jesus Christ to suffer death upon the cross
for our redemption, who made there (by his one oblation once
offered) a full, perfect, and sufficient sacrifice, oblation, and
satisfaction, for the sins of the whole world, and did institute,
and in his holy Gospel command us, to celebrate a perpetual
memory of that his precious death, until his coming again:
Hear us (O merciful Father) we beseech thee; and with thy
Holy Spirit and word, vouchsafe to bless [✠] and sanctify [✠]
these thy gifts, and creatures of bread and wine, that they
may be unto us the body and blood of thy most dearly beloved

son Jesus Christ. Who in the same night that he was betrayed: took bread [*Here the priest must take the bread into his hands*], and when he had blessed, and given thanks, he brake it, and gave it to his disciples, saying, Take, eat, this is my body which is given for you; do this in remembrance of me.

Likewise after supper he took the cup [*Here the priest shall take the Cup into his hands*], and when he had given thanks, he gave it to them, saying, Drink ye all of this, for this is my blood of the new Testament, which is shed for you and for many, for remission of sins; do this as oft as you shall drink it, in remembrance of me.

These words before rehearsed are to be said, turning still to the Altar, without any elevation, or showing the Sacrament to the people.

Wherefore, O Lord and heavenly Father, according to the institution of thy dearly beloved son, our savior Jesus Christ, we thy humble servants do celebrate, and make here before thy divine majesty, with these thy holy gifts, the memorial which thy son hath willed us to make, having in remembrance his blessed passion, mighty resurrection, and glorious ascension, rendering unto thee most hearty thanks for the innumerable benefits procured unto us by the same, entirely desiring thy fatherly goodness, mercifully to accept this our sacrifice of praise and thanksgiving; most humbly beseeching thee to grant that by the merits and death of thy son Jesus Christ, and through faith in his blood, we and all thy whole church, may obtain remission of our sins, and all other benefits of his passion. And here we offer and present unto thee (O Lord) our self, our souls, and bodies, to be a reasonable, holy, and lively sacrifice unto thee; humbly beseeching thee, that whosoever shall be partakers of this holy Communion, may worthily receive the most precious body and blood of thy son Jesus Christ and be fulfilled with thy grace and heavenly benediction and made one body with thy son Jesus Christ, that he may dwell in them, and they in him. And although we be unworthy (through our manifold sins) to offer unto thee any sacrifice, yet we beseech thee to accept this our bounden duty and service, and command these our prayers and supplications, by the ministry of thy holy angels, to be brought up into thy holy taberna-

cle before the sight of thy divine majesty; not weighing our
merits, but pardoning our offences, through Christ our Lord,
by whom, and with whom, in the unity of the Holy Ghost, all
honor and glory be unto thee, O Father almighty, world
without end. Amen.

The Eucharistic Prayer was followed by the Lord's
Prayer (with Protocol), the Pax, and an Anthem, "Christ
our Pascall lambe is offred up for us." At this point, preparatory to Communion, the Invitation, General Confession, Absolution, Comfortable Words, and Prayer of Humble Access
were said. The Agnus Dei was to be sung during the Communions, and one or more of a selection of Scriptural Sentences afterward. The rite ended with an earlier version of
the second of the post-Communion prayers of later Prayer
Books and a blessing which owes something to the *Consultation*. The 1549 book had specified that the Bread be put into
people's mouths to prevent its being taken away and put to
superstitious uses. The subsequent books had ordered that
it be delivered into their hands.

The Liturgical Year—The Prayer Books retained the general structure of the Church Year but reduced the Holy
Days to those typically retained in the German Church Orders (p. 109). Propers for St. Mary Magdalene, retained in
1549, were dropped in 1552. The 1552 book restored to the
Calendar three "Black Letter Days," and the number of
"Black Letter Days" (of which no further notice is taken in
the Prayer Books) was increased further in Elizabeth's
reign. (The reason for their inclusion was probably for convenience in identifying dates found in old documents, etc.)[17]

A significant aspect of the revision of the Church Year in
1549 was the attempt to restore something of the unitive
baptismal nature to the Easter-Pentecost cycle. Following
Ambrosian precedent, propers were provided for Easter
Even, thereby pushing the "vigil" back to Easter itself.
Proper "Anthems" and a collect were to precede Matins on
Easter Day. Exodus 12 (an account of the Passover and cir-
cumcision) and Romans 6 (Pauline teaching on baptism)

were appointed as the lections for Matins, and Acts 2 (the story of Pentecost) as the New Testament lection for Evensong. Precedents for some of these and of other provisions of the liturgy for Easter Day are found in the Mozarabic Rite.

From Elizabeth's reign special "State Services" (Propers for Daily Offices and/or the Eucharist) were occasionally provided for times of civil distress or thanksgiving. Eventually four became a regular part of the annual cycle and remained so until 1859—November 5 (Gunpowder Treason), January 30 (the Martyrdom of King Charles), May 29 (the Restoration), and the day of the Accession of the reigning monarch.

Music—Coverdale published a collection of *Goostly Psalmes and Spirituall Songes* based upon the Wittenberg hymnals, and in 1549 Sternhold published a small collection of metrical Psalms which was later enlarged by Hopkins. Merbecke provided musical settings for the rites of the 1549 Prayer Book (See *The Hymnal 1940* 702-707). In larger churches plainsong, motets, and new polyphonic service music were used by the choirs, but the staple musical diet from early in Elizabeth's reign was the Sternhold and Hopkins Psalter, further enlarged (See *The Hymnal 1940* 278), to which were appended a few hymns and metrical settings of the Creed, the Decalogue, the Lord's Prayer, and some of the canticles. When the Psalms or canticles or other portions of the Services were sung in most churches, they were sung in these metrical versions, being precented by the parish clerk. Anglican chants and verse anthems came into being during the seventeenth century, and in 1696 a new metrical version of the Psalter by Tate and Brady (See *The Hymnal 1940* 390, 439, 450) was published. It was soon provided with a small appendix of hymns (See *The Hymnal 1940* 13), and it gradually gained in popularity, displacing Sternhold and Hopkins in many places. It was not until the nineteenth century that hymns were used freely within the Church of England. Organs were accepted in the larger churches to lead the congregation in Psalms, hymns, and chants, to accompany the choir, and to provide a short voluntary between the Psalms and the Old Testament lection. In less affluent situations, leadership was provided by the parish clerk, village instrumentalists (or barrel organs), and/or "singers."[18]

THE SANCTIFICATION OF SPACE

Buildings—At the Reformation, as among some of the Continental and Scottish churches, the old chancels were often treated as rooms for the Eucharist (centered about the Table, which was covered with a rich, expensive "carpet" which extended to the floor on all sides, and over which for the Eucharist was placed a white linen cloth which covered the "carpet"). The nave was treated as a room for the Liturgy of the Word, and it was centered about the (double or triple decker) pulpit. The 1549 Prayer Book had ordered that those intending to communicate move from the nave into the chancel at the offering, and this practice was continued. Typically the third liturgical center, the font, was prominently situated near the West door. Until after the Restoration new churches were typically built with such a two-room, three-center arrangement. Economic necessity forced the emergence of one-room churches. In some of these churches the pulpit was placed near the front of the nave, in the center, for convenience in seeing and hearing, and the Table was placed behind it against the East wall (or in a shallow apse) with space about it for the communicants to "draw near." Some of the space could be economically used for both the Liturgy of the Word and the Liturgy of the Table, for people could conveniently see and hear what went on at either pulpit or Table. A yet more economical provision for seating was provided in other churches by placing the pulpit over the Table against the East wall, and the people remained in the same places throughout the rite. In other churches the seating was arranged "choir-fashion," and the Table was placed at one end and the pulpit at the opposite end. In these newer, less spacious churches rails enclosed the Table, and the people began to move up to the rails to receive. The choir, organ, and/or instrumentalists were usually placed in the West end, generally in a gallery. These arrangements, which fostered active congregational participation in the liturgy, remained normal within Anglicanism until well into the nineteenth century. As in the medieval church and among Continental Protestants, until the last few decades, the naves were normally made available for a variety of parish and community functions.[19]

The Consecration of Churches—Though various forms for the consecration of a church from as far back as the reign of Elizabeth are extant, a particular form has never been given official acceptance within the Church of England.[20]

Colors—Not until the late nineteenth century did Anglicans begin to make use of seasonal colors. The Table (and oftentimes the pulpit) had typically been provided with expensive, rich hangings, often red, which drew attention to these centers and gave expression to their importance. Skimpy "frontals," "super-frontals," or "pulpit falls," or leaving the Table bare, became acceptable within Anglicanism only within the late nineteenth century.

CHAPTER **VIII**

THE BOOK OF
COMMON
PRAYER
(AMERICAN)

The American Revolution and the independence of the States made some revision of the 1662 English Prayer Book for American use inevitable. The 1662 revision, however, had been a conservative one. Many proposals had been made by Puritans and by Laudians which had not been accepted, and these proposals had not died with the passing of the Act of Uniformity. Within the next decades there were various attempts at Prayer Book revision in the interest of comprehending more of the people within the Church of England, the most significant of which were the proposals of 1668 and 1689. Prayer Books printed in the eighteenth century for use in Ireland had been supplemented with additional Offices. From early in the seventeenth century certain Anglicans had begun to have a high respect for Eastern liturgies (especially the *Apostolic Consti-*

tutions, which had become available in print in 1563) and for certain aspects of two Prayer Books which had been little more than Trial Uses in their days, the first Book of Common Prayer of 1549 and the Scottish book of 1637. Stephens, Whiston, and Henley, and others, had published and put into use with small groups liturgies based upon these models. In 1718 some of the Non-Jurors published, and put into use, Offices for the Eucharist, Confirmation, and Visitation of the Sick, revised along Eastern lines. In 1734 Thomas Deacon published his *Compleat Collection of Devotions,* which he later put into use with his splinter group of Non-Jurors. Scottish nonjuring Episcopalians, from 1722, published a series of "Wee Bookies," which were editions of the Eucharistic rite of 1637 with some modifications, for use in conjunction with the 1662 book. The most important influences upon these Offices were the English Non-Juror rites and Bishop Thomas Rattray's reconstruction of the Jerusalem Liturgy of St. James. Also, early in the eighteenth century, sentiment for revision began to grow among those of Latitudinarian sympathies, and a number of proposed revisions and arguments for revisions´were published. The most significant of these were *Free and Candid Disquisitions* (a collection of anonymous essays by different authors, edited anonymously by John Jones of Alconbury and published in 1749), *The Expediency and Necessity of Revising and Improving the Publick Liturgy* (another anonymous 1749 publication, to which was appended a proposed *A New Liturgy*), and *Reasons Humbly Offered for Composing a New Set of Articles of Religion* (an anonymous 1751 publication, which included twenty-one specimen Articles). Alongside the Latitudinarian proposals came a series of "Arian" proposals, some of which took as their starting point a copy of the Prayer Book amended by Samuel Clarke, whose Christology had been censured by Convocation early in the century. The most influential of these was the revision made by Theophilus Lindsey for the chapel which he set up in London after leaving the Church of England over the issue of subscription to the Articles of Religion. Even Benjamin

Franklin, then living in England, got his hand into the business of Prayer Book revision, collaborating with Sir Francis Dashwood in a revision published in London in 1773. Soon after the end of the Revolution John Wesley published a revised liturgy for the use of American Methodists, and a Boston congregation, that of King's Chapel, adopted a liturgy based upon the revision of Theophilus Lindsey. Persons who were to exercise leadership in a revision of the Prayer Book for the American Church were sympathetic with various proposals which were being made.[1]

The possibility of a revision which would find general acceptance was complicated not only by liturgical and theological issues but also by political enmities and personal animosities. As the only hope of unity seemed to lie in making only those changes necessitated by political independence, the first interstate convention adopted this stance as a "fundamental principle," but in August 1785 a committee which was appointed by Seabury and on which he served prepared proposals for revision for Connecticut along Latitudinarian lines and sent these on to Boston for a convention from other New England States. That convention added to these proposals and sent them on to Philadelphia for a convention of the States south of New England. The Philadelphia convention of 1785 also received proposals for revision from a Virginia State convention and from a number of individuals, so it set aside the "fundamental principle" and authorized a revision for trial use. In the meantime, Seabury, finding it politically expedient to do so in a diocese dominated by liturgically and politically reactionary Tories, did an about face and set himself against the Proposed Book. The use of the book (which came off the press in April 1786) was authorized in all the States represented at Philadelphia except New Jersey and in the New England States except for Connecticut, and it served as the basis for the book which was authorized in 1789.[2]

The revisers of 1789 used the Proposed Book of 1786 as their basis, returning to the 1662 English book at certain points, adopting some proposals from State conventions, go-ing back again to *Free and Candid Disquisitions* and to *The Expediency and Necessity of Revising* (both of which had contributed to the 1786 Proposed Book), and incorporating other ideas from Jeremy Taylor's *Holy Dying*, and from Bishop Edmund Gibson's *Family Devotion*, and from a manuscript notebook of Seabury's, in which he had inscribed various forms from sources as diverse as the writings of Bishop Wilson of Sodor and Man, the Scottish Communion Office, and the King's Chapel liturgy.

Contemporaneous with the 1789 revision was the French Revolution. The fright created by this brought in a period of reaction, of looking to the past for models, of antiquarianism, of romanticism. The supposed order and stability of the Middle Ages and of the classical eras of Greece and Rome began to have a great appeal (neo-classic and neo-Gothic architecture; romantic music and poetry; the Gothic novel). In Anglicanism there was a revival and consolidation of old-fashioned high churchmanship (for example, William Jones of Nayland in England; Hobart in America). This came at the time of a gradual loss of fire among Anglican evangelicals, a reaction in some circles against Calvinism, and a growing distaste for puritan plainness. Churchmen were further frightened by the multiplication of denominations, the toleration of Romanism in the British Isles (Keble's sermon on *National Apostasy*), and the wave of Roman immigrants to America. In reaction, Anglicans began to work hard to prove their catholicism. Medieval rationales were forced upon Prayer Book rites. Medieval rites were printed and studied, and Anglicans began to imitate and incorporate Baroque vesture and ceremonies. Though done supposedly as a liturgical revival, there was more emphasis upon allegorization, aesthetics, and antiquarianism in much of what began to be done than on liturgical participation (compare such parallel movements in the mid-nineteenth century as Ultramontanism among French Romanists and the work of such men as the Mercersburg theologians and Charles W. Shields among American Protestants).[3]

Muhlenberg, in his efforts in hymnody, his innovations in

the parish he established, and the recommendations for Prayer Book revision of the Muhlenberg Memorial (1853), represents an effort at comprehension and enrichment with a missionary aim.[4] The pamphlets providing for "Mission Services" or "Third Services" and the Prayer Books for the Armed Forces of the 1850s and 1860s generally present materials for the simplification and/or enrichment of Prayer Book rites along pietistic or evangelical lines.

In the last decades of the nineteenth century the Prayer Book was revised in Ireland, with some concessions along evangelical lines and some tightening against the growing "ritualism" (ceremonialism) of the period and against certain "advanced" interpretations of the rites. Though there were many proposals for revision in England, the political situation and the strife within the church were such that the only successful revision was that of the lectionary for the Daily Offices (1871). William Reed Huntington, who had proposed the Chicago Quadrilateral, was the leading figure in a movement toward Prayer Book revision in America in the interest of "liturgical enrichment and increased flexibility of use," which issued in the very conservative revision of 1892.[5]

The early decades of the twentieth century saw World War I, Rauschenbusch and the Social Gospel, Liberal Protestantism, and further changes in patterns of parish life. The provision of supplementary material for use with the Prayer Book in Scotland in 1912, and the revisions for Canada (1922), Ireland (1927), England (1928), the United States (1928), and Scotland (1929) (as also the liturgical changes among Roman Catholics and Protestants during this period) were principally in the interest of "enrichment" and "flexibility." These same aims seem to underlie the revision of the lectionary in 1943 and the Prayer Book Studies of the 1950s and the changes within the rites of other American churches up into that decade. There was little questioning of principles or approach.[6]

Changes throughout this period within the rites themselves are not so drastic as the changes within the ceremonies which accompanied the rites, the piety with which they were approached, and the theology which was read into or out of the rites.

THE SANCTIFICATION OF LIFE

Initiation—The 1790 Prayer Book, which came out of the 1789 convention, allowed parents to serve as sponsors for the baptism of their children. It also allowed the omission of either of the first two prayers. The word "sin" was substituted for "sins" at two places within the rite, implying that baptism remits original sin but does not suffice for the remission of actual sins. A question about belief in the faith was substituted for the repetition of the Apostles' Creed. Permission was given to omit the Signation. The rubric which stated that baptized children are "undoubtedly saved" was omitted. These changes, retained from the Proposed Book, had been frequently proposed. Some of them date as far back as the early days of Puritanism. The 1790 book also deleted the word "elect," probably because of Calvinistic associations, and permitted the omission of a substantial portion of the rite if it were included once within the month.[7]

The last half of the nineteenth century was wracked by controversy over baptismal regeneration (for example, the Gorham Judgment in England; the formation of the Reformed Episcopal Church in America), with both sides often straining the meanings of Prayer Book texts. The only important change in the baptismal rites at the 1892 revision, however, was the addition of a form for Conditional Baptism. An author writing in 1911 could rejoice that, due to the hard work of the last generation of clergy, baptisms were now normally in private. The 1928 revision omitted Luther's "Flood Prayer," thereby omitting references to the Old Testament types of Baptism and to the Baptism of our Lord, and weakened some of the statements on original sin. This revision again required the use of the Sign of the Cross and allowed for any baptized person to baptize "if a Minister cannot be procured."

The principal change in the catechism in the 1790 book (following the Proposed Book) was the substitution of the words "spiritually taken" for "verily and indeed taken" in the answer to the question concerning the "inward part, or thing signified" in the Lord's Supper. During the nineteenth century the old custom of catechizing at Sunday Evening Prayer was superseded by the Sunday School. In the 1928 revision, the content of the catechism was largely duplicated in two Offices of Instruction, which also provided additional questions and answers on the ministry, the church, and the duties and privileges of membership.

In the "confirmation" rite, the question was revised in 1789 to take into account situations in which the candidate had been baptized as an adult or in which parents had served as sponsors. In 1826 Hobart proposed a revision of the preface and of the first prayer which made explicit that "all the blessings of thy covenant of grace and mercy" were conferred in baptism. In the last decades of the nineteenth century, several authors (notably Mason and Hall) attempted, often making use of mistaken or strained readings of the Fathers and early liturgies, to establish the laying-on-of-hands or anointing as necessary to the "completion" of baptism. The 1892 revision provided a presentation of the candidates reminiscent of those of the ordination rites and added, apparently intending it as Scriptural warrant for the rite, the option of reading Acts 8:14–17. The 1928 revision dropped the preface to the rite and added a promise to follow Jesus Christ as Lord and Saviour. Within the last century the typical age for "confirmation" has dropped several years, so that it has come to be associated with entrance into puberty rather than with entrance into adulthood.[8]

Penance—The 1790 book (following the Proposed Book) retained only the two prayers and the anthem from the Commination Office (printing them with the Ash Wednesday Propers) to be said before the General Thanksgiving at Morning Prayer. Whereas (except for the canonical discipline of clergy and of persons remarried after divorce) the exercise of public penance fell into total disuse within Anglicanism in the nineteenth century, the understanding of Lent as a public penance, which had been played down somewhat in eighteenth century proposals and revisions, was possibly again heightened in the 1892 revision by the provision of "A Penitential Office for Ash-Wednesday." This Office was constructed by prefacing the special prayers for Ash Wednesday (which had been retained from the English Commination Office) with Psalm 51 and the Preces and Blessing from that Office and by adding an Occasional Prayer from the English Book (which had been consciously rejected at the 1789 revision) which goes back to the old Maundy Thursday reconciliation rite.[9]

In 1892 permission was given to omit the General Confession and Absolution at Morning Prayer if Holy Communion was immediately to follow, and at Evening Prayer on any day except Sunday. In 1928 this permission to omit the General Confession and Absolution was extended to include Sundays at Evening Prayer and any day not a day of fasting or abstinence at Morning Prayer (and even on those days if the Litany or Holy Communion was to follow immediately).

The 1790 book dealt more radically with private confession than had the Proposed Book. Following precedents as diverse as proposals of Non-Jurors and "Arians", it struck the reference to absolution from the Communion Exhortation and deleted all reference to "special Confession" from the Visitation of the Sick. Provision for a private confession was, however, retained in the rite for the Visitation of Prisoners. In the later decades of the nineteenth century, largely as a result of the work of those under Tractarian influence, its use was somewhat revived. This revival, coupled with insights of psychology, led to the restoration of the acceptance of the principle of a "special confession" in the 1928 revision (See the Book of Common Prayer, p. 313), though the minister is not to "absolve" the penitent but to "assure him of God's mercy and forgiveness."

Marriage—The 1790 book deleted from the exhortation

at the beginning of the marriage rite "the causes for which Matrimony was ordained." From the form associated with the giving of the ring the words "with my body I thee worship" were deleted. The procession to the Table and all that follows it were omitted. This abridged rite represents the old civil espousals, being cut short prior to the sacramental crowning of the civil rite. The 1892 revision restored to the exhortation the references to marriage as instituted of God, as signifying the union between Christ and His church, and as "adorned and beautified" by the miracle at Cana. The 1928 revision deleted the promise of the woman to "obey," the use of Old Testament types of marriage, and the phrase "with all my worldly goods I thee endow." It added an optional form for the blessing of the ring, a prayer for children, and another prayer for the couple, and it provided Eucharistic Propers.

Pregnancy and Childbirth—In the churching rite the Psalm was abbreviated at the 1789 revision, and the prayer was revised along lines suggested by *A New Liturgy* (1749). The prayer was also printed among the Occasional Prayers, for use instead of the whole office at the minister's discretion. The 1928 revision added an optional prayer for the child, thereby continuing a trend which makes this office less concerned with the reincorporation of the woman into the life of the community and more of a thanksgiving for the birth of a child.

Ordination—The significant change in the Ordinal at its revision in 1792 was the provision of an alternative form for use with the laying-on-of-hands at the ordination of a presbyter. Lying behind this change were difficulties in this period with the use of the word "priest" and the concept of priestly absolution. Non-Juror, Scottish, and Latitudinarian revisions of the period had typically substituted the words "presbyter" or "minister" throughout the rites for the word "priest," and had omitted or revised absolutions. The 1790 book made use of the word "priest" much less frequently than the 1662 book, and it omitted the reference to absolution from the Exhortation, the word "Absolution" from the rubric prior to the form in the Eucharistic rite, and the "special Confession" from the Visitation of the Sick. The 1928 revision provided a different translation for the Veni Creator and a shorter alternative litany for use at ordinations. During the nineteenth century the parish clerk disappeared. His functions were taken over by layreaders, choirs, altar guilds, and servers.[10]

Institution of Ministers—In the eighteenth century ministers instituted themselves (before a witness) by reading the Articles of Religion, the proclamation of the inductor, and the Prayer Book Service for the Day. The 1799 Connecticut convocation adopted a special service for the purpose prepared by the younger William Smith, then rector at Norwalk. This was slightly revised in 1802 for use in New York. This version was accepted (with additional slight revisions) by the General Convention of 1804. Further minor amendments were made in 1808 and 1844.[11]

Vestments—Within the last half of the nineteenth century Eucharistic Vestments and mitres were re-introduced within Anglicanism, and the use of copes gained in popularity. The use of tippets and of stoles became normal, and the gown fell into disuse. From as early as the 1780s some choirs began to make use of surplices.[12]

Sick Rites—In the 1790 book the provision for a "special Confession" was dropped from the Visitation of the Sick, and Psalm 130 was substituted for Psalm 71. The precedent for this substitution was the Visitation Office of Jeremy Taylor's popular devotional manual, *Holy Dying*, Chapter V, Section 7, which also furnished a number of phrases for two of the three additional prayers which were appended to the rite at that time. The 1928 revisers reworked the Visitation Office, eliminating the exhortation and examination and making other substitutions to make it less grim. It was restructured so that it consists of an introductory portion (which includes a Greeting, an Antiphon, the Lord's Prayer, Preces, and a Collect), followed by a choice from among several units (each of which consists of an Antiphon, a Psalm, and a Collect), and ending with an Anthem, prayers, and a

Blessing. The 1928 revisers also provided a Litany for the Dying and, in accord with a revival of the practice, a form for anointing or laying-on-of-hands.

The 1892 book made provision for the abbreviation of the Communion of the Sick "in the times of contagious sickness or disease," and for the use of this shortened office "with aged and bed-ridden persons" as well as with the sick. The 1928 revisers added alternative Propers and alternative forms for the General Confession and Absolution. In actual practice, while not sanctioned by the Prayer Book, Communion of the Sick from the Reserved Sacrament began to grow in frequency during the last half of the nineteenth century.

Visitation of Prisoners—The forms for the Visitation of Prisoners included in Irish Prayer Books from 1711 were incorporated into the Proposed Book and retained in the books of 1790 and 1892. They were dropped in 1928, except for one prayer (revised) which was placed among the Occasional Prayers.

Burial—The rubric on the use of the Burial Office was changed in 1790, so that it was no longer denied all unbaptized persons but only unbaptized adults. A cento taken from Psalms 39 and 90 was substituted for the use of the whole of these Psalms, and the Committal was revised. These changes stem from the Proposed Book. The controversial first prayer was revised (along lines suggested by the Pennsylvania State convention of 1786) in a manner which owes something to the Scottish Prayer for the Whole State of Christ's Church. The words "as our hope is this our brother doth" were deleted from the second prayer, thereby deleting one of the last vestiges of prayer for the departed from the book.

By the mid-nineteenth century the Psalmody and the lection provided for use in the church were no longer being set within the context of a Daily Office. The 1892 revisers, therefore, provided for the optional addition of a hymn or anthem, the creed, and fitting prayers, thereby providing a burial office analogous to a shortened form of the Daily Offices. Three additional prayers were also printed at the end of the rite.

In 1928 a statement that "this Office is appropriate to be used only for the faithful departed in Christ" was substituted for the old rubric restricting the use of the Office. Alternatives were provided for the Psalms, lections, and Sentences at the grave, and additional prayers were provided. A special Office was also provided for use at the burial of a child. Among the prayers of the Offices of the 1928 book are specific petitions for the departed. This had long been advocated among the Tractarians, and the practice had found a much wider response at the time of World War I when such petitions were typically included in Prayer Books for the Armed Forces and in Special Services authorized by the bishops. The 1928 book reintroduced Eucharistic Propers for use "At a Burial."

THE SANCTIFICATION OF TIME

The Liturgical Day—In the 1790 book the obligation to say the Offices daily was no longer explicitly spelled out, but it was certainly implied in the retention of the titles "Daily Morning Prayer" and "Daily Evening Prayer." The Ornaments Rubric (long a dead-letter law) was dropped. Additional Opening Sentences were retained from the Proposed Book, and another was added. The title "The Declaration of Absolution" was substituted for "The Absolution." The form from the Eucharistic rite was also printed as an alternative. The wording of the Lord's Prayer, and of many of the other texts in the book, was slightly updated. Most of the verbal updatings came from the Proposed Book. The second of the Opening Versicles and Responses ("O God, make speed to save us . . .") was dropped. Latitudinarian and "Arian" revisions of the period (and Seabury's liturgical notebook) had retained only the first seven verses of the Venite. The 1790 book dropped the other verses, rounding off the canticle by adding Psalm 96:7 and 13. Substitutes for the Venite for use

on several major days were retained from the Proposed
Book. The many repetitions of the Gloria Patri within a Service had been frequently criticized, and the 1790 book did
not require its use after any of the canticles of the Daily
Offices, and only after the last of the Psalms. Following the
precedent of Eastern liturgies (and of Deacon and Rattray
and the Proposed Book), the 1790 book restored the use of
the Gloria in excelsis to Morning Prayer, as an alternative
to the Gloria Patri after the Psalms. Following the precedent of the Proposed Book, and of various eighteenth-cen-
tury revisions prior to it, the 1790 book provided "Selections
of Psalms" for use as an alternative to the "promiscuous"
use of the whole of the Psalter. The Table of Proper Psalms
for six major days of the 1662 book was slightly revised.
The Old Testament lectionary for the weekdays of the Proposed Book, which had eliminated readings from the Apocrypha and made a few other changes, was adopted. The Proposed Book's revisions of the Te Deum (with slight changes)
and of the Benedicite were used. The New Testament lectionary of the Proposed Book, which was arranged so that
the New Testament (except for Revelation) would be read
twice rather than thrice a year, was adopted. Many revisions of the period had omitted or shortened the Benedictus
(it was shortened in Seabury's notebook), and only the first
four verses were retained in 1790, and these were placed
after rather than before the Jubilate Deo. In Evening
Prayer, Psalm 92:1–4 was substituted for the Magnificat and
Psalm 103:1–4, 20-22 for the Nunc dimittis. The Gospel canticles (Magnificat, Benedictus, and Nunc dimittis) had been
omitted from many revisions of the period (though not from
the Proposed Book). They evidently had been a source of
controversy as far back as 1552 when a Psalm had been provided as an alternative for each of them. The phrase "He
descended into hell" had been omitted from the Proposed
Book, but it had been restored by the interstate convention
of 1786. The 1789 convention gave permission for "any
Churches" (that is, those of a State convention) to omit the
phrase or to substitute "He went into the Place of departed
Spirits." Following the interstate convention of 1786, permis-

sion was given to substitute the Nicene Creed for the Apostles'. The controversial Athanasian Creed was not retained. Following the precedent of many revisions (including the Proposed Book), the Kyrie and the second use of the Lord's Prayer were dropped. Only the first and the last of the Versicles and Responses were retained. As in the Proposed Book and many other revisions, the saying of the Collect for the Day in Morning Prayer was no longer required if it were to be said in Ante-Communion immediately afterward. The Third Collect of Evening Prayer was revised along lines suggested by *A New Liturgy* (1749), making it parallel to the Collect for Grace of Morning Prayer. The permission to sing an anthem after the Fixed Collects was dropped. Following the Proposed Book and many prior revisions, "A Prayer for all Conditions of Men" (as revised in the Proposed Book) and "A General Thanksgiving" were printed within the Daily Offices, to be used "when the Litany is not said." A new lectionary for the Daily Offices which included readings from the Apocrypha, given approval in the Church of England in 1871, was approved for alternative use in America in 1877.[13]

The 1892 and 1928 revisions made some provisions for shortening the Daily Offices. In 1892 the anthems included in the 1790 book to take the place of the Venite on special days were dropped (but not the older Easter Anthems), and the permission to omit the phrase from the Apostles' Creed was withdrawn. Proper Opening Sentences were provided, and also a fuller set of Preces for Evening Prayer. The Magnificat and the Nunc dimittis and the full text of the Benedictus were restored. In the 1928 revision, permission was given to the congregation to join in the General Thanksgiving.

Several Occasional Prayers were revised, and additional ones were provided, in 1790. The principal sources for these changes and additions were the Proposed Book, *A New Liturgy* (1749), and Seabury's notebook. Several of the prayers were revised, and their number was increased at the revisions of 1892 and 1928.

The "Sea Forms" were retained up until the 1928 revision, basically in the revised version of the Proposed Book.

Included in the 1790 book were forms for daily Morning and Evening Prayer for families, abbreviated from the popular forms of Bishop Gibson, which had been printed in some thirty editions by 1789. The 1928 revisers added shorter alternative forms for Family Prayer, and also a number of "Additional Prayers" for use with that Office.

In the mid-nineteenth century, simplified forms of the Daily Offices ("Mission Services" or "Third Services") came into use in many places. The General Convention of 1856 authorized bishops to provide for simplified services for use in congregations not "capable" of making use of the Daily Offices of the Prayer Book. The 1892 book allowed a third daily service, constructed from the contents of the Prayer Book, subject to the discretion of the Ordinary. The 1928 book incorporates both provisions within the directions "Concerning the Service of the Church."

The Liturgical Week—Despite many proposals to shorten the Sunday Service, the 1790 book retained the old pattern of Morning Prayer, Litany, and Holy Communion (or Ante-Communion if there were not sufficient communicants) for Sunday mornings and of Evening Prayer and catechizing for Sunday afternoons. Pressure to shorten the Morning Service mounted during the nineteenth century, and the General Convention of 1856, rather than dealing with the issue by allowing omission of secondary elements, gave permission to the bishops to allow clergy to use the three rites separately (compare the English Shortened Services Act of 1872). Continued pressure over the next decades resulted in a general permission in the 1892 revision. The patterns for the principal Sunday Services which resulted robbed some parishes of the weekly Ante-Communion which at least pointed toward the Eucharist as the normal Sunday rite, the climactic rite in the ritual pattern, and robbed other parishes of the Psalmody, Old Testament lections, and other valuable portions of their liturgical heritage which were enshrined in Morning Prayer. Morning Prayer and Eucharist began to be treated as viable options served up cafeteria style rather than as rites which served different functions within a ritual pattern. The 1928 revisers attempted to deal with the problem by allowing Morning Prayer to end with the canticle after the Old Testament lection if the Eucharist were immediately to follow, but few places seem to have taken advantage of this opportunity to restore wholeness to the Sunday Morning Service.

Wednesdays and Fridays were continued as Litany days up until the 1928 revision, which marks those Fridays which are days of fasting or abstinence by requiring either the General Confession or the Litany at Morning Prayer, if Holy Communion is not immediately to follow, and marks Fridays in Lent (since 1943) by the use of Psalm 95 in place of the Venite. Possibly the most significant of the changes in the Litany in the 1790 book was the substitution of "From all inordinate and sinful affections" for "From fornication, and all other deadly sin." Objections to the phrase "deadly sin" had been raised from at least as far back as the Lords' Committee of 1641. Permission was given for the omission of everything from the Agnus Dei to the final prayer of the Litany, a portion which many revisers considered to be needless duplication.

Carrying further the changes in the Sunday lectionary of the Proposed Book, the number of lections from the Prophets appointed for Sundays was substantially increased in the 1790 book, and the provisions for proper New Testament lections for all the Sundays (new to the Proposed Book) were adopted. Some changes were made in the Sunday lections in 1892 and 1928, and the number of choices was substantially increased in 1943.

The Eucharist—The revision of the Eucharistic rite in the Proposed Book had been especially conservative. The requirement that communicants signify their intention the day before had been dropped. The initial Lord's Prayer, the prayer for the King, and the Nicene Creed had been deleted. Some phrases had been dropped from the Exhortations, and the Gloria in excelsis had been abbreviated. Ante-Communion was to end with the Gospel. The "Black Rubric" (which Wheatly had said denied a doctrine so ridiculous that it was "needless to offer any confutation of it") was omitted.[14]

Some of the Scottish clergy in America, from the time that they no longer felt bound to the 1662 book, had been making use of the Scottish Communion Office (which had restored some of the features of the 1549 book and approximated its order more closely than other Prayer Books) or, at least, of the Eucharistic Prayer from that Office, which contained an initial exclamation of praise (from 1764), an *anamnesis*, an oblation (from 1735), and an *epiclesis*. When the Proposed Book was fresh off the press, before any copies could even be bound, the sheets were sent to the Maryland State convention. Two of the powerful figures in that convention were Scotsmen, both of whom were named William Smith. Among the proposals of that convention was the insertion within the Eucharistic Prayer of the Proposed Book of an excerpt from the *epiclesis* of the 1637 book (which was the form of the *epiclesis* found in the "Wee Bookies" up to 1764, though it had been moved to a position after the oblation in 1755). This proposal was sent to Pennsylvania and adopted by that State convention as well. It was also sent to Boston, and Samuel Parker, the most prominent of the clergy of that area, put himself on record as desiring the adoption of the whole of the Scottish Eucharistic Prayer. Manuscripts now available have caused a reassessment of Seabury's part in the whole procedure. A year and a half prior to this, Seabury had signed a concordat with the Scottish bishops pledging to attempt to introduce the Scottish Communion Office, but up to this time all his suggestions for liturgical revision had been along Latitudinarian lines. After the State conventions of Maryland and of Pennsylvania and Parker of Boston had committed themselves to a revision of the Eucharistic Prayer along Scottish lines, Seabury had a revised version of the Scottish Office printed for presentation to the Connecticut convocation. This convocation, however, according to a contemporary account, "with *a noble spirit rejected*" this Office. Seabury, at some point, copied the Eucharistic Prayer from his revision of the Scottish Office (revising it slightly in the process) into his manuscript notebook which he later took with him to the 1789 convention at Philadelphia. Just prior to the convention, the younger William Smith, now rector at Newport, Rhode Island, wrote to an indeterminable number of delegates to that convention urging them, as a safeguard against the Romish error of Transubstantiation, to adopt a Eucharistic Prayer based upon ancient models.

Except for the restoration of the initial Lord's Prayer (for permissive use) and the full text of the Gloria in excelsis, the changes of the Proposed Book were incorporated into the 1789 revision. A rubric allowed the reading of Ante-Communion from where Morning Prayer was read, which had been a common custom from the reign of Queen Elizabeth. The Summary of the Law, in the eighteenth century, had frequently been used instead of the Decalogue (as in the Non-Juror rite and among those of other schools of thought as well), or in addition to it (as in Scottish usage). The 1790 book permitted its use after the Decalogue. The Scottish nonjuring clergy (and possibly others as well) had substituted the "Decalogue Collect" for the prayer for the King, and it was printed in that place in the 1790 book. The Collects for the Day of the Proposed Book were retained, with a few additional verbal changes. The use of the Gloria tibi at the announcement of the Gospel was restored. This usage had been common, and it had been included in revisions as diverse as the Non-Juror Offices of 1718 and the revision of William Hopkins, the anti-Trinitarian. A rubric provided that either the Apostles' or the Nicene Creed was to be read if a Creed had not been said immediately before in Morning Prayer. Almost all of the small changes made in the rubrics and texts associated with the offering and the Penitential Order were derived from the Proposed Book. The 1790 book gave permission to omit the Proper Preface for Trinity Sunday, and it provided an alternative form which set forth the doctrine in terms less metaphysical than the traditional Preface. The Proposed Book had required the use of the Trinity Proper Preface, though many liturgies of the period (including that of Deacon the Non-Juror as well as those of Whiston, Lindsey, and the King's Chapel) had omitted it. The people were to say the Sanctus with the priest, beginning with the words "Therefore with angels and archangels." This was probably a legalization of a common practice. The Eucharistic Prayer was formed by revising that of Seabury's notebook to conform in the *epiclesis* to the proposal of the Maryland and Pennsylvania State conventions of 1786. Additional elements were to be consecrated by repeating a substantial portion of the Prayer (following the liturgies of 1689, of Whiston, of Wesley, and the 1764 Scottish Office), in contrast to a mere repetition of the pertinent Words of Institution, which was the 1662 form. The singing of a hymn was ordered after the Eucharistic Prayer, and (apparently new to this revision) permission was given to substitute a hymn for the Gloria in excelsis. The rubric which required thrice yearly Communion (retained in the Proposed Book) was dropped from the 1790 book, more frequent communions having by now been firmly established.

In the 1892 revision, the use of the Decalogue was required only once each Sunday. The Kyrie was added for use after the Summary of the Law, "if the Decalogue hath been omitted." The use of the Nicene Creed was required on five major feasts. Some additional Offertory Sentences were added, largely from the Andrewes—Non-Juror—Scottish tradition. The Exhortation was required only once a month, and the Communion hymn was no longer obligatory. Because non-communicating rites had been instituted in some places, it was made explicit that "sufficient opportunity shall be given to those present to communicate."

In the 1928 revision, the use of the Decalogue is required only one Sunday a month, and the Exhortation only three times a year. Several enrichments were provided: permission to use a hymn or anthem after the Epistle and the Laus tibi after the Gospel, and three additional Proper Prefaces (Epiphany; Purification, Annunciation, and Transfiguration; and All Saints). The principal changes, and the most controversial, were the inclusion of a petition for the departed and some changes in the order which brought it more into line with the 1549 and Scottish traditions (the Lord's Prayer was placed after the Eucharistic Prayer, and the Prayer of Humble Access after that, as a Communion devotion).

After the restoration in 1789 of a more adequate Eucharistic Prayer, the significant changes have been in the Eucharistic ceremonial and piety rather than in the text. From the mid-nineteenth century certain practices were imported or revived. The justifications for the changes tended to be allegorical, aesthetic, or antiquarian. The changes often tended to promote an individualistic, pietistic approach, to make seeing and hearing the liturgy more difficult for the congregation, and to curtail actual congregational participation. Such changes included a shift in the position of the officiant at the Eucharist so that his back was to the people, the substitution of round wafers for broken bread and sometimes of a ciborium for a more significatory paten, the substitution of sips of ("sacramental") white wine for substantial drinks of the more significatory red wine (often homemade), and also the imposition of ceremonial appropriate to the Western Roman type Eucharistic Prayer upon an Eastern West Syrian type Eucharistic Prayer. The service patterns which developed (sometimes with a multiplication of small weekday Communions as extensions of or preparations for a principal Sunday Service of Morning Prayer or a non-communicating Mass) did much to break down the last vestiges of understanding of a liturgical week.

The Liturgical Year—The Black Letter Days were eliminated from the calendar of the 1790 book, and one State Service (for Thanksgiving Day) was included in the place of the four of the English book. The marking of the eves of Sundays and Holy Days was also done away. The 1892 book included readings from the Apocrypha and from Revelation in the weekday lectionary, and it provided Propers for the Feast of the Transfiguration and a table of alternative lections for Lent, the Ember Days, and the Rogation Days. It also allowed the use of the Collect for a Sunday or Holy Day on its eve. The 1928 revision rearranged the lectionary for the Daily Offices according to the Church Year rather than the calendar year (associating particular Biblical books with appropriate seasons), and that principle was followed in the 1943 revision of the lectionary, which also arranged the Psalms so that they could be used selectively. The 1928 book also provided proper lections for the eves of saint's days and included Propers for a Saint's Day, the Feast of the Dedication of a Church, the Ember Days, the Rogation Days, and Independence Day. The rites for the great feasts have, however, in the 1892, 1928, and 1943 revisions, tended to lose the unitive baptismal nature which was to some extent restored in the first Book of Common Prayer of 1549.

Music—During the eighteenth century Isaac Watts had provided Christianized metrical versions of the Psalms (See *The Hymnal 1940* 277, 289, 300, 319, 542), and hymns (See *The Hymnal 1940* 127, 242, 337, 369, 550, 586), which had found a ready reception among nonconformists. John and Charles Wesley wrote over 6000 hymns (See *The Hymnal 1940* 1, 5, 27, 85, 95, 104, *et al.*), and made great use of hymnody in their evangelistic work. Selections of verses from the Psalter of Sternhold and Hopkins or of Tate and Brady (chosen for subject matter or arranged as an "in course" system) provided the staple musical diet of the typical Anglican parish, but from the mid-eighteenth century some parishes began to bring into use small parochial collections of additional hymns. Those of Watts, Doddridge, and Addison were particularly favored. The Proposed Book included a selection of verses from the Tate and Brady Psalter, arranged according to subject matter, and a collection of fifty-one (Psalms and) hymns. The 1790 Prayer Book included the whole of the Tate and Brady Psalter and twenty-seven of the hymns from the Proposed Book, thus giving to hymnody a greater recognition than it had previously been accorded within Anglicanism. During the eighteenth and nineteenth centuries, organs and choirs gradually displaced clerks and village instrumentalists as leaders of congregational singing. From the late eighteenth century, the use of

Anglican chants in parish churches began to spread. The Tate and Brady Psalter was displaced in 1832 by a Psalter which drew upon other metrical versions as well. The "Prayer Book Collection" of hymns was increased in 1808, 1826, and 1865. During the mid-nineteenth century a great many hymns were translated into English from Latin, Greek, and German, and many new hymns were written. There was also the beginning of a revival of the use of plainsong tunes and of the importation of tunes from the Continent and of the writing of tunes in a new style. Metrical Psalms and Scriptural paraphrases, and the old Psalm tunes, fell into disfavor. The General Convention of 1871 authorized a hymnal twice the size of its predecessor which incorporated only a few of the metrical Psalms and drew heavily upon the new hymns and translations. This hymnal, which was divorced from the Prayer Book, was revised in 1874, 1892, 1916, and 1940. During the last decades of the nineteenth century and the first decades of the twentieth, the increased use of professional choirs or quartets and of choir tunes for hymns and anthem settings for canticles and service music tended to reduce the opportunities for congregational participation in the rites.[15]

THE SANCTIFICATION OF SPACE

Buildings—The first churches built in America (for example, St. Luke's, near Smithfield, Virginia) provided two rooms—one for the Word, centered in the pulpit, and one for the Eucharist, centered about the Table. Eighteenth and early nineteenth century churches were typically one room buildings, arranged so that people could easily see and hear the clergyman in the pulpit and at the Table (after having drawn near). But in the mid-nineteenth century the principle that form follows function in the building of churches was largely abandoned. Rather than being constructed for the liturgy, the buildings began to determine what went on inside. The medieval cathedral (which had been a functional

setting for the worship and the church and community life of
its day) began to be accepted as the model. The Table was
removed from the people. The choir was brought up from
the back of the church and placed on a stage erected between the congregation and the Table. The pulpit, the lectern, and the reading desk were typically placed on the
sides in positions which made seeing and hearing the liturgies of the Word more difficult. Side aisles (which had functioned in early basilicas as passageways and in medieval
churches as spaces for additional Altars) began to be used
for seating. Victorian builders with their love of vistas were
concerned to keep the central alley clear, and they replaced
"honest Tables" with impressive sideboards (which began to
be equipped with crosses, flowers, and candles) to create an
artificial numinous effect and to impress all who entered the
main door. But the placement of the Table, the pulpit, the
lectern, and the choir, the rearrangement of the seating in
military rows, and the intrusion of rood screens began to
obstruct the view of the Table from the communicants and
to make access to it difficult. In many churches fonts were
tucked away in a narthex or a side aisle. In the 1880s and
1890s buildings built prior to the Cambridge Movement began to be remodeled according to the ideals of the ecclesiologists, so that now there are probably less than a dozen
church buildings left in America with the older, more functional liturgical arrangements intact. Within the late nineteenth and early twentieth centuries, the provision of the
parish house for functions which had formerly taken place in
the nave became the norm.[16]

During the late nineteenth and early twentieth centuries,
the ceremonial use of candles and the placing of crosses and
flowers on or above the Table came into general use, as did
the use of a processional cross. Processional candles and incense also came into use in some parishes. This same period
witnessed, in some places, a re-introduction of the public reservation of the Sacrament, either in an aumbry, for which
there is abundant pre-Reformation precedent, or in a tabernacle above the Altar.

The Consecration of Churches—Though the Church of England did not have an official form for the Consecration of Churches, the General Convention in 1799 adopted Bishop Provoost's revision of a Convocation form of 1712, which he had used in the State of New York. This form provided for an entry of the bishop and clergy during the recitation of Psalm 24, a presentation of Instruments of Donation and Endowment, "setting apart this place in solemn manner, for the performance of the several offices of religious worship," with prayers related to the various offices, the reading of the Sentence of Consecration and placing it upon the Table, and Propers for Morning Prayer and the Eucharist.

Colors—During the late nineteenth and early twentieth centuries, the Baroque Roman color sequence was gradually brought into general use for vestments and for super-frontals and/or frontals which gradually displaced the traditional Anglican "Laudian" ("Jacobean") frontals. Small corporals replaced the large white tablecloths which had covered the Laudian frontals for the Eucharistic rite, and the new stiff palls and colored communion veils came into use.

CHAPTER IX

THE PERIOD OF PAPERBACK LITURGIES

The beginning of World War I marked in Europe the end of an age of Romanticism, Neo-Gothicism, Liberal Protestantism, and rabid denomination-alism. It marked the beginning of a new or renewed emphasis upon Biblical theology, Patristics, and ecumenism, and of historical-critical study of liturgy, renewed lay participation with a rediscovery of the corporate nature of the church and the role of the laity, and different directions in iconography and architecture. The Liturgical Movement can be traced back to the first Liturgical Week for laymen at the Abbey of Maria Laach in 1914. In the period between the two World Wars the movement gained significant followings in Germany, Belgium, Austria, Holland, and France. Outstanding among those whose writings have contributed to the movement, or whose scholarship has fostered it, have been Ilde-

fons Herwegan, Odo Casel, Romano Guardini, Josef A. Jungmann, Theodor Klauser, Pius Parsch, Louis Bouyer,
Bernard Botte, and Jean Daniélou. The progress of the
movement in America can be traced back to the beginning
of the periodical *Orate Fratres* (now *Worship*) by the Bene-
dictines of St. John's Abbey, Collegeville, Minnesota, under
the leadership of Virgil Michel. Some of the changes of
the 1950s (such as, the restoration of the Easter Vigil and
reform of the Holy Week rites, the simplification of rubrics,
relaxation of regulations in regard to the Eucharistic fast
and the hours of celebrations, and efforts to promote more
congregational participation in the music) were in the spirit
of the Liturgical Movement. Vatican II promulgated the
Constitution on the Sacred Liturgy which underlined the
fact that liturgy demands "full, conscious, and active participation" and called for a return to the sources and for adapta-
tion of the liturgy to present conditions. This paved the way
for a thorough revision of the liturgical books.[1]

Though the Liturgical Movement originated within the
Roman Catholic Church, Continental Protestants and the
Eastern Orthodox gradually became aware of its potentiali-
ties and began to respond to it. The works of such Continental Protestants as Yngve Brilioth, Dietrich Bonhoeffer, J.-J.
von Allmen, and Max Thurian have been informed by the
ideals of the Liturgical Movement and have contributed to
its spread. The Protestant monastery at Taizé has functioned as a center and place of pilgrimage for people from all
over the world. Among the Eastern Orthodox, the work of
Alexander Schmemann has been outstanding, and one mark
of the Liturgical Movement among Roman Catholics and Protestants has been a heightened appreciation for many aspects of the Eastern heritage and a better perspective concerning it. One mark of this period has been a growing
consensus among liturgical scholars. A concrete result of
this can be seen in the new rites of the Church of South
India, which incorporated fruits of the new knowledge in
rites which were adapted to the particular culture and to
the pastoral needs of its people. That liturgy has contrib-

uted to later revisions of various churches. In the 1960s and 1970s most of the major Protestant Churches have been involved in revisions of their liturgical books.[2]

It was not until the 1930s that the Liturgical Movement began to have some effect among Anglicans. The writings of Father Hebert, Dean Ladd, and Walter Lowrie began to make people aware of the movement. Its first fruits were the "Parish Communion" which was established in some places, the restoration of baptisms to public services, and the return to the congregation of some parts of the rites which had been preempted by choirs. Despite these trends, the Prayer Book revision proposals within Anglicanism in the 1950s were still, by and large, directed toward enrichment and elaboration, following the patterns of the late nineteenth and early twentieth century revisions. In the 1950s, however, there was a gradual awakening to new directions within Romanism (particularly through the early writings of Bouyer and Jungmann) and within Continental Protestantism (particularly Taizé), and to the new revisions for the Church of South India. The Lambeth Conference 1958 acknowledged that the time for more drastic Prayer Book revisions had come and set forth certain guidelines which were more fully developed by the Anglican Congress 1963. From that point, liturgical revision within Anglicanism seemed to enter a new phase. Most of the provinces of Anglicanism are currently engaged in a process of revision, making use of a method of "trial use" (pioneered in America 1786–1789), which allows both clergy and laity to respond after appreciable use of proposed rites.[3]

The revisions of the various churches now in process are being carried out with the expressed aim of returning to the sources, the Biblical and Patristic heritage, incorporating the results of liturgical scholarship, and adapting to present conditions and missionary and pastoral needs. There have been attempts to make the language more intelligible, to incorporate the social concerns of the day, and to allow for more flexibility to meet the needs of particular worshiping communities. There have been attempts to restore to the liturgies something of the missionary, proclamatory, educational, and pastoral aspects, which have been missing or overclouded for some centuries. The various denominations have cooperated or consulted with each other (for example, International Consultation on English Texts [ICET]; Joint Liturgical Group), in order that in the process of revising they might be drawn closer to each other rather than being pushed further apart. One book influenced by the concerns, insights, and aims of the Liturgical Movement is the 1979 revision of the American Book of Common Prayer. First published in 1976, as a paperback, under the title the Draft Proposed Book of Common Prayer, it was presented for preliminary approval to the Church's General Convention of that same year. Its form and contents were the result of extensive trial use of particular rites since 1967, and its provisions and changes are in many ways typical of the period.[4] The Convention accepted the book, with a number of amendments, in 1976, authorized it for trial use for three years, and adopted it as the Book of Common Prayer in 1979.

THE SANCTIFICATION OF LIFE

Initiation—Underlying the revision of the rites of initiation were a number of factors. For centuries the rites had not been effective in separating the initiate from the world and incorporating him into the church. Problems associated with "indiscriminate baptism" had multiplied. Infant baptism, often interpreted in sentimental terms, had in people's thinking replaced adult baptism (following catechesis, and symbolizing repentance and confession of faith) as the norm. The rites had been largely divorced from any integral relationship with the congregation, with the bishop, and with the Church Year, and earlier Prayer Book rites were sparse in their use of Biblical types and analogies. "Confirmation" ("a rite looking for a theology") had sometimes been exalted at the expense of downgrading the primary sacrament of baptism. It had been used as a gateway to Communion. Bishops were associated with "confirmation" rather than baptism. The 1928 Prayer Book rite made what is probably illegitimate use of a text (Acts 8:14–17) as scriptural warrant for the rite.[5]

The baptismal rite of the 1979 Book of Common Prayer, in the light of new knowledge and of the problems involved, is a rather conservative revision. It simply attempts to restore the centrality of initiation to the ritual pattern, the public nature of the rite and congregational involvement in it, the bishop as the normal minister, the relationship to the Church Year, and admission to the Family Table as the climax. The rubrics assume adult baptism as the norm, while making provision for infants and children. The context is that of a Sunday Liturgy of the Word and Eucharist. Promises are phrased in terms which are more easily grasped. The Baptismal Confession of Faith (the Apostles' Creed) is restored to the rite. The Promises also constitute a rite of renewal of baptismal vows for the whole congregation. Use is made of the principal Biblical types of baptism (Creation, the Exodus, and the Baptism of Jesus) in the Blessing of the Water. Provision is made for chrismation, and references are made to baptism as the anointing of kings and priests. Explicit reference is made to the Seal of the Spirit. The rite includes the Peace (which allows the congregation to welcome the newly baptized) and First Communion.

A rite of "confirmation" is retained. It is expected that those baptized in infancy "when they are ready and have been duly prepared . . . make a mature public affirmation of their faith and commitment to the responsibilities of their Baptism; and . . . receive the laying-on of hands by the Bishop," and it is seen as appropriate that such affirmations also be made by those who come under the bishop's jurisdiction from another church and by others who wish to reaffirm their baptismal vows. It is expected that this rite will normally take place within the context of the service of Holy Baptism. In the rite the bishop prays for a renewal of the baptismal covenant with these persons, and that they might be sent forth "in the power of the Spirit to perform the service you set before *them*." Separate forms are provided for use in conjunction with the laying-on-of-hands "for confirmation," "for reception," and "for reaffirmation." It is obvious from the content of the rite that it is not appropriate for use with an adult who has been recently baptized, and that it does not supplant baptism as the gateway to communion.

Penance—Emphasis upon Lent as a season of penitence is maintained in the new revisions. That of the 1979 Book of Common Prayer provides a suitable Proper for the Liturgy of the Word for Ash Wednesday, and it follows the sermon on that day with an exhortation which sets forth the baptismal and penitential aspects of Lent, Psalm 51, and a Litany of Penitence; and it provides for the distribution of ashes.

The Daily Office and the Eucharistic rite provide for a General Confession and Absolution, and its use is required within the Eucharistic rite except "on occasion," which permits it to be omitted in Easter Season. In addition, to meet a need which has often been dealt with through the use of forms which have lacked approval, a Penitential Order has been provided for occasional use in preparation for the Eucharist, which consists of an Opening Acclamation, (a sermon or exhortation), (the Decalogue,) Sentences, a General Confession and Absolution, (appropriate prayers, and the grace). On occasion (except for the sermon and concluding devotions), the Order may be used as an introduction to the Eucharistic rite.

Following the lead of some recent Anglican revisions, a form for private confession, "The Reconciliation of a Penitent," is provided. Following ancient and Eastern precedents, provision is made for confession to a deacon or a lay person when a priest is not available.[6]

Marriage—The problems of pluralism and mixed marriages and of mobility have caused a loss of a sense of the public nature and significance of marriage rites, and they have come to be looked upon by many as private rites to be determined by personal taste, in which the church building functions only as a setting rented for the occasion and the clergyman as an official paid for the job. The fact that the distinctive things about a Christian marriage are its setting within the Christian community and the blessing of the church has been largely lost sight of. The new rite includes a pledge on the part of the congregation to support and uphold this couple, and the marriage rite is set within the context of a Liturgy of the Word and Eucharist within which the members of the congregation are given a chance to express their concern and good wishes, and the couple begin their married life by presenting the bread and wine and by receiving Communion as husband and wife within the setting of a Eucharistic Meal of the Family of God. An order of elements of a marriage rite is also provided, which can be fleshed out for the particular occasion.[7]

Pregnancy and Childbirth—The old Churching rite had fallen into disuse. A rite is provided in the new Book of Common Prayer which can appropriately be used for public giving of thanks for the gift of a living child, one of the functions which was sometimes served within the more complex historic Churching rites. It includes an optional prayer for use if the child is not yet baptized (compare forms for the admission of a catechumen) which does not imply that the baptism is to take place in the immediate future. The new rite is also designed for use upon the adoption of a child.[8]

Ordination—It has been recognized that the historic ordination rites of Anglicanism did not give sufficient expression to the voice of the people nor sufficient emphasis upon their prayers, and that they allowed little or no opportunity for the lay order to participate as presenters or readers or for the congregation to welcome and congratulate the newly ordained. The first Anglican Ordinal rightly restored the laying-on-of-hands with prayer as the essential action of the rites, but the laying-on-of-hands was separated from the prayers of the people and the "consecration" prayer of the bishop, and it was associated with forms which have only late medieval Western precedent. Within the historic Prayer Book rites, it was only at the ordination of a deacon that the newly ordained was given any opportunity to function in his new role at the climactic Eucharist. The prayers themselves did not enunciate clearly the function of the order being conferred. Since the rites were originally preceded by Morning Prayer, there was no Old Testament lection and no Psalmody. Since the rites were cast in the plural, the assumption seems to have been that they would not take place within the congregation immediately concerned.[9]

The new rites for each of the three orders, which follow essentially the same format, provide for a Presentation, a Litany, and a full Liturgy of the Word, followed by an Examination, a hymn invoking the Holy Spirit, a period of silent prayer, the laying-on-of-hands with a prayer which depicts the order being conferred, the donning of insignia and delivery of instruments appropriate to the order, the Peace, and a Eucharist within which the newly ordained person functions in his new office. Provision is made within the rites for the members of various orders (laity as well as deacons, presbyters, and bishops) to function in manners appropriate to their orders.

The Celebration of a New Ministry—The American Prayer Book had provided no form for the celebration of the beginning of a new ministry of anyone who was not being instituted as rector of a parish, even though in the American Church the purpose of the rite of Institution of Ministers was devotional and edifying rather than legal. The rite of the 1979 Book of Common Prayer may be used, with adaptations where necessary, not only for rectors of parishes but also for assistants, vicars of missions, deans and canons of cathedrals, chaplains of institutions, or non-stipendiary clergy. It may be used for deacons and lay vicars as well as for priests. The rubrics are designed to allow for a large measure of flexibility and localization. At the beginning of the rite the new minister vocalizes commitment, and the congregation pledges its support. The Liturgy of the Word (for which appropriate lections and Psalms are suggested) follows. Representatives of the congregation then present to the new minister instruments symbolic of various aspects of the new ministry. The rite is concluded with a Eucharist at which the bishop serves as principal celebrant.[10]

Vestments—Within the last decades the use of Eucharistic Vestments and of copes and mitres has come to be generally acceptable throughout the Episcopal Church. There has been a general return to pre-Baroque forms of these vestments and to fuller and longer surplices. More creativity is being applied to the ornamentation of vestments. At the same time, there has developed a new feeling of freedom to omit the use of vestments when such use might be awkward, incongruous, or inappropriate.[11]

Commitment to Christian Service—In some current revisions questions have been included within baptismal rites which spell out the commitment in more concrete terms, or a "confirmation" rite has been framed as an "ordination of the laity" or commitment to Christian service, for responsible adult candidates. The 1979 Book of Common Prayer includes a very flexible rite suitable for use as a public expression of commitment at any number of critical points within the life of an individual.[12]

Sick Rites—The grim aspect of the Sick rites of the historic Prayer Books and their lack of flexibility led to general disuse of them except for an occasional collect. At the same time, something of a revival of spiritual healing, and of anointing or laying-on-of-hands, has drawn attention to the need for different and/or additional provisions in this area.[13]

The new Book of Common Prayer provides for the ministry to the sick a form which includes suggested Psalms and readings from the New Testament, prayers, which normally include a confession of sin, (the blessing of oil,) and the laying-on-of-hands with or without anointing. Provisions are made for a private Communion for the Sick or for Communion from the Reserved Sacrament. Provision is also made for the inclusion of the laying-on-of-hands or anointing at a public celebration of the Eucharist. Prayers for use by a sick person are also provided.[14]

Ministry at the Time of Death—The contents are as follows: a prayer for a person near death, a litany for the dying, a commendation at the time of death, suggested devotions for a vigil or a wake, a form for the reception of the body which may be used immediately prior to the burial rite or prior to the vigil if the vigil is held in the church.

Burial—Within the age of Romanticism a sentimental approach to burial was fostered which essentially denied the reality of death and substituted the assurance of immortality for the proclamation of resurrection. It was natural that in this climate the Funeral Home should develop as an institution, and that drastic changes should be made in the conduct of the rite. The connection of the burial rite with a Daily Office died out in the nineteenth century, and burial came to be thought of as a private rite. Sentimental music, excessive flowers, exorbitant expenditures upon coffins and vaults, and even the postponement of the actual lowering of the body and covering of the grave became commonplace.[15]

The 1979 Book of Common Prayer provides burial rites in traditional and contemporary language with rubrics and texts which are aimed at diminishing the sentimental, immortality-of-the-soul approach, and which provide for more congregational participation. The full rite consists of Opening Anthems, a Liturgy of the Word (with suitable lections, Psalmody, and prayers), the Eucharist (for which a Proper Preface is provided), a brief commendation, suggested anthems for use as the body is borne from the church, and a rite of committal. "An Order of Burial" is also provided which is to be filled out by the celebrant in a manner appropriate to the particular situation. A form is also provided for the consecration of a grave if the burial is in a place which has not previously been set apart for Christian burial. Cremation is expressly permitted.

THE SANCTIFICATION OF TIME

The Liturgical Day—The working hours of the laity, at least from the time of the Industrial Revolution, the geographical spread of typical parishes, and other factors have worked against the continued congregational use of both of the Daily Offices. A number of the clergy have found burdensome the daily use of the Offices and have abandoned the use of one or both. Yet the Offices are useful or needful in a great variety of situations—individual devotions, seminary or monastic communities, small groups which meet periodically or groups which are together only for a limited period of time, and small congregations which represent the parish in microcosm. It is also desirable that the offices be used on occasion as alternative Liturgies of the Word for use in conjunction with the Eucharist. The variety of these situations demanded greater flexibility than was provided by earlier Prayer Book rites.[16]

The 1979 Book of Common Prayer includes Daily Offices for morning and evening (in both traditional and contemporary language) which provide for abbreviation, variety, and enrichment while holding to the historic structure of the Prayer Book rites. Invitatory Antiphons are provided for all seasons and festivals, and their use is made more flexible. The ancient candlelighting hymn *Phos hilaron* is restored to the Daily Office for optional use (as a *lucernarium* hymn) prior to the Psalmody at the Evening Office. The Jubilate Deo is used as an alternative to the Venite. Either is to be used in the morning and may now be used in the evening. "Christ our Passover" may now be used at this place from Easter until the Day of Pentecost. More flexibility is allowed at the core of the Office, the Proclamation of the Word. Only one reading is required, but there may be as many as three. Readings may be followed by a period of silence. A greater variety of canticles is provided, allowing them to be used more meaningfully as responses to particular lections. Canticles are no longer limited to morning use or evening use. Certain canticles are appropriately designated as suitable for use after Old Testament readings, and others for use after New Testament readings. Canticles particularly appropriate for Lent and for the Easter season are provided. An appended table suggests a distribution of the canticles by the days of the week. In special circumstances, a hymn may now be substituted for a canticle. A sermon or meditation is allowed, and it is appropriately placed immediately following the lections. The Creed is now omissible, and the Lord's Prayer is placed in a climactic position. Alternative forms are provided for the Suffrages. In order that the Office may be more closely tied in with the liturgical week, special collects are provided for Fridays, Saturdays, and Sundays at both Morning and Evening Prayer. Additional prayers are provided for use after the collect when a Form of Intercession is not used.

A need has been felt by many for an evening service, apart from the regular Daily Office, which might be used as a complete rite, or as the introduction to Evening Prayer or some other service, or to an evening meal or other activity. Several traditional elements of Christian evening worship have been brought together in a simple and flexible Order of Worship for the Evening, which includes a lighting of candles with a Prayer for Light and the traditional lamplighting hymn, *Phos hilaron*.

Within some situations a need has been felt for a short Office for use at noonday along the lines of the monastic Hour of Sext, and another for use at the close of the day along the lines of the Hour of Compline, and the 1979

Book of Common Prayer provides forms with which many Anglicans can be more comfortable than with many of the forms which have been used in these circumstances.

The eighteenth century forms for Family Prayer having fallen out of general use, the 1979 Prayer Book provides brief, flexible forms which may prove more viable in our day.

The Liturgical Week—The new Book of Common Prayer attempts to restore the primacy of Sunday within the liturgical week by providing Proper Prefaces for the Lord's Day which stress this as the Day of Creation, of Resurrection, and of the outpouring of the Holy Spirit and Baptism, and also by giving normative precedence to Sundays over Saints' Days.

Except for those within the Easter and Christmas seasons and those on which Major Feasts of the Lord occur, Fridays are designated as days to be observed "by special acts of discipline and self-denial."

In a number of ways attempts are made to open up possibilities for a recovery of more sense of the liturgical week with its Daily Offices culminating in a congregational Sunday Eucharist. Among these changes are the provision of more adequate lections and Psalmody, more use of canticles and hymns, and greater flexibility in the prayers within the Eucharistic rite. The permission to substitute the Daily Office for the Liturgy of the Word may also contribute to the recovery of some sense of the pattern of the liturgical week. The provision for use within the Daily Office of additional canticles and for the use of a collect particularly appropriate to the day on Fridays, Saturdays, and Sundays, and provisions in the Proper for Various Occasions designated as appropriate to certain weekdays, may also aid in this recovery. Another helpful step is the fact that Passion Psalms are assigned to Fridays and that Creation and Paschal Deliverance Psalms are assigned to Saturday nights and Sundays in the new Daily Office Lectionary.

The Eucharist—Many criticisms had been aimed at the

Eucharistic rite because of the paucity of its lectionary (particularly in regard to Old Testament lections), the lack of flexibility, the lack of opportunities for congregational participation, its invariable length, its separation of the essential actions, and its failure to provide for a real breaking of the bread. The Eucharistic Prayer itself was criticized for not sufficiently giving thanks for the Mighty Acts of God in Creation, Incarnation, and the sending of the Holy Spirit as well as in Redemption, and for its lack of eschatological reference. In comparison to Morning Prayer, what was supposedly a festal, eucharistic service seemed overly penitential to many.[17]

The 1979 Book of Common Prayer provides Eucharistic rites in both traditional and contemporary language. A hymn, Psalm, or anthem may be sung at the entrance of the ministers. The rite proper begins (optionally in Rite One) with an Opening Acclamation which is varied in Lent and the Easter Season. Rite One has a penitential introduction consisting of the Collect for Purity, the Decalogue and/or the Summary of the Law, and the Kyrie. On festal days the Gloria in excelsis or some other song of praise is to be used. Rite Two provides for the use of the Gloria in excelsis or some other song of praise as an immediate response to the Acclamation on festal days or for a more subdued response of (the Collect for Purity and) the Kyrie or Trisagion on other occasions. On occasions when it seems appropriate, either rite may begin with the Penitential Order (see page 165). Several new Collects of the Day have been provided, and some have been placed more appropriately in the Church Year. Old Testament lections have been provided, as well as Psalms which make appropriate responses to the Old Testament lections. Epistles and Gospels appropriate to the major feasts and seasons are provided, and the Epistles and Gospels are to be read in course over a three-year period on the other Sundays of the year. The lections must be read from an appropriate place. The sermon is placed immediately after the lections (with neither a hymn nor announcements intervening). The

Nicene Creed (which is a formulation of the church's faith, not an individual profession) is again appropriately introduced with the words "We believe," and it is placed as the climax of and response to the Liturgy of the Word. The Prayers of the People follow, for which several forms are provided. Printed within Rite One is a revised form of the Prayer for the Whole State of Christ's Church, with the provision that appropriate responses may be made after each paragraph. Among the other forms are litanies, responsive reading type prayers, a bidding prayer, and a form (for use on Good Friday) modeled after the ancient Roman Solemn Prayers, which consists of a series of biddings each of which is to be followed by silence and a collect by the celebrant. Normally the Prayers of the People (which are appropriately led by a deacon or assisting priest or by a layperson) are concluded with a collect by the celebrant. Then, except on occasion (such as a time of great festivity), and if it was not said at the beginning of the rite, a General Confession and Absolution follow. Before entering into the Liturgy of the Table the fellow guests appropriately greet each other with the Peace. From a practical standpoint this provides an opportunity to welcome strangers and put them at ease and to express one's Christian concern for other members of the Family. The attention of the congregation is then shifted from the pulpit to the Table, which is appropriately prepared at this time (by a deacon or some person other than the officiating priest, if possible) so that the bread, wine, and other offerings may be brought forward (by representatives of the congregation) and placed upon it (by a deacon or assisting clergyman, rather than by the officiating priest, if possible). The congregation stands (though permission is given, for those who must, to kneel after the Sanctus) for the Eucharistic Prayer, the Great Thanksgiving, within which (within most of the forms) praise is offered for God's work in Creation and Redemption, the Words which constitute our warrant for the celebration are recited, *anamnesis* is made, the gifts are offered, the Holy Spirit is invoked upon the gifts and the people, and prayer is made for a worthy participation. The congregation's participation in the Great Thanksgiving is symbolized by its standing posture and by its vocal participation in the Sanctus, (Acclamation,) and Amen. Among the authorized texts is that produced by the Committee for a Common Eucharistic Prayer which is based upon the ancient Anaphora of St. Basil (See pp. 65–67). The Eucharistic Prayer is followed by the Lord's Prayer. Then, after a period of silence during which the initial fraction is made, the Bread is broken for the administration of Communion, and if more than one chalice is needed wine is poured from the flagon into the additional chalice(s). At this point, "Christ our Passover" and/or some other appropriate anthem may be sung. Rite One provides for the use of a preparatory prayer (the Prayer of Humble Access) after the Breaking of the Bread. The rubrics allow the communicants to receive standing, in accordance with ancient catholic tradition. A new briefer form for use when additional elements must be consecrated is provided. Provisions are made so that the ablutions need not be obtrusive or assume undue attention or importance. The congregation is allowed to join in the post-communion prayer, which may be preceded or followed by a hymn. The congregation is then sent on its way with a blessing and/or a dismissal.

The revised Book of Common Prayer also provides a "Rite Three," "An Order for Celebrating the Holy Eucharist," which is not itself a rite but a listing of essential elements which can with "careful preparation by all the worshipers" be fleshed out for use "on occasions other than the principal service on Sundays and other feasts of our Lord." This order gives a definition of the "essential parts" of a Eucharistic rite. Any of the Eucharistic Prayers from Rite One or Rite Two may be used in this Order, or either of two forms which allow for a great deal of extemporization.

The Administration of Communion Under Special Circumstances—Specific directions are given for the private administration of Communion to those who for any reason cannot be present at the public celebration. In its fullest form it consists of the celebration of the Eucharist according to one of the authorized rites. When circumstances require, however, the service may begin with the Offertory. When Communion is to be administered from the Reserved Sacrament, the service normally includes a reading from Scripture (and commentary), prayers concluding with a collect praying for worthy reception of the Sacrament, confession and absolution, (the Peace,) the Lord's Prayer, administration of the Sacrament, a post-communion prayer, and a blessing.

The period of paperback liturgies has been marked by significant changes in Eucharistic ceremonial and piety. A concern for the significatory value of the signs has shown itself in a return to the use of real broken bread, of red wine, of plate-like patens in place of ciboriums, of Table-like Altars. Ceremonial practices which allegorized or mystified are being replaced by practices which dramatize or elucidate the texts. The individualistic piety which saw the Eucharistic rite primarily as medicine for one's soul and as a setting for one's private devotions is being replaced by a piety which has recaptured something of the family aspect of the feast, its basic Eucharistic nature, its kerygmatic function, and its eschatological implications.[18]

The Liturgical Year—The 1979 Book of Common Prayer attempts to give emphasis to the baptismal nature of the Church Year, the centrality of the Great Fifty Days and the primacy of the Proper of Time over the Proper of Saints.[19]

Provision is made for the inauguration of the Great Fifty Days with a Baptismal Vigil which includes the lighting of the Paschal Candle, lections which recall God's Mighty Acts in Creation and Redemption, baptism with the renewal of baptismal vows, and the Eucharist. "Christ our Passover" may be used as the invitatory anthem at the Daily Offices from Easter until the Day of Pentecost. Proper lections for a Vigil of Pentecost are also provided. No longer is fasting required within the Great Fifty Days. The Sundays which follow are designated as Sundays after Pentecost.

The First Sunday after the Epiphany is designated "The Baptism of our Lord Jesus Christ." The Rogation Days, which had come to rest within the Easter Season, are freed from the Temporale, so that they may be celebrated at times which meet local needs. The Ember Days may also be moved so that their celebration may be related to local times of ordinations. Special rites are provided to mark certain special days in addition to Easter: Ash Wednesday, Palm Sunday, Good Friday, and Thanksgiving Day. Seven Red Letter Days are added to the calendar: the Confession of Saint Peter, Saint Joseph, the Visitation of the Blessed Virgin Mary, Saint Mary Magdalene, Saint Mary the Virgin, Holy Cross, and Saint James of Jerusalem. Black Letter Days (basically those for which Propers had been provided in *Lesser Feasts and Fasts)* are also noted in the calendar, and several sets of collects, Psalms, and lections, "The Common of Saints," are provided which may be used on these days or on patronal festivals. Octaves and the use of a second "seasonal collect" have been eliminated. Propers for Various Occasions ("Votives") are also provided which may be used on days other than Sundays or Holy Days.

Music—Prior to World War II there was some movement to return to the congregation some of the canticles and Service Music which rightly belonged to them rather than to the choir. Steps also began to be taken to encourage more active congregational participation in the music through a return to speech-rhythm chanting, the replacement of organs imitative of the orchestra with organs better adapted not only for organ repertoire but also for providing a precise lead and firm support for congregational singing, and the publication of hymnals which included the music and were basically designed for the congregation rather than for the choir. Musicians began to produce simple hymn-anthems and hymn tune-preludes which provided a subtle, painless way of exposing a congregation to new hymn tunes and of enlarging the repertoire. *The Hymnal 1940* (following a precedent set by *The English Hymnal* of 1906) reached out to include folksongs native to the land. While the general thrust over the past forty years has been toward the encouragement of congregational participation, this has in many smaller places been somewhat handicapped by the replacement of pianos or reed organs by the new electronic instruments which have typically been modeled upon the older theater organs rather than upon organs better adapted to liturgical usage. The Joint Committee on Church Music prepared in 1960 a *Supplement to the Hymnal 1940* which provided some additional canticles and service music. Since then the doors have been opened to the use of guitars and other instruments, there has been a revival of folk singing, and some use has begun to be made of electronic tapes. The Standing Commission on Church Music and the publisher of "Music for Liturgy," in particular, have sponsored the publication of new texts and tunes, and greater use of local musical resources is being encouraged.[20]

THE SANCTIFICATION OF SPACE

Buildings—Within the last few years, in the building of churches, there has been something of a recovery of the architectural (and liturgical) principle that form follows function, that the liturgy should determine the building rather than being determined by the building. Many of the older churches which had been Gothicized during the late nineteenth or early twentieth century have been restored to something approximating their former, more functional, liturgical arrangements. There was a fad in the 1950s of building churches "in the round," but these were found not to function well for purposes other than the Liturgy of the Table. Ideally the congregation must be able to see and hear easily what goes on at each of three liturgical centers: the font, which must speak by means of its size, dignity, and placement, of the centrality of baptism in the life of the Christian; the pulpit (lectern, ambo), which symbolizes the

Word read and proclaimed and its importance in the life of the church; and the Table, where the life of the family is continually nourished. No center should be so designed or placed that it is difficult for the congregation to focus its attention there at the appropriate times, or so that it overpowers or diverts attention at a time when it is not serving as the functional liturgical center. The choir and organ should be placed so that they give maximal leadership and support to the participation in the liturgy of the congregation. Flexibility is desirable within the space occupied by the congregation, because of the various functions and the varying sizes of groups which this space serves, and sufficient space must be provided for processionals and for efficient movement to and from the liturgical centers.[21]

There is a general return to the significatory and the practical in terms of appurtenances, and away from the fussy and the overly elaborate which diverts attention away from the liturgy itself or from the liturgical centers. There is a growing realization that the offerings of local resources and artists are often more liturgically appropriate than what can be procured from a commercial church supply house.[22]

The Dedication and Consecration of a Church—The rite for the consecration of churches of the older American Prayer Books was limited to situations in which the premises were owned by the church and the building free of debt. This had in some cases discouraged the use of any ceremonies in connection with the opening of a church or chapel, and in other instances it led to curious duplications of ceremonies. The rite of the 1979 Book of Common Prayer may be used to dedicate and consecrate a church or chapel at any time after the building is ready for regular use as a place of worship. The rite does not imply that the building will not also be used for educational or social purposes or for other suitable activities. The clergy and people enter the building after the opening of the doors. After the Prayer for the Consecration of the Church, the font is dedicated and water poured into it for a Blessing of

Water (and baptism). After the dedication of lectern and/or pulpit comes the Ministry of the Word. Prior to the Peace, the Altar is set apart and prepared for the Liturgy of the Table. The service may be adapted for special circumstances, and relevant portions of it may be used for the blessing of alterations, additions, or new furnishings, or for the dedication of a private or institutional chapel or oratory.[23]

FOR FURTHER REFERENCE

CHAPTER I.

[1]*The Roots of Ritual*, ed. by J. D. Shaughnessy (Grand Rapids: William B. Eerdmans Publishing Company, 1973).

[2]L. Bouyer, *Liturgical Piety* (Notre Dame: University of Notre Dame Press, 1955), pp. 272-81. See also J. A. Jungmann, *Pastoral Liturgy* (New York: Herder and Herder, 1962).

[3]A. van Gennep, *The Rites of Passage* (Chicago: University of Chicago Press, 1961).

[4]E. Norbeck, *Religion in Primitive Society* (New York: Harper & Row, 1961), pp. 138ff.

[5]M. Eliade, *The Sacred and the Profane: The Nature of Religion* (New York: Harper & Row [Harper Torchbooks], 1961). See also his *Patterns in Comparative Religion* (Cleveland: World Publishing Company [Meridian Books], 1963).

[6]V. W. Turner, *The Ritual Process: Structure and Anti-Structure* (Chicago: Aldine Publishing Company, 1969). See also his *The Forest of Sym-*

bols: *Aspects of Ndembu Ritual* (Ithaca: Cornell University Press [Cornell Paperbacks], 1970); *Dramas, Fields, and Metaphors: Symbolic Action in Human Society* (Ithaca and London: Cornell University Press, 1974); *The Drums of Affliction: A Study of Religious Processes Among the Ndembu of Zambia* (Oxford: Clarendon Press, 1968); *Revelation and Divination in Ndembu Ritual* (Ithaca and London: Cornell University Press, 1975).

[7]Turner, *The Forest of Symbols*, pp. 131-50.

[8]*Ibid.*, pp. 50ff.

[9]R. Otto, *The Idea of the Holy*, 2d ed., (London: Oxford University Press, 1950), pp. 210-14.

[10]J.-J. von Allmen, *Worship: Its Theology and Practice* (New York: Oxford University Press, 1965), pp. 86-95.

[11]M. Eliade, *Rites and Symbols of Initiation: The Mysteries of Birth and Rebirth* (New York: Harper & Row [Harper Torchbooks], 1965); Turner, *The Forest of Symbols*, pp. 151-279.

[12]G. E. Howard, *A History of Matrimonial Institutions Chiefly in England and the United States with an Introductory Analysis of the Literature and the Theories of Primitive Marriage and the Family*, 3 vols., reprint, (New York: Humanities Press, 1964).

[13]Norbeck, *op. cit.*, pp. 101-24.

[14]A. Kiev, ed., *Magic, Faith, and Healing: Studies in Primitive Psychiatry Today* (New York: The Free Press of Glencoe, 1964); C. Hudson, " 'Sociosomatic' Illness," (paper presented at the seventh annual meeting of the Southern Anthropological Society, February 24, 1972, Columbia, Missouri).

[15]J. Goody, *Death, Property and the Ancestors: A Study of the Mortuary Customs of the Lodagaa of West Africa* (Stanford: Stanford University Press, 1962).

[16]J. Pieper, *In Tune with the World: A Theory of Festivity* (Chicago: Franciscan Herald Press, 1965).

[17]Eliade, *The Sacred and the Profane*, pp. 20-65; G. van der Leeuw, *Religion in Essence and Manifestation*, 2 Vols., (New York: Harper & Row [Harper Torchbooks], 1963), pp. 393-402.

[18]E. B. Koenker, *Secular Salvations: The Rites and Symbols of Political Religions* (Philadelphia: Fortress Press, 1965); R. N. Bellah, "Civil Religion in America," *Religion in America*, ed. by W. G. McLoughlin and R. N. Bellah (Boston: Beacon Press, 1968), pp. 3-23.

[19]J. F. White, *New Forms of Worship* (Nashville: Abingdon Press, 1971), pp. 15-79. See also P. W. Hoon, *The Integrity of Worship: Ecumenical and Pastoral Studies in Liturgical Theology* (Nashville: Abingdon Press, 1971).

[20]A. Schmemann, *Introduction to Liturgical Theology* (London: Faith Press, 1966).

²¹F. W. Dillistone, *Christianity and Symbolism* (London: Collins, 1955); P. Tillich, *The Protestant Era* (Chicago: University of Chicago Press, 1948), pp. 94-112; P. Tillich, "The Religious Symbol," *Symbolism in Religion and Literature*, ed. by Rollo May (New York: George Braziller, 1960), pp. 75-97. See also G. Cope, *Symbolism in the Bible and the Church* (London: S. C. M. Press, 1959); J. E. Cirlot, *A Dictionary of Symbols* (New York: Philosophical Library, 1962).

²²K. Jaspers, *Truth and Symbol* (New York: Twayne Publishers, 1959), pp. 49ff.

²³W. H. Frere, *The Principles of Religious Ceremonial* (London: Longmans, Green, and Co., 1912).

CHAPTER II

¹Schmemann, *op. cit.;* J. Dupont, "Jesus and Liturgical Prayer," *Worship* XLII (April, 1969), 198-213.

²C. F. D. Moule, *Worship in the New Testament* (Richmond: John Knox Press, 1961); G. Delling, *Worship in the New Testament* (Philadelphia: Westminster Press, 1962); F. Hahn, *The Worship of the Early Church* (Philadelphia: Fortress Press, 1973).

³H.-J. Kraus, *Worship in Israel: A Cultic History of the Old Testament* (Richmond: John Knox Press, 1966); H. H. Rowley, *Worship in Ancient Israel: Its Forms and Meaning* (Philadelphia: Fortress Press, 1967); R. de Vaux, *Ancient Israel* (New York: McGraw-Hill Book Company, 1965); A. E. Millgram, *Jewish Worship* (Philadelphia: Jewish Publication Society of America, 1971); L. Finkelstein, *Pharisaism in the Making: Selected Essays* (New York: Ktav Publishing House, Inc., 1972).

⁴A. Guilding, *The Fourth Gospel and Jewish Worship: A Study of the Relation of St. John's Gospel to the Ancient Jewish Lectionary System* (Oxford: Clarendon Press, 1960); J. C. Kirby, *Ephesians, Baptism and Pentecost: An Inquiry into the Structure and Purpose of the Epistle to the Ephesians* (London: S. P. C. K., 1968); F. L. Cross, *I Peter: A Paschal Liturgy* (London: A. R. Mowbray, 1954); M. H. Shepherd, Jr., *The Paschal Liturgy and the Apocalypse* (Richmond: John Knox Press, 1960); J. van Goudoever, *Biblical Calendars* (Leiden: E. J. Brill, 1959).

⁵Check in scholarly journals reviews of the books listed in the preceding note.

⁶F. Gavin, *The Jewish Antecedents of the Christian Sacraments* (London: S. P. C. K., 1928), pp. 26-58.

⁷G. R. Beasley-Murray, *Baptism in the New Testament* (London: Macmillan, 1962); W. F. Flemington, *The New Testament Doctrine of Baptism* (London: S. P. C. K., 1957); O. Cullmann, *Baptism in the New Testament* (Chicago: Henry Regnery Company, 1950); R. Schnackenburg, *Baptism in the Thought of St. Paul: A Study in Pauline Theology* (Oxford: Basil Black-

well, 1964); G. W. H. Lampe, *The Seal of the Spirit*, rev. ed., (London: S. P. C. K., 1967).

[8]E. Ferguson, "Laying on of Hands: Its Significance in Ordination," *The Journal of Theological Studies* [New Series] XXVI Part 1 (April, 1975), 1-12.

[9]*Ibid.;* D. N. Power, *Ministers of Christ and His Church: the Theology of Priesthood* (London: Geoffrey Chapman, 1969), pp. 13-29; B. Gerhardsson, *Memory and Manuscript: Oral Tradition and Written Transmission in Rabbinic Judaism and Early Christianity* (Uppsala, 1961); E. Schweizer, *Church Order in the New Testament* (London: S. C. M. Press, 1961).

[10]I. Levy, *The Synagogue: Its History and Function* (London: Valentine, Mitchell & Co., 1963).

[11]C. W. Dugmore, *The Influence of the Synagogue upon the Divine Office* (London: Faith Press, 1964).

[12]A. Jaubert, *The Date of the Last Supper* (Staten Island: Alba House, 1965); T. Maertens, *A Feast in Honor of Yahweh* (Notre Dame: Fides Publishers, Inc., 1965).

[13]D. Hedegard, *Sedar R. Amran Gaon: Part I. Hebrew Text with Critical Apparatus, Translation with Notes and Introduction* (Lund, 1951).

[14]H. B. Porter, Jr., *The Day of Light: The Biblical and Liturgical Meaning of Sunday* (Greenwich: Seabury Press, 1960); W. Rordorf, *Sunday: The History of the Day of Rest and Worship in the Earliest Centuries of the Christian Church* (Philadelphia: Westminster Press, 1968).

[15]Gavin, *op. cit.*, pp. 59-97.

[16]E. Schweizer, *The Lord's Supper according to the New Testament* (Philadelphia: Fortress Press, 1967); K. G. Kuhn, "The Lord's Supper and the Communal Meal at Qumran," *The Scrolls and the New Testament*, ed. by K. Stendahl (New York: Harper & Brothers, 1957); H. Lietzmann, *Mass and Lord's Supper: A Study in the History of the Liturgy* (Leiden: E. J. Brill [in process of publication in fascicles]); E. J. Kilmartin, *The Eucharist in the Primitive Church* (Englewood Cliffs: Prentice-Hall, Inc., 1965).

[17]E. L. Mascall, *Corpus Christi: Essays on the Church and the Eucharist* (London: Longmans, 1953), pp. 49-55.

[18]J. B. Segal, *The Hebrew Passover from the Earliest Times to A.D. 70* (London: Oxford University Press, 1963).

[19]J. A. Lamb, *The Psalms in Christian Worship* (London: Faith Press, 1962), pp. 1-22; E. Werner, *The Sacred Bridge: The Interdependence of Liturgy and Music in Synagogue and Church during the First Millennium* (London: Dennis Dobson; New York: Columbia University Press, 1959); M. Patrick, *The Story of the Church's Song*, rev. for American use, (Richmond: John Knox Press, 1962), pp. 11-23.

[20]R. Patai, *Man and Temple: In Ancient Jewish Myth and Ritual*, 2d ed. (New York: Ktav Publishing House, 1967).

CHAPTER III

[1]C. C. Richardson, ed., *Early Christian Fathers* (New York: Macmillan Company, 1970), pp. 157-79.

[2]B. Botte, *Hippolyte de Rome: La tradition apostolique* (Paris: Les Éditions du Cerf, 1968); B. S. Easton, *The Apostolic Tradition of Hippolytus*, reprint, (Archon Books, 1962); G. Dix, *The Treatise on the Apostolic Tradition by St. Hippolytus of Rome*, reissued with corrections by H. Chadwick, (London: S. P. C. K., 1968).

[3]R. H. Connolly, *Didascalia Apostolorum* (Oxford: Clarendon Press, 1929).

[4]F. X. Funk, *Didascalia et constitutiones apostolorum* (Padeborn: Schöningh, 1905-06); A. Roberts and J. Donaldson, ed., *The Ante-Nicene Fathers*, American ed., (Grand Rapids: Wm. B. Eerdmans Publishing Company), VII, 385-508.

[5]K. Lake, *The Apostolic Fathers with an English Translation*, 2 vols., (Cambridge, Massachusetts: Harvard University Press, 1912).

[6]E. Hennecke and W. Schneemelcher, *New Testament Apocrypha*, 2 vols., (Philadelphia: Westminster Press, c. 1965); A. F. J. Klijn, *The Acts of Thomas* (Leiden: E. J. Brill, 1962).

[7]Richardson, *op. cit.*, pp. 225-89.

[8]Roberts and Donaldson, *op. cit.*

[9]F. Cumont, *The Mysteries of Mithra* (New York: Dover Publications, 1956), pp. 150-74.

[10]E. C. Whitaker, *Documents of the Baptismal Liturgy*, 2d ed. (London: S. P. C. K., 1970), Chapter I; L. L. Mitchell, *Baptismal Anointing* (London: S. P. C. K., 1966), pp. 1-50; Lampe, *op. cit.*; S. Brock, "Studies in the Early History of the Syrian Orthodox Baptismal Liturgy," *The Journal of Theological Studies*, New Series, XXIII (April, 1972), 16-64; *Studies on Syrian Baptismal Rites*, Vol. VI of *The Syrian Churches Series*, ed. by J. Vellian (Kottayam: C. M. S. Press, 1973).

[11]Whitaker, *op. cit.*, Introductory Essay.

[12]J. Gunstone, *The Liturgy of Penance* (London: Faith Press, 1966), pp. 26-40; W. Telfer, *The Forgiveness of Sins* (London: S. C. M. Press, 1959), pp. 7-74; B. Poschmann, *Penance and the Anointing of the Sick* (New York: Herder and Herder, 1964), pp. 1-80; C. Vogel, "Sin and Penance: A Survey of the Historical Evolution of the Penitential Discipline in the Latin Church," *Pastoral Treatment of Sin*, ed. by P. Delhaye (New York: Desclée Co., 1968).

[13]K. Ritzer, *Le mariage dans les Eglises chrétiennes du Ier au XIe siècle*, Lex orandi 45 (Paris: Les Éditions du Cerf, 1970).

[14]H. B. Porter, Jr., *The Ordination Prayers of the Ancient Western Churches* (London: S. P. C. K., 1967) with permission; Power, *op. cit.*, pp.

30-52. (The translations of the ordination prayers from the *Apostolic Tradition* of Hippolytus are by H. Boone Porter, Jr.)

[15]F. W. Puller, *The Anointing of the Sick in Scripture and Tradition* (London: S. P. C. K., 1910).

[16]A. C. Rush, *Death and Burial in Christian Antiquity* (Washington: Catholic University of America Press, 1941).

[17]Dugmore, *op. cit.*

[18]Shepherd, *op. cit.*, pp. 70-74.

[19]Porter, *The Day of Light;* Rordorf, *op. cit.*

[20]Lietzmann, *op. cit.;* J. Quasten, *Monumenta eucharistica et liturgica vetustissima Collegit notis et prolegomenis instruxit* (Bonnae: Sumptibus Petri Hanstein, 1935); G. W. H. Lampe, "The Eucharist in the Thought of the Early Church," *Eucharistic Theology Then and Now*, Theological Collections 9 (London: S. P. C. K., 1968), pp. 34-58; J. H. Srawley, *The Early History of the Liturgy*, 2d ed., (Cambridge University Press, 1947); M. J. Hatchett, "Seven Pre-Reformation Eucharistic Liturgies: Historic Rites Arranged for Contemporary Celebration," *St. Luke's Journal of Theology*, XVI (June, 1973), 13-23.

[21]Didache 9-10, 14; Acts of John 85, 109; Apostolic Tradition 4; Acts of Thomas 49-50, 133, 158; Addai and Mari; Serapion; Apostolic Constitutions VIII, 12.

[22]A. A. McArthur, *The Evolution of the Christian Year* (New York: Seabury Press, 1955).

[23]E. Wellesz, *A History of Byzantine Music and Hymnography*, 2d ed., rev., (Oxford: Clarendon Press, 1961); Werner, *op. cit.;* Lamb, *op. cit.*, pp. 24-45.

[24]J. G. Davies, *The Origin and Development of Early Christian Church Architecture* (London: S. C. M. Press, 1952); R. Krautheimer, *Early Christian and Byzantine Architecture* (Harmondsworth, Middlesex: Penguin Books, 1965); J. G. Davies, *The Architectural Setting of Baptism* (London: Barrie and Rockliff, 1962).

[25]W. Lowrie, *Art in the Early Church* (New York: Pantheon Books, 1947); F. van der Meer and C. Mohrmann, *Atlas of the Early Christian World* (London: Nelson, 1966), pp. 33-57; A. Grabar, *Le Premier Art Chrétien (200-395)* (Gallimard, 1966).

CHAPTER IV

[1]Schmemann, *op. cit.;* M. H. Shepherd, Jr., "Liturgical Expressions of the Constantinian Triumph," *Dunbarton Oaks Papers*, XVI (Washington: Dunbarton Oaks Center for Byzantine Studies, 1967), pp. 57-78; J. G. Davies, "The Introduction of the Numinous into the Liturgy: An Historical Note," *Studia Liturgica*, VIII (1971/1972), 216-23.

[2]A. Schmemann, *Sacraments and Orthodoxy* (New York: Herder and Herder, 1965); S. Salaville, *An Introduction to the Study of Eastern Liturgies* (London: Sands & Co., 1938); J. Goar, *Euchologion*, 2d ed. (Venice, 1730); J. G. King, *The Rites and Ceremonies of the Greek Church, in Russia* (London: W. Owen, 1772).

[3]J. Wordsworth, *Bishop Sarapion's Prayer-Book: An Egyptian Sacramentary Dated Probably about A. D. 350–356*, reprint, (Hamden, Connecticut: Archon Books, 1964); F. E. Brightman, *Liturgies Eastern and Western* (Oxford: Clarendon Press, 1896), pp. lxiii-lxxii, 111-88; R. M. Woolley, *Coptic Offices* (London: S. P. C. K., 1930).

[4]G. Gerster, *Churches in Rock: Early Christian Art in Ethiopia* (New York: Phaidon, 1970); Brightman, *op. cit.*, pp. lxxii-lxxvi, 189-244; S. A. B. Mercer, *The Ethiopic Liturgy* (Milwaukee: Young Churchman Co.; London: A. R. Mowbray, 1915); J. M. Harden, *The Anaphoras of the Ethiopic Liturgy* (London, 1928); E. Hammerschmidt, *Studies in the Ethiopic Anaphoras* (Berlin: Akademie-Verlag, 1961).

[5]Brightman, *op. cit.*, pp. lxxvii-lxxxi, 245-305.

[6]F. L. Cross, *St. Cyril of Jerusalem's Lectures on the Christian Sacraments* (London: S. P. C. K., 1960); J. Wilkinson, *Egeria's Travels* (London: S. P. C. K., 1971); A. Renoux, *Le Codex Arménien Jérusalem 121*, Patrologia Orientalis, XXXV-1, No. 163 (1969), XXXVI-2, No. 168 (1971); R. H. Miller, *Enlightenment through the Bath of Rebirth: The Experience of Christian Initiation in Late Fourth Century Jerusalem* (unpublished Ph.D. dissertation, Fordham University, 1972); Brightman, *op. cit.*, pp. xlviii-lv, 31-68; M. H. Shepherd, Jr., "The Formation and Influence of the Antiochene Liturgy," *Dunbarton Oaks Papers* XV (Washington: Dunbarton Oaks Research Library and Collection, 1961), pp. 25-44.

[7]P. W. Harkins, *St. John Chrysostom: Baptismal Instructions* (Westminster, Maryland: Newman Press, 1963); Brightman, *op. cit.*, pp. xvii-lxiii, lxxxi-ci, 1-110, 307-457; J. F. Mathews, *The Early Churches of Constantinople: Architecture and Liturgy* (University Park and London: The Pennsylvania State University Press, 1971).

[8]H. G. J. Beck, *The Pastoral Care of Souls in South-East France during the Sixth Century* (Rome: Analecta Gregoriana, 1950); H. B. Porter, Jr., *The Liturgical Reforms of Charlemagne* (unpublished D. Phil. dissertation, Oxford, 1954); A. A. King, *Liturgies of the Past* (Milwaukee: Bruce Publishing Co., 1959), pp. 77-185.

[9]For references, see K. Gamber, *Codices Liturgici Latini Antiquiores* (Universitätsverlag Freiburg Schweiz, 1968), pp. 56-66, 153-93.

[10]W. C. Bishop, *The Mozarabic and Ambrosian Rites: Four Essays in Comparative Liturgiology* (London: A. R. Mowbray, 1924); A. A. King, *Liturgies of the Primatial Sees* (London: Longmans, Green and Co., 1957), pp. 457-631.

[11]Gamber, *op. cit.*, pp. 67-72, 194-225.

[12]F. E. Warren, *Liturgy and Ritual of the Celtic Church* (Oxford: Clarendon Press, 1881); King, *Liturgies of the Past*, pp. 186-275.

[13]Gamber, *op. cit.*, pp. 130-52.

[14]Bishop, *op. cit.;* King, *Liturgies of the Primatial Sees*, pp. 286-456.

[15]Gamber, *op. cit.*, pp. 259-86.

[16]E. Bishop, "The Genius of the Roman Rite," *Liturgica Historica: Papers on the Liturgy and Religious Life of the Western Church* (Oxford: Clarendon Press, 1918), pp. 1-19.

[17]F. van der Meer, *Augustine the Bishop* (London and New York: Sheed and Ward, 1961); G. G. Willis, *St. Augustine's Lectionary* (London: S. P. C. K., 1962); Gamber, *op. cit.*, pp. 29-55.

[18]J. A. Jungmann, *The Early Liturgy to the Time of Gregory the Great* (Notre Dame: University of Notre Dame Press, 1959); A. A. King, *Liturgy of the Roman Church* (London: Longmans, Green and Co., 1957); L. Eisenhofer and J. Lechner, *The Liturgy of the Roman Rite* (New York: Herder and Herder, 1961); A. G. Martimort, ed., *L'Église en Prière* (Paris: Desclée & Cie, 1961); G. G. Willis, *Essays in Early Roman Liturgy* (London: S. P. C. K., 1964); G. G. Willis, *Further Essays in Early Roman Liturgy* (London: S. P. C. K., 1968; T. Klauser, *A Short History of the Western Liturgy: An Account and Some Reflections* (London: Oxford University Press, 1969), pp. 45-93.

[19]Willis, *Further Essays in Early Roman Liturgy*, pp. 189-243.

[20]Gamber, *op. cit.;* D. M. Hope, *The Leonine Sacramentary: A Reassessment of Its Nature and Purpose* (Oxford: Oxford University Press, 1971); A. Chavasse, *Le sacramentaire gélasien* (Tournai: Desclée, 1958); J. Deshusses, *Le Sacramentaire grégorien* (Fribourg: Édit. Universitaires, 1971).

[21]E. Yarnold, *The Awe-Inspiring Rites of Initiation: Baptismal Homilies of the Fourth Century* (St. Paul Publications, 1972); *Studies on Syrian Baptismal Rites.*

[22]J. D. C. Fisher, *Christian Initiation: Baptism in the Medieval West* (London: S. P. C. K., 1965); Whitaker, *op. cit.;* Miller, *op. cit.;* Mitchell, *op. cit.*, pp. 51-175; T. C. Akeley, *Christian Initiation in Spain c. 300-1100* (London: Darton, Longman and Todd, 1967); T. M. Finn, *The Liturgy of Baptism in the Baptismal Instructions of St. John Chrysostom* (Washington: Catholic University of America Press, 1967); Brock, *op. cit.*

[23]J. T. McNeill, *A History of the Cure of Souls* (New York: Harper & Row [Harper Torchbooks], 1965), pp. 88-111; Telfer, *op. cit.*, pp. 75-94; Poschmann, *op. cit.*, pp. 81-121.

[24]Gunstone, *op. cit.*, pp. 26-40; H. B. Porter, Jr., "The Ash Wednesday Rites," *Holy Cross Magazine*, LXV (February, 1954), 35-37.

[25]McNeill, *op. cit.*, pp. 112-35; Gunstone, *op. cit.*, pp. 41-48; Telfer, *op. cit.*, pp. 95-106; Poschmann, *op. cit.*, pp. 122-54; R. C. Mortimer, *The Origins of Private Penance in the Western Church* (Oxford: Clarendon Press, 1939); J.T. McNeill and H. M. Gamer, *Medieval Handbooks of Penance* (New York: Columbia University Press, 1938).

[26]Ritzer, *op. cit.*

[27]Whitaker, *op. cit.*, pp. 73-74.

[28]Porter, *The Ordination Prayers of the Ancient Western Churches*, pp. 12-77; Power, *op. cit.*, pp. 53-88.

[29]C. E. Pocknee, *Liturgical Vesture: Its Origins and Development* (Westminster, Maryland: Canterbury Press, 1961); B. M. Ramsey, *The Chasuble: Its History and Development to the Present Day* (unpublished M. S. thesis, University of Tennessee, 1972), pp. 5-26.

[30]E. G. C. F. Atchley, *A History of the Use of Incense in Divine Worship* (London: Longmans, Green and Co., 1909); D. R. Dendy, *The Use of Lights in Christian Worship* (London: S. P. C. K., 1959); C. E. Pocknee, *Cross and Crucifix in Christian Worship and Devotion* (London: A. R. Mowbray, 1962).

[31]H. B. Porter, Jr., "The Origins of the Medieval Rite for Anointing," *Journal of Theological Studies*, New Series, VII (October, 1956), 211-25; Puller, *op. cit.*

[32]Rush, *op. cit.*

[33]Jungmann, *Pastoral Liturgy*, pp. 105-214; J. Mateos, "The Origin of the Divine Office," *Worship*, XLI (October, 1967), 477-85; J.Mateos, "The Morning and Evening Office," *Worship*, XLII (January, 1968), 31-47; W. J. Grisbrooke, "A Contemporary Liturgical Problem: The Divine Office and Public Worship," *Studia Liturgica*, VIII (1971/1972), 129-68, IX (1973), 3-18, 81-106.

[34]Lamb, *op. cit.*, pp. 54-60, 99-104.

[35]J. Doresse and E. Lanne, *Un témoin archaïque de la liturgie copte de saint Basile*, Bibliothèque du Muséon 47 (Louvain, 1960); A. Hänggi and I. Pahl, Prex eucharistica, Textus e variis liturgiis antiquioribus selecti (Fribourg: Éditions Universitaires, 1968), pp. 230-43, 347-57.

[36] R. F. Taft, *The Great Entrance: A History of the Transfer of Gifts and Other Pre-anaphoral Rites of the Liturgy of St. John Chrysostom*, Orientalia Christiana Analecta 200 (Rome: Pontifical Oriental Institute, 1975); J. Mateos, *La Célébration de la Parole dans la Liturgie Byzantine: Étude historique*, Orientalia Christiana Analecta 191 (Rome: Pontifical Oriental Institute, 1971); J. Mateos, "The Evolution of the Byzantine Liturgy," *John XXIII Lectures Vol. I: 1965 Byzantine Christian Heritage* (New York: John XXIII Center for Eastern Christian Studies, Fordham University, 1966), pp. 76-112; R. Taft, "Some Notes on the Bema in the East and West Syrian Traditions," *Orientalia Christiana Periodica*, XXXIV (1968), 326-59; R. Taft, "On the Use of the Bema in the East-Syrian Liturgy," *Eastern Churches Review*, III (Spring, 1970), 30-39; R. Taft, "Towards the Origins of the Offertory Procession in the Syro-Byzantine East," *Orientalia Christiana Periodica*, XXXVI (1970), 73-107; R. Taft, "Evolution historique de la liturgie de saint Jean Chrysostome," *Proche-Orient chrétien*, XXII (1972), 241-87; XXIV (1974, 3-33; Mathews, *op. cit.;* Srawley, *op. cit.*, pp. 41-119, 187-234; Hatchett, "Seven Pre-Reformation Eucharistic Liturgies," pp.

24-42; J. Doresse and E. Lanne, *op. cit.*; M. M. Solovey, *The Byzantine Divine Liturgy: History and Commentary* (Washington: Catholic University of America Press, 1970); C. Kucharek, *The Byzantine-Slav Liturgy of St. John Chrysostom: Its Origin and Evolution* (Allendale, New Jersey: Alleluia Press, 1971).

[37]W. C. Bishop, *op. cit.*; W. S. Porter, *The Gallican Rite* (London: A. R. Mowbray, 1958); F. Cabrol, *The Mass of the Western Rites* (St. Louis: B. Herder Book Co., 1934); Srawley, *op. cit.*, pp. 120-234; Hatchett, "Seven Pre-Reformation Eucharistic Liturgies," pp. 52-61.

[38] *Ibid.*, pp. 43-51; J. A. Jungmann, *The Mass of the Roman Rite: Its Origins and Development*, 2 vols., (New York: Benziger Brothers, 1950).

[39] E. G. C. F. Atchley, *Ordo Romanus Primus* (London: De La More Press, 1905).

[40]J. Gunstone, *Christmas and Epiphany* (London: Faith Press, 1967).

[41]Jungmann, *The Early Liturgy*, pp. 175-87; N. M. Denis-Boulet, *The Christian Calendar* (New York: Hawthorn Books, 1960), pp. 51-69.

[42]J. G. Davies, *Holy Week: A Short History* (Richmond: John Knox Press, 1963).

[43]J. Gunstone, *The Feast of Pentecost: The Great Fifty Days in the Liturgy* (London: Faith Press, 1967).

[44]J. A. Jungmann, *Public Worship* (Collegeville: Liturgical Press), pp. 219-29; T. J. Talley, *The Development of the Ember Days to the Time of Gregory VII* (unpublished Th.D. dissertation, General Theological Seminary, 1969).

[45]Patrick, *op. cit.*, pp. 31-51; W. Apel, *Gregorian Chant* (Bloomington: Indiana University Press, 1958); Lamb, *op. cit.*, pp. 46ff.

[46]Davies, *The Origin and Development of Early Christian Church Architecture;* Krautheimer, *op. cit.;* van der Meer and Mohrmann, *op. cit.*, pp. 58-215; R. Krautheimer, "The Constantinian Basilica," *Dunbarton Oak Papers*, XXI, 115-40; A. Grabar, *L'âge d'or de Justinien* (Gallimard, 1966).

[47]A. Grabar, *Martyrium: Recherches sur le culte des reliques et l'art chrétien antique*, 2 vols., (London: Variorum Reprints, 1972).

[48]Davies, *The Architectural Setting of Baptism*, pp. 1-42.

[49]Willis, *Further Essays in Early Roman Liturgy*, pp. 133-73.

CHAPTER V

[1]Klauser, *op. cit.*, pp. 94-116; S. J. P. van Dijk and J. H. Walker, *The Origins of the Modern Roman Liturgy: The Liturgy of the Papal Court and the Franciscan Order in the Thirteenth Century* (London: Darton, Longman & Todd, 1960).

[2]Deshusses, *op. cit.*

[3]A. A. King, *Liturgies of the Religious Orders* (London: Longmans, Green and Co., 1955); R. W. Pfaff, *New Liturgical Feasts in Later Medieval England* (Oxford: Clarendon Press, 1970), pp. xvii-xviii, 1-12.

[4]Pfaff, *op. cit.*, pp. xvii-xviii, 1-12; King, *Liturgies of the Past,* pp. 276-374.

[5]Peter Lombard, *Sentences*, Book IV; Hugh of St. Victor, *De sacramentis;* Thomas Aquinas, *Summa Theologica*, Part III, Questions 60-90 and Supplement.

[6]Fisher, *op. cit.*

[7]See any Book of Common Prayer from 1552, the text used in connection with the signation after the application of water.

[8]M. J. Hatchett, "The Rite of 'Confirmation' in the Book of Common Prayer and in *Authorized Services 1973*," *Anglican Theological Review*, LVI (July, 1974), 292-310.

[9]Porter, "The Ash Wednesday Rites."

[10]Gunstone, *The Liturgy of Penance*, pp. 49-66; Telfer, *op. cit.*, pp. 95-106; McNeill, *op. cit.*, pp. 132-62; Poschmann, *op. cit.*, pp. 154-93.

[11]J.-B. Molina and P. Mutembe, *Le Rituel du Mariage en France du XIIe au XVIe siècle* (Paris: Beauchesne, 1974).

[12]W. B. Fitch, "The Churching of Women," unpublished paper delivered in a seminar, School of Theology, University of the South, February 10, 1971.

[13]Porter, *The Ordination Prayers of the Ancient Western Churches*, pp. 78-93; P. F. Bradshaw, *The Anglican Ordinal: Its History and Development from the Reformation to the Present Day* (London: S. P. C. K., 1971), pp. 1-7; M. J. Hatchett, "Initiation: Baptism or Ordination?," *The St. Luke's Journal of Theology*, XII (September, 1969), 17-22; Power, *op. cit.*, pp. 89-126; J. Bligh, *Ordination to the Priesthood* (London: Sheed and Ward, 1956).

[14]Pocknee, *op. cit.;* Ramsey, *op. cit.*, pp. 27-54.

[15]Porter, "The Origins of the Medieval Rite for Anointing"; W. K. L. Clarke, ed., *Liturgy and Worship* (London: S. P. C. K., 1932), pp. 487-505.

[16]Clarke, *op. cit.*, pp. 616-22.

[17]P. Salmon, *The Breviary through the Centuries* (Collegeville: The Liturgical Press, 1962); van Dijk and Walker, *op. cit.;* E. Bishop, *op. cit.*, pp. 211-37; G. J. Cuming, *A History of Anglican Liturgy* (London: Macmillan, 1969), pp. 292-317 (the Sarum Office of the First Sunday in Advent); E. Hoskins, *Horae Beatae Mariae Virginis or Sarum and York Primers with Kindred Books and Primers of the Reformed Roman Use together with an Introduction* (London: Longmans, Green, and Co., 1901).

[18]N. Cabasilas, *A Commentary on the Divine Liturgy* (London: S. P. C. K., 1960); R. F. Taft, *The Great Entrance;* J. Mateos, *La Célébration de la*

192) SANCTIFYING LIFE, TIME AND SPACE

Parole dans la Liturgie Byzantine; J. Mateos, "The Evolution of the Byzantine Liturgy"; R. Taft, "Evolution historique de la liturgie de saint Jean Chrysostome"; Solovey, *op. cit.;* Kucharek, *op. cit.*

[19]Jungmann, *The Mass of the Roman Rite;* J. D. Crichton, "An Historical Sketch of the Roman Liturgy," *True Worship,* ed. by L. Sheppard (Baltimore: Helicon Press, 1963), pp. 45-72; Cuming, *op. cit.,* pp. 269-91 (the Sarum Mass of the First Sunday in Advent); Hatchett, "Seven Pre-Reformation Eucharistic Liturgies," pp. 62-115.

[20]Jungmann, *Pastoral Liturgy,* pp. 251-77.

[21]Pfaff, *op. cit.*

[22]Patrick, *op. cit.,* pp. 52-69; Apel, *op. cit.;* G. Reese, *Music in the Middle Ages with an Introduction on the Music of Ancient Times* (New York: W. W. Norton & Company, 1940).

[23]G. H. Cook, *The English Mediaeval Parish Church* (London: Phoenix House, 1954); J. G. Davies, *The Secular Use of Church Buildings* (New York: Seabury Press, 1968), pp. 36-95; Davies, *The Architectural Setting of Baptism,* pp. 43-90; B. Clarke and J. Betjeman, *English Churches* (London: Vista Books, 1964), pp. 7-30.

[24]A. G. Martimort, *The Church at Prayer: Introduction to the Liturgy* (New York: Desclée Company, c. 1968), pp. 174-78.

[25]Turner, *The Forest of Symbols,* pp. 59-92; Ramsey, *op. cit.,* pp. 36-39; G. Cope, "Liturgical Colors," *Studia Liturgica,* VII (1970), 40-49.

CHAPTER VI

[1]Cuming, *op. cit.,* pp. 32-48, 318-57; B. Thompson, *Liturgies of the Western Church* (Cleveland: World Publishing Company, 1962); N. Micklem, *Christian Worship* (London: Oxford University Press, 1936); P. Edwall, E. Hayman, and W. D. Maxwell, ed., *Ways of Worship: The Report of a Theological Commission of Faith and Order* (New York: Harper & Brothers, 1951).

[2]H. T. Lehmann, *Luther's Works,* Vol. LIII, U.S. Leupold, ed. (Philadelphia: Fortress Press, 1965); L. D. Reed, *The Lutheran Liturgy,* rev. ed., (Philadelphia: Muhlenberg Press, 1959); V. Vajta, *Luther on Worship* (Philadelphia: Fortress Press, 1958); D. S. Armentrout and J. E. Lenhardt II, "Martin Luther's Theology of Worship and a Reconstruction of His 1523 'Order of Mass and Communion'," *St. Luke's Journal of Theology,* XVI (March, 1973), 65-85.

[3]G. J. van de Poll, *Martin Bucer's Liturgical Ideas* (Assen: van Gorcum, 1954).

[4]J. H. Nichols, *Corporate Worship in the Reformed Tradition* (Philadelphia: Westminster Press, 1968); J. M. Barkley, *The Worship of the Reformed Church: An Exposition and Critical Analysis of the Eucharistic,*

Baptismal, and Confirmation Rites in the Scottish, English-Welsh, and Irish Liturgies (Richmond: John Knox Press, 1967); H. G. Hageman, *Pulpit and Table: Some Chapters in the History of Worship in the Reformed Churches* (Richmond: John Knox Press, 1962); R. S. Wallace, *Calvin's Doctrine of the Word and Sacrament* (Edinburgh: Oliver and Boyd, 1953); H. Davies, *Worship and Theology in England*, 5 vols., (Princeton: Princeton University Press, 1961ff.); W. D. Maxwell, *The Liturgical Portions of the Genevan Service Book* (Edinburgh: Oliver and Boyd, 1931); W. D. Maxwell, *A History of Worship in the Church of Scotland* (London: Oxford University Press, 1955).

[5]G. H. Williams, *The Radical Reformation* (Philadelphia: Westminster Press, 1962).

[6]Klauser, *op. cit.*, pp. 117-52; Bouyer, *op. cit.*

[7]I. F. Hapgood, *Service Book of the Holy Orthodox-Catholic Apostolic Church*, 4th ed., rev., (Brooklyn: Syrian Antiochian Orthodox Arch-diocese, 1965); I.-H. Dalmais, *Eastern Liturgies* (New York: Hawthorn Books, 1960).

[8]S. Mayor, *The Lord's Supper in Early English Dissent* (London: Epworth Press, 1972); Reed, *op. cit.*; N. G. Harmon, Jr., *The Rites and Ritual of Episcopal Methodism with Particular Reference to the Rituals of the Methodist Episcopal Church and the Methodist Episcopal Church, South, Respectively* (Nashville: Publishing House of the M. E. Church, South, 1926); J. Melton, *Presbyterian Worship in America: Changing Patterns Since 1787* (Richmond: John Knox Press, 1967); D. Macleod, *Presbyterian Worship: Its Meaning and Method* (Richmond: John Knox Press, 1965); K. Watkins, *The Breaking of Bread: An Approach to Worship for the Christian Churches (Disciples of Christ)* (St. Louis: Bethany Press, 1966).

[9]W. M. S. West, "The Anabaptists and the Rise of the Baptist Movement," *Christian Baptism*, ed. by A. Gilmore (London: Lutterworth Press, 1959), pp. 223-72; J. D. C. Fisher, *Christian Initiation: The Reformation Period* (London; S. P. C. K., 1970); P. J. Jagger, *Christian Initiation 1552-1969* (London: S. P. C. K., 1970); Barkley, *op. cit.*; Davies, *The Architectural Setting of Baptism*, pp. 91-161; B. G. Holland, *Baptism in Early Methodism* (London: Epworth Press, 1970).

[10]Hatchett, "The Rite of 'Confirmation' in the Book of Common Prayer and in *Authorized Services 1973*"; A. C. Repp, *Confirmation in the Lutheran Church* (St. Louis: Concordia Publishing House, 1964).

[11]M. Thurian, *Confession* (London: S. C. M. Press, 1958); Telfer, *op. cit.*, pp. 107-26; McNeill, *op. cit.*, pp. 163-217, 247-330; Poschmann, *op. cit.*, pp. 194-209.

[12]Howard, *op. cit.*

[13]Maxwell, *The Liturgical Portions of the Genevan Service Book*, pp. 58-60, 165-74; P. De Puniet, *The Roman Pontifical: A History and Commentary* (London: Longmans, Green and Co., 1932); Bligh, *op. cit.*

[14]Pocknee, *Liturgical Vesture;* Ramsey, *op. cit.*, pp. 51-52, 56-59.

[15]Poschmann, *op. cit.*, pp. 233-57.

[16]Maxwell, *The Liturgical Portions of the Genevan Service Book*, pp. 58-59, 160-64.

[17]Jungmann, *Pastoral Liturgy*, pp. 200-14; Salmon, *op. cit.*, pp. 95-121; Lamb, *op. cit.*, pp. 107-20, 137.

[18]G. B. Burnet, *The Holy Communion in the Reformed Church of Scotland 1560-1960* (Edinburgh: Oliver and Boyd, 1960).

[19]Thompson, *op. cit.;* W. D. Maxwell, *An Outline of Christian Worship* (London: Oxford University Press, 1936); Y. Brilioth, *Eucharistic Faith & Practice: Evangelical & Catholic* (London: S. P. C. K., 1930); C. W. Dugmore, "The Eucharist in the Reformation Era," *Eucharistic Theology Then and Now*, pp. 59-75.

[20]Denis-Boulet, *op. cit.*, pp. 97-107.

[21]Patrick, *op. cit.*, pp. 70-173; Lamb, *op. cit.*, pp. 133-63; E. Routley, *The Music of Christian Hymnody* (London: Independent Press, 1957); J. Riedel, *The Lutheran Chorale: Its Basic Traditions* (Minneapolis: Augsburg, 1967); E. Liemohn, *The Chorale Through Four Hundred Years of Musical Development as a Congregational Hymn* (Philadelphia: Muhlenberg Press, 1953); L. F. Benson, *The English Hymn: Its Development and Use in Worship*, reprint, (Richmond: John Knox Press, 1962); A. Hutchings, *Church Music in the Nineteenth Century* (New York: Oxford University Press, 1967); L. Ellinwood, *The History of American Church Music* (New York: Morehouse-Gorham Co., 1953); G. P. Jackson, *White Spirituals in the Southern Uplands*, reprint, (New York: Dover Publications, 1965); H. W. Foote, *Three Centuries of American Hymnody*, reprint, (Hamden, Connecticut: Shoe String Press, 1961); R. Stevenson, *Protestant Church Music in America: A Short Survey of Men and Movements from 1564 to the Present* (New York: W. W. Norton, 1966).

[22]J. F. White, *Protestant Worship and Church Architecture* (New York: Oxford University Press, 1964), pp. 78-117; G. Hay, *The Architecture of Scottish Post-Reformation Churches 1560-1843* (Oxford: Clarendon Press, 1957); Davies, *The Architectural Setting of Baptism*, pp. 91-161.

[23]Davies, *The Secular Use of Church Buildings*, pp. 96-204.

CHAPTER VII

[1]Cuming, *op. cit.*, pp. 49-167, 358-74; F. E. Brightman, *The English Rite: Being a Synopsis of the Sources and Revisions of the Book of Common Prayer with an Introduction and an Appendix*, 2 vols., (London: Rivingtons, 1915); *The First and Second Prayer Books of Edward VI* (Everyman's Library edition); E. C. Ratcliff, *The Booke of Common Prayer of the Churche of England: Its Making and Revisions M.D.xlix—M.D.clxi. Set Forth in Eighty Illustrations, with Introduction and Notes* (London: S. P. C. K., 1949); *The English Prayer Book 1549-1662* (London: S. P. C. K.,

For Further Reference (195

1963); H. Davies, *op. cit.;* Clarke, *op. cit.,* pp. 145-97; C. Wheatly, *A Rational Illustration of the Book of Common Prayer* (various editions from 1710); E. Daniel, *The Prayer Book: Its History, Language, and Contents* (London: Wells Gardner, Darton and Co., 1913); E. C. Whitaker, *Martin Bucer and the Book of Common Prayer* (Great Wakering: Mayhew-McCrimmon, 1974).

[2]W. P. Haugaard, *Elizabeth and the English Reformation* (Cambridge: University Press, 1968); E. Cardwell, *A History of Conferences and Other Proceedings Connected with the Revision of the Book of Common Prayer; from the Year 1558 to the Year 1690,* 3d ed., (Oxford: University Press, 1849); H. Davies, *The Worship of the English Puritans* (Westminster: Dacre Press, 1948).

[3]G. W. O. Addleshaw, *The High Church Tradition: A Study in the Liturgical Thought of the Seventeenth Century* (London: Faber and Faber, 1941); G. W. Sprott, *Scottish Liturgies of the Reign of James VI,* rev. ed., (Edinburgh: William Blackwood and Sons, 1901); G. Donaldson, *The Making of the Scottish Prayer Book of 1637* (Edinburgh: University Press, 1954).

[4]T. Leishman, *The Westminster Directory* (Edinburgh: William Blackwood and Sons, 1901).

[5]R. S. Bosher, *The Making of the Restoration Settlement: The Influence of the Laudians 1649-1662,* reprinted with slight revision, (Westminster: Dacre Press, 1957); G. J. Cuming, *The Durham Book: Being the First Draft of the Revision of the Book of Common Prayer in 1661 Edited with an Introduction and Notes* (London: Oxford University Press, 1961); E. C. Ratcliff, "The Savoy Conference and the Revision of the Book of Common Prayer," *From Uniformity to Unity 1662-1962,* ed. by G. F. Nuttall and O. Chadwick (London: S. P. C. K., 1962), pp. 89-148.

[6]Fisher, *Christian Initiation: The Reformation Period;* Jagger, *op. cit.;* M. J. Hatchett, *Thomas Cranmer and the Rites of Christian Initiation* (unpublished S. T. M. thesis, General Theological Seminary, 1967); G. W. Bromily, *Baptism and the Anglican Reformers* (London: Lutterworth, 1953); Hatchett, "The Rite of 'Confirmation' in the Book of Common Prayer and in *Authorized Services 1973.*"

[7]Gunstone, *The Liturgy of Penance,* pp. 67-75; Telfer, *op. cit.,* pp. 127-40; McNeill, *op. cit.,* pp. 218-46; Porter, "The Ash Wednesday Rites."

[8]Howard, *op. cit.;* Clarke, *op. cit.,* pp. 463-71.

[9]Bradshaw, *op. cit.,* pp. 1-104.

[10]Ramsey, *op. cit.,* pp. 57-59; H. Gee, *The Elizabethan Prayer-Book & Ornaments: With an Appendix of Documents* (London: Macmillan and Co., 1902); M. MacColl, *The Royal Commission and the Ornaments Rubric* (London: Longmans, Green, and Co., 1906).

[11]C. W. Gusmer, *The Ministry of Healing in the Church of England: An Ecumenical-Liturgical Study* (Great Wakering: Mayhew-McCrimmon, 1974).

[12]Clarke, *op. cit.,* pp. 622-24.

[13]Lamb, *op. cit.*, pp. 145-46; Clarke, *op. cit.*, pp. 266-92.

[14]C. C. Butterworth, *The English Primers, 1529-1545: Their Publication and Connection with the English Bible and the Reformation in England* (Philadelphia: University of Pennsylvania Press, 1953); E. Hoskins, *op. cit.*

[15]Clarke, *op. cit.*, pp. 247-48, 282-87; Reed, *op. cit.*, pp. 623-38, 736-50.

[16]B. Wigan, *The Liturgy in English*, 2d ed., (London: Oxford University Press, 1964); C. W. Dugmore, *The Mass and the English Reformers* (London: Macmillan, 1958); C. W. Dugmore, *Eucharistic Doctrine in England from Hooker to Waterland* (New York: Macmillan, 1942); A. H. Couratin, *Church Quarterly Review*, CLXIV (April-June, 1963), 148-59; CLXIII (October-December, 1962), 431-42; J. A. Devereaux, S. J., "Reformed Doctrine in the Collects of the First Book of Common Prayer," *Harvard Theological Review*, LVIII (January, 1965), 49-68.

[17]Gunstone, *The Feast of Pentecost;* Gunstone, *Christmas and Epiphany;* Clarke, *op. cit.*, pp. 215-39.

[18]Patrick, *op. cit.*, pp. 94-100; Lamb, *op. cit.*, pp. 145-51; Benson, *op. cit.;* Routley, *op. cit.;* P. Le Huray, *Music and the Reformation in England 1549-1660* (New York: Oxford University Press, 1967); C. Dearnley, *English Church Music 1650-1750 in Royal Chapel, Cathedral and Parish Church* (London: Barrie & Jenkins, 1970); C. H. Phillips, *The Singing Church: An Outline History of the Music Sung by Choir and People* (London: Faber and Faber, 1945); M. Frost, *Historical Companion to Hymns Ancient & Modern* (London: Printed for the Proprietors by William Clowes & Sons, 1962).

[19]G. W. O. Addleshaw and F. Etchells, *The Architectural Setting of Anglican Worship* (London: Faber and Faber, 1948); Davies, *The Architectural Setting of Baptism*, pp. 91-118; Davies, *The Secular Use of Church Buildings*, pp. 96-204; Clarke and Betjeman, *op. cit.*, pp. 31-54; J. S. Rawlings, *Virginia's Colonial Churches: An Architectural Guide* (Richmond: Garrett & Massie, 1963).

[20]J. W. Legg, *English Orders for Consecrating Churches*, Henry Bradshaw Society Vol. XLI (London, 1911); Davies, *The Secular Use of Church Buildings*, pp. 249-64; Cuming, *A History of Anglican Liturgy*, pp. 380-85.

CHAPTER VIII

[1]M. J. Hatchett, *The Making of the First American Prayer Book* (unpublished Th. D. dissertation, General Theological Seminary, 1972); Cuming, *A History of Anglican Liturgy*, pp. 168-90; H. Davies, *op. cit.*, Vol. III; J. W. Legg, *English Church Life from the Restoration to the Tractarian Movement* (London: Longmans, Green and Co., 1914); T. J. Fawcett, *The Liturgy of Comprehension 1689: An Abortive Attempt to Revise the Book of Common Prayer* (Southend-on-sea: Mayhew-McCrimmon, 1973); George Every, *The High Church Party 1688-1718* (London: S. P. C. K., 1956); F.

R. Bolton, *The Caroline Tradition of the Church of Ireland* (London: S. P. C. K., 1958); Henry Broxap, *The Later Non-Jurors* (Cambridge: University Press, 1924); A. C. Don, *The Scottish Book of Common Prayer 1929* (London: S. P. C. K., 1949); A. E. Peaston, *The Prayer Book Reform Movement in the XVIIIth Century* (Oxford: Basil Blackwell, 1940).

²M. J. Hatchett, "The First American Trial Liturgy," *The St. Luke's Journal of Theology*, XIV (September, 1971), 20-29; W. McGarvey, *Liturgiae Americanae: or the Book of Common Prayer As Used in the United States of America Compared with the Proposed Book of 1786 and with the Prayer Book of the Church of England, and an Historical Account and Documents* (Philadelphia: Philadelphia Church Publishing Company, 1907); C. O. Loveland, *The Critical Years* (Greenwich: Seabury Press, 1956); W. White, *Memoirs of the Protestant Episcopal Church*, ed. by B. F. DeCosta (New York: E. P. Dutton & Company, 1880).

³R. C. D. Jasper, *Prayer Book Revision in England 1800-1900* (London: S. P. C. K., 1954); Cuming, *A History of Anglican Liturgy*, pp. 191-212; W. W. Manross, *The Episcopal Church in the United States 1800-1840: A Study in Church Life* (New York: Columbia University Press, 1938); G. E. DeMille, *The Catholic Movement in the American Episcopal Church*, 2d ed., (Philadelphia: Church Historical Society, 1950); A. E. Peaston, *The Prayer Book Revisions of the Victorian Evangelicals* (Dublin, 1963).

⁴A. W. Skardon, *Church Leader in the Cities: William Augustus Muhlenberg* (Philadelphia: University of Pennsylvania Press, 1971).

⁵J. F. Woolverton, "W. R. Huntington: Liturgical Renewal and Church Unity in the 1880s," *Anglican Theological Review*, XLVIII (April, 1966), 175-99; W. R. Huntington, *A Short History of the Book of Common Prayer Together with Certain Papers Illustrative of Liturgical Revision 1878-1892* (New York: Thomas Whittaker, [1893]).

⁶Cuming, *A History of Anglican Liturgy*, pp. 213-44; Clarke, *op. cit.;* E. C. Chorley, *The New American Prayer Book: Its History and Contents* (New York: Macmillan Company, 1930); E. L. Parsons and B. H. Jones, *The American Prayer Book: Its Origins and Principles* (New York: Charles Scribner's Sons, 1937); M. H. Shepherd, Jr., *The Oxford American Prayer Book Commentary* (New York: Oxford University Press, 1950).

⁷Jagger, *op. cit.*

⁸*Confirmation or the Laying on of Hands*, 2 vols., (London: S. P. C. K., 1926).

⁹Gunstone, *The Liturgy of Penance*, pp. 74-75; McNeill, *op. cit.*, pp. 239-46; Porter, "The Ash Wednesday Rites."

¹⁰Bradshaw, *op. cit.*, pp. 96-171.

¹¹Clarke, *op. cit.*, pp. 714-21.

¹²Ramsey, *op. cit.*, pp. 60-68.

¹³B. H. Jones, *The American Lectionary* (New York: Morehouse-Gorham Co., 1944).

[14]Wigan, *op. cit.*; W. J. Grisbrooke, *Anglican Liturgies of the Seventeenth and Eighteenth Centuries* (London: S. P. C. K., 1958); J. Dowden, *The Scottish Communion Office 1764*, ed. by H. A. Wilson (Oxford: Clarendon Press, 1922); A. D. Calcote, *Word and Spirit: The Prayer of Consecration in Anglican Thought and Practice 1604-1740* (unpublished S. T. M. thesis, General Theological Seminary, 1963); *Prayer Book Studies IV: The Eucharistic Liturgy* (New York: Church Pension Fund, 1953); A. Härdelin, *The Tractarian Understanding of the Eucharist* (Uppsala, 1965); A. Härdelin, "The Eucharist in the Theology of the Nineteenth Century," *Eucharistic Theology Then and Now*, pp. 76-89; J. Wilkinson, "Liturgy in the Twentieth Century," *Eucharistic Theology Then and Now*, pp. 90-105.

[15]Patrick, *op. cit.*, pp. 114-92; Benson, *op. cit.*; Routley, *op. cit.*; Phillips, *op. cit.*; Frost, *op. cit.*; Foote, *op. cit.*; Ellinwood, *op. cit.*; M. D. Gable, Jr., "The Hymnody of the Church—1789-1832," *Historical Magazine of the Protestant Episcopal Church*, XXXVI (September, 1967), 249-70; B. Rainbow, *The Choral Revival in the Anglican Church (1839-1872)* (New York: Oxford University Press, 1970); *The Hymnal 1940 Companion*, 3d ed., rev., (New York: Church Pension Fund, 1958).

[16]Addleshaw and Etchells, *op. cit.*; H. W. Rose, *The Colonial Houses of Worship in America* (New York: Hastings House, 1963); S. P. Dorsey, *Early English Churches in America 1607-1807* (New York: Oxford University Press, 1952); J. F. White, *The Cambridge Movement: The Ecclesiologists and the Gothic Revival* (Cambridge: University Press, 1962); P. B. Stanton, *The Gothic Revival and American Church Architecture: An Episode in Taste, 1840-1856* (Baltimore: Johns Hopkins Press, 1968); Davies, *The Architectural Setting of Baptism*, pp. 91-161; Davies, *The Secular Use of Church Buildings*; Rawlings, *op. cit.*

CHAPTER IX

[1]E. B. Koenker, *The Liturgical Renaissance in the Roman Catholic Church*, rev. ed., (St. Louis: Concordia Publishing House, 1966); *The People Worship: A History of the Liturgical Movement*, ed. by L. Sheppard (New York: Hawthorn Books, 1967); M. H. Shepherd, Jr., *The Reform of Liturgical Worship: Perspectives and Prospects* (New York: Oxford University Press, 1961).

[2]White, *New Forms of Worship*; Hoon, *op. cit.*

[3]P. G. Craighill, *Liturgy and Piety: A Study of Three Trial Eucharistic Rites in the Episcopal Church* (unpublished Th. D. dissertation, Princeton Theological Seminary, 1972); A. R. Shands, *The Liturgical Movement and the Local Church*, rev. ed., first American printing (New York: Morehouse-Barlow Co., 1966); D. E. Babin, *The Celebration of Life: Our Changing Liturgy* (New York: Morehouse-Barlow, 1969); A. R. Shands and H. B. Evans, *How & Why: An Introduction to the Three New Trial Eucharists and the Daily Office of the Episcopal Church* (New York: Seabury Press, 1971), pp. 13-32; *The Lambeth Conference 1958: The Encyclical Letter from the Bishops together with the Resolutions and Reports* (London: S. P. C. K.;

New York: Seabury Press, 1958); *Prayer Book Studies*, 28 vols. (New York: Church Pension Fund, 1950-73).

⁴L. L. Mitchell, *Liturgical Change: How Much Do We Need?* (New York: Seabury Press, 1975).

⁵Jagger, *op. cit.; Crisis for Baptism: The Report of the 1965 Ecumenical Conference Sponsored by the Parish and People Movement*, ed. by B. S. Moss (London: S. C. M. Press, 1965); *Confirmation Crisis* (New York: Seabury Press, 1968); *Prayer Book Studies 18;* "Documentation and Reflection: Confirmation Today," *Anglican Theological Review*, LIV (April, 1972), 106-19; Hatchett, "The Rite of 'Confirmation' in the Book of Common Prayer and in *Authorized Services 1973*"; L. Weil, "Christian Initiation: A Theological and Pastoral Commentary on the Proposed Rites," *St. Luke's Journal of Theology*, XVIII (March, 1975), 95-112; U. T. Holmes, *Confirmation: The Celebration of Maturity in Christ* (New York: Seabury Press, 1975); *Prayer Book Studies 26*.

⁶*Prayer Book Studies 24*, pp. 15-16, 58-60.

⁷*Ibid.*, pp. 1-8, 24-36; H. Kirschenbaum and R. Stensrud, *The Wedding Book: Alternative Ways to Celebrate Marriage* (New York: Seabury Press, 1974); P. H. Biddle, Jr., *Abingdon Marriage Manual* (Nashville: Abingdon Press, 1974).

⁸*Prayer Book Studies 24*, pp. 8-9, 37-39.

⁹*Prayer Book Studies 20;* Bradshaw, *op. cit.*, pp. 172-211; H. B. Porter, Jr., "The Theology of Ordination and the New Rites," *Anglican Theological Review*, LIV (April, 1972), 69-81; Power, *op. cit.*, pp. 127-89.

¹⁰*Prayer Book Studies 28*, pp. 41-61.

¹¹Ramsey, *op. cit.*, pp. 69-129; G. Cope, "Vestments," *A Dictionary of Liturgy and Worship*, ed. by J. G. Davies (New York: Macmillan Company, 1972), pp. 365-83.

¹²*Prayer Book Studies 24*, pp. 9-11, 40-41; Jagger, *op. cit.*, pp. 315-16; M. Thurian, *Consecration of the Layman: New Approaches to the Sacrament of Confirmation* (Baltimore: Helicon, 1963).

¹³*Prayer Book Studies 24*, pp. 11-19, 42-77.

¹⁴*Ibid.*, pp. 17-18, 64-74.

¹⁵*Ibid.*, pp. 19-23, 78-131; J. Mitford, *The American Way of Death* (New York: Simon and Schuster, 1963); *Dying, Death and Disposal*, ed. by G. Cope (London: S. P. C. K., 1970); The Church of England Liturgical Commission, *Alternative Services: Second Series* (London: S. P. C. K., 1965), pp. 99-141; P. H. Biddle, Jr., *Abingdon Funeral Manual* (Nashville: Abingdon Press, 1976).

¹⁶*Prayer Book Studies 22; The Daily Office by the Joint Liturgical Group*, ed. by R. C. D. Jasper (London: S. P. C. K. and Epworth Press, 1968); *The Taizé Office* (London: Faith Press, 1966); Shands and Barry, *op. cit.*, pp. 79-88; H. B. Porter, Jr., "What Does the Daily Office Do?," *Anglican Theological Review*, LVI (April, 1974), 170-81.

[17]*Prayer Book Studies XVII; Prayer Book Studies 21;* C. O. Buchanan, *Modern Anglican Liturgies 1958-1968* (London: Oxford University Press, 1968); M. J. Hatchett, "Recent Anglican Revisions of the Eucharistic Rite," *American Church Quarterly: A Theological Review,* VI (1969-70), 203-11; J. C. Kirby, *Word and Action: New Forms of the Liturgy* (New York: Seabury Press, 1969). Wilkinson, "Liturgy in the Twentieth Century"; C. B. Naylor, "Eucharistic Theology Today," *Eucharistic Theology Then and Now,* pp. 106-16; Shands and Evans, *op. cit.,* pp. 33-78; D. E. Babin, *Doing the Eucharist: A Guide to Trial Use* (New York: Morehouse-Barlow Co., 1971); Craighill, *op. cit.;* T. W. Guzie, *Jesus and the Eucharist* (New York: Paulist Press, 1974); J. M. Powers, *Eucharistic Theology* (New York: Seabury Press, 1967); J. H. McKenna, "Eucharistic Epiclesis: Myopia or Microcosm?," *Theological Studies,* XXXVI (June, 1975), 265-84. J. H. McKenna, *Eucharist and Holy Spirit: The Eucharistic Epiclesis in Twentieth Century Theology (1900-1966)* (Great Wakering: Mayhew-McCrimmon, 1975); C. O. Buchanan, *Further Anglican Liturgies 1968-1975* (Bramcote, Nottingham: Grove Books, 1975).

[18]M. J. Hatchett, "A Manuale of Ceremonial," *St. Luke's Journal of Theology,* XVII (March, 1974), 19-84.

[19]*Prayer Book Studies 19.*

[20]E. Routley, *Church Music and Theology* (London: S. C. M. Press, 1959); E. Routley, *Twentieth Century Church Music* (New York: Oxford University Press, 1964); E. Routley, *Hymns Today and Tomorrow* (New York: Abingdon Press, 1964); E. Routley, *Words, Music and the Church* (Nashville: Abingdon Press, 1967); *Crisis in Church Music?* (Washington: The Liturgical Conference, 1967); *Music for Holy Week,* edited by Mason Martens (New York: Music for Liturgy, 1972); The Passion Gospels (RSV) set to the traditional passion tone (New York: Music for Liturgy, 1977-79); *Settings for the Common Texts of the Eucharist* (New York: Church Hymnal Corp., 1976); *Music for Ministers and Congregation* (New York: Church Hymnal Corp., 1978); *The Book of Canticles* (New York: Church Hymnal Corp., 1979); *Hymns III* (New York: Church Hymnal Corp., 1979); *Gradual Psalms, Alleluia Verses, and Tracts* (New York: Church Hymnal Corp., 1980–82); *Congregational Music for Eucharist* (New York: Church Hymnal Corp., 1980).

[21]White, *Protestant Worship and Church Architecture;* F. DeBuyst, *Modern Architecture and Christian Celebration* (Richmond: John Knox Press, 1968); E. A. Sovik, *Architecture for Worship* (Minneapolis: Augsburg Publishing House, 1973); R. Gieselmann, *Contemporary Church Architecture* (London: Thames and Hudson, 1972).

[22]Ramsey, *op. cit.,* pp. 36-39, 79, 92-93.

[23]*Prayer Book Studies 28,* pp. 7-39.

INDEX

Bishops' Book, 113.
Black, 43, 112.
Black Letter Days, 114, 132, 155, 176.
Black Rubric, 130, 151.
Bless, 24.
Blessing, At Eucharistic rite, 70, 107–8, 129, 132, 174, 175; at marriage, 60, 120, 165; other rites, 45, 62, 63, 86, 103, 118, 122, 124, 143.
Blood, 9; *see* Eucharist.
Bobbio Missal, 55, 82.
Bohemian Brethren, 101; *see* Moravian.
Bonhoeffer, Dietrich, 161.
Bonner, Edmund, 114.
Book of Common Order (1562), 98, 115.
Book of Common Prayer, 12, 71, 162–63; English, 113–135; *1549*, 113–137 *passim*, 152, 154, 156; *1552*, 114–132, 148; *1559*, 114, 122, 123, 125, 126, 127; *Latin version* (1560), 115, 123; *1604*, 115, 118, 122, 124, 127; *1637* (for Scotland), 115, 137, 152; *1662*, 116–132, 136, 137, 138, 144, 148, 152, 154; *1928*, 140; American, 136–59; *1786, see* Proposed Book; *1790*, 141, 142–56; *1892*, 140, 142–46, 149, 150, 151, 154–56; *1928*, 140–56, 163, 166, 167–69, 172, 178–79; *1979*, 163–79; other, 140.
Book of Homilies, 113; *see* Homily.
Book of Hours, 90; *see* Primer.
Books, Liturgical, 81, 83, 161.
Booths, Feast of, *see* Tabernacles.
Boston, 138.
Botte, Bernard, 160.
Bouyer, Louis, 160, 162.
Brady, Nicholas, 156.
Brandenburg, 98, 104, 121, 122.
Bread, 9, 21, 23, 27, 63, 88, 92, 128, 155, 175; Blessed, 63, 88.
Breaking of Bread, 23, 27, 47, 75, 172, 174; *see* Fraction.
Breathing on Candidates, 34, 56, 100.
Brenz, Johann, 98.
Breviary, 83, 97, 99, 105, 113.
Brilioth, Yngve, 161.

Bucer (Butzer), Martin, 98, 101, 103, 114, 121, 127.
Buildings, 78–79, 95–96, 111–12, 134–35, 157–8, 160, 177–8; *see* House-church.
Burial, 8–9, 21–2, 43, 52, 62, 89–90, 96, 105, 122–3, 146–7, 168–9.

Caesarius of Arles, 54.
Calenburg, 98.
Calvin, John, 98, 101, 102, 106, 108, 110, 114, 127.
Calvinism, 139, 140.
Candidate, 16, 18, 33–35, 56–58, 84.
Candle, 57, 61, 68, 72, 85, 100, 158, 170, 171, 175.
Canon (New Testament), 45.
Canon (Prayer), 71, 91–92, 95, 107–8, 130; *see* Eucharistic Prayer.
Canons, of Hippolytus, 60; *1604*, 127; *1640*, 115.
Cantate Domino, 124.
Canterbury, 55.
Canticles, 133, 170, 172, 176; *see* by title.
Carlstadt, Andreas, 97.
"Carpet," 134.
Cassel, 98.
Casel, Odo, 161.
Cassian, John, 63.
Catechesis, 32–33, 53, 85, 106, 125, 142, 150.
Catechism, 98, 101, 118, 163; "Cranmer's," 113.
Catechumen, 32, 33, 45, 48, 56–58, 60, 64, 68, 84, 166.
Catechumens, Liturgy of the, 45; *see* Eucharist.
Cathedra, 49, 79.
Celebration of a New Ministry, 167; *see* Institution of Ministers.
Ceremonies, 4, 10–11, 13–14, 92, 108, 139, 140–41, 155, 175.
Chabûrah Meal, 23.
Chalice, 92, 96, 121, 127, 174; *see* Cup.
Chancel, 111, 130, 134.
Charles I, 115, 133.
Chasuble, 61, 88–89, 104, 121.
Chicago Quadrilateral, 140.

Maryland, 152, 154.
Mason, A. J., 142.
Mass, 91, 92, 94–95, 96, 98, 105, 107, 114, 126, 155; *see* Eucharist.
Masses of Mone, 54.
Matins, 62, 89, 90, 105, 123–4, 133; *see* Morning Prayer.
Matthias, St., 94.
Maundy Thursday, 59, 77, 122, 143.
Meal, 9, 23–24, 25–26, 40, 171; *see* Agape; Eucharist.
Meat, 9; *see* Eucharist.
Medievalism, 139.
Melancthon, Philip, 98.
Merbecke, John, 133.
Mercersburg theologians, 139.
Methodists, 102, 109, 138.
Michael and All Angels, St., 109.
Michel, Virgil, 161.
Milan, 55.
Milk and Honey, 38; *see* Honey.
Millenary Petition, 115.
Ministry at the Time of Death, 168.
Miracles, Eucharistic, 93.
Missal, 82–83, 86, 94.
Missale Francorum, 54.
Missale Gallicanum vetus, 54, 117.
Missale Gothicum, 54, 69–70.
Missale Mixtum, 97, 117.
"Mission Services," 140, 150.
Mithraism, 31.
Mitre, 89, 104, 145, 167.
Modes, 78.
Mohar, 19.
Monasticism, 52; *see* Franciscan Order; Friars; Monks.
Monday, 23, 94.
Mone, Masses of, 54.
Monks, 59, 63, 75, 81; *see* Monasticism.
Monstrance, 93.
Moravians, 102, 109.
Morning Prayer, 124, 125–26, 142–43, 147–50, 151, 153, 155, 159, 166, 170–71, 172.
Motet, 133.
Muhlenberg, William Augustus, 139–40.
Music, 28, 48–49, 78, 94–95, 109, 110, 133–34, 156–57, 161, 169, 176–77.
Mysterion, 12.

Mystery Religions, 31, 46, 51, 68, 71.
Myth, 4, 7.

Name of Jesus, Feast of the, 94.
Naming, 100.
Narsai, 53.
Narthex, 158.
Nationalism, 97.
Nave, 111, 112, 134–35, 158.
Neo-Gothic, 160, 177.
Neophyte, 57.
New England, 138.
New Fire, 56.
New Jersey, 138.
New Liturgy, A, 137, 144, 149.
New Testament, 16; *see* Lection.
New Testament Apocrypha, 31.
New Year, 109.
New York, 145, 159.
Nicea, Council of, 58.
Nonconformists, 156.
None, 63; *see* Hours of Prayer.
Non-Jurors, 137, 143, 144, 153, 154.
Norbeck, Edward, 5.
Norfolk Rebels, 114.
Norwalk, Connecticut, 145.
Nowell, Alexander, 118.
Nunc dimittis, 28, 88, 105, 123–24, 148–49.
Nuptial Eucharist, *see* Eucharist, at Marriages.
Nuremburg, 98.

Oblation, 46–47, 64, 66, 69, 71–72, 73–74, 129, 152, 174.
Oblation, Self-, 130, 131.
Occult, 5.
Octave, 57–8, 77, 90, 114, 128, 176.
Offering, 37, 45, 64, 68, 72, 77, 92, 95, 107, 127, 128, 130, 134, 154, 174, 175.
Office, Daily, *see* Daily Office.
Office Hymns, 94.
Office of Our Lady, 90, 106.
Office of the Dead, 90, 106.
Offices of Instruction, 142.
Oil, 35–37, 42–43, 57, 77, 85, 100, 168; *see* Anointing.
Old Testament Worthies, 76.
"Orans" Position, 45.
Orate Fratres, 161.

212) SANCTIFYING LIFE, TIME AND SPACE